Rural Development and Bureaucracy in Tanzania:
the Case of Mwanza Region

James R. Finucane

Rural Development and Bureaucracy in Tanzania: the Case of Mwanza Region

AFRICANA PUBLISHING COMPANY

A Division of Holmes & Meier Publishers, Inc.
101 Fifth Avenue, New York, N.Y. 10003

Printed in Sweden by
Bohusläningens AB, Uddevalla 1974

For Helen, Jeane, Thomas, Jr.
and Don, and in memory of Thomas, Sr.

Development brings freedom, provided it is development of people. But people cannot be developed; they can only develop themselves ... A man develops himself by joining in free discussion of a new venture and participating in the subsequent decision; he is not being developed if he is herded like an animal into a new venture.

Julius K. Nyerere
"Freedom and Development"

Contents

Tables

Preface

From September, 1968 to November, 1970 I was the development administration specialist on the four member Rural Research Project of the University of Dar es Salaam. The Project, funded by a grant from the Danish aid agency to the University for research on rural agricultural development, was a multidisciplinary enquiry into the problems and patterns of development in the rural areas of Mwanza Region and Shinyanga District. My particular approach, an examination of the balance struck between hierarchy and participation in organizational structures in relation to the Tanzanian government's rural development goals of increasing both equality and economic output, was initially presented to a seminar of the Dar es Salaam Faculty of Arts and Social Sciences in December, 1968, at the outset of the study.

The conflict between increasing both output and equality often seems intransigent in rural agricultural development. Peasants using low productivity routines and technology, and producing largely for home consumption, must somehow change or be induced to change their methods. In spite of much experimentation and decades of experience in many countries with different organizational approaches to rural development, each with a different mix of the organizing principles of hierarchy and participation, we are as yet largely unable to reasonably estimate the probable effectiveness and efficiency of one form or another in terms of goals such as output and equality. And sometimes even the basis of the principles themselves seem threatened with hierarchical, bureaucratic approaches leading at times to reductions in output, and participatory approaches, co-operatives for instance, leading to greater inequality. In general however the practice in most countries has been to rely on a hopefully modernizing bureaucracy as the agent of change in rural areas, a practice prolifically underwritten in scholarly works on the need for the "modernization of traditional societies", and a practice not noticeably successful in that rural development remains the urgent priority of most of the world.

Tanzania's organizational strategy for rural development was of interest to me because it seemed to be a different approach, one which involved a sincere reliance upon 'the people' as their own vehicle for change. Arising from a "development of underdevelopment" view of the process of social change the theme in Tanzania's ideology has been that if the people do not participate in decision making then there can be no development and what limited economic growth might occur will not be in their interests. The Tanzanian leaders have specifically rejected the approach of a modernizing bureaucracy, and their attempt to find another way is of relevance to all who are interested in the efficacy of rural development administration.

As this study shows Tanzania in practice has not presented as different an approach as I had initially thought. One finds in rural Tanzania, at least in the economically and politically important areas in which this study was conducted, much the same bureaucratic method which one finds in other parts of the underdeveloped world today and two decades ago. There are differences to be sure—the consumption patterns of Tanzania's bureaucracy have been seriously curtailed by the leadership, persuasion is a more revered art, the peasant has a respectable status in the society, the bureaucrats themselves are industrious, responsive to the government's wishes, and well-intentioned in their efforts. But the basic, familiar pattern remains—an elite, ensconced in a state bureaucracy, trying with varying degrees of detachment to convince the masses to change their ways; what participation there is remains an arena in which those who know the route to modernity—by self-identification the bureaucrats—try to educate their less enlightened fellows. The major decentralization measures implemented during 1972 and 1973 have been the government's response to the set of problems which this bureaucratic method has engendered. As I explain, however, the measures are designed not to increase participation of the people in decisions but rather to produce a better bureaucratic method for increasing agricultural production.

The description of this bureaucratic pattern and some of the difficulties and contradictions which the Tanzanian leaders have faced in attempting to alter it is the burden of this book. Tanzania's leaders have attacked their nation's problems with a seriousness of purpose unparalled by that of many of their colleagues in other underdeveloped countries. What is being done in Tanzania's rural areas is thus an experience well worthy of observation. The limited conclusion of this study, that Tanzania's organizational arrangements are in fact fairly common should be construed not as a setback for efforts to find a productive and people-oriented approach to rural development, but as an indication of some of the obstacles involved.

Many individuals deserve acknowledgements for their assistance only a few of who I can name. Colin Leys, Carl Rosberg, and D. Cruise O'Brien criticized early outlines of my research. In the field I benefited from the insights of Tanzanians and students of Tanzania. I mention especially Antony Ellman, Gottfried Lang, R. G. Saylor, Bill Sutherland, Brian van Arkadie, and my fellow members of the Rural Research Project—Tom Hankins, Robert Hulls, and Arne Larsen. At various times Charles Bayeka, Daudi Masija, Mbeti Musiyi and Aloys Rutaihwa were my diligent research assistants. In 1964—1966 I had spent twenty-one months working in rural development administration in Swahili speaking areas of Kenya and thus had some ability in Tanzania's national language when I arrived in Dar es Salaam. While in Tanzania my fluency was greatly increased through the assistance of friends including S. K. Msuya and M. Mwambara. Two close friends of mine, M. Baregu and C. Rwechungura, contributed greatly to my understanding of Tanzania and continue to do so.

I took up an appointment as Lecturer in Public Administration at the University of Zambia early in 1971 and later that year the University authorities financed a short return visit to East Africa. C. Gertzel, V. Subramaniam, Malcolm Wallis, Göran Hydén, Anthony Rweyemamu, and Raymond Hopkins, made helpful comments on draft chapters. The extensive critiques of Ilsa Schuster, Keith Pantar-Brick, my doctoral examiner at the London School of Economics, and William Tordoff who served as the external examiner, were of great assistance in preparing this study for publication. Jeane Finucane suffered all the pains of an author's wife while simultaneously carrying out her own studies; without her patience and support I fear nothing would have been produced.

Lusaka
February, 1974

J. R. F.

Introduction

The Problem

The leaders of Tanzania today desire to develop their nation economically, they want increased material output and a greater capacity for self-sustaining growth. These economic production goals are similar to those of the leaders of most other countries, developed and underdeveloped alike. The Tanzaphilia[1] which has been demonstrated by social scientists has not been induced by such commonplace goals. Rather it has been brought about by the sincerity which many of them have been willing to attribute to the efforts of the Tanzanian leadership, and particularly President Julius Nyerere, to achieve their other main objective, the creation of a just and egalitarian society.[2]

The problem which has confronted the Tanzanian leadership in its pursuit of these objectives of increased production of wealth and human equality, which we take together as defining development in the Tanzanian context, has been that they have often appeared to stand in opposition to each other. Students of development, and especially those who see development as the 'modernization of traditional societies',[3] have argued that "the quest for greater social justice, for more equality of participation in the making of decisions and for a fair share of what is produced seems often to be incompatible with the desire for increasing productivity, for more efficiency and larger outputs".[4] This incompatibility presents a dilemma for statesmen as well as scholars. Nyerere in describing it in terms of "the sacrifice in the interests of the society" which an individual makes in the hope of gaining material rewards has referred to its "inevitable and inescapable" nature.[5]

The essence of this 'sacrifice' is that each of us concedes to society some authority to decide what we will do and how we will do it. This sacrifice becomes larger as our society increases in size and employs more complex technology to better the natural environment. We know that when work is organized rationally we can gain an increase in the amount of wealth produced, and that it is possible to distribute this wealth fairly equitably so as to do away with certain economic inequalities. Unfortunately this "rational organization of work" which makes us able to win a satisfactory life from nature "cannot be achieved without a hierarchy in which man has authority over man",[6] that is, without an inegalitarian distribution of power.

Once a society develops non-traditional or "autonomous" goals having to do ultimately with increased economic production there is a need for centralized bureaucracies[7]—hierarchies which recruit their members on the basis of some sort of qualification, have a differentiation of tasks, and compartmentalized decision making process.[8] The economic problems and aspirations of all present-day states have required the use of bureaucracies in their attempts to increase output, specifically so as to achieve the order and discipline needed by high productivity technology and to allocate scarce resources. But it is not only economic goals which hierarchies have been employed to achieve. Nation-states have found that bureaucracies are also essential in successfully meeting basic political requirements for the maintenance of national independence and unity.[9]

In using bureaucracies to deal with these political and economic problems leadership groups are confronted with the difficulty of reconciling the strain between "the organization's needs and the participant's needs".[10] This is an objective difficulty which all management or leadership groups face regardless of their particular set of goals and the Tanzanian leaders are quite aware of the tensions involved.[11] In the case of any state the penetration of official hierarchies into the society to exact and sometimes to change a specific pattern of behaviour must be balanced with the opposing need for participation if such penetration is to be effective and efficient.

At the minimum participation can improve organizational performance through improving communications[12] and hence ward off expensive mistakes. The difficulty however is larger than the sometimes technical one of information flow. The basis of the management problem in using hierarchies is that given the psychological needs of human beings a hierarchy to be viable cannot give the appearance to its members of being too hierarchical.[13] Power must not be, or at least must not appear to be, distributed as unequally as the notion of a pure hierarchy suggests. Particularly for non-military bureaucracies, in order to realize their objectives without recourse to a large amount of coercion, the individuals who form their membership and the larger society into which they penetrate must perceive that they will realize a share of the material benefits brought about by the hierarchical arrangement of power and they must have, or more precisely they must believe that they have, some influence on the decisions affecting the activities of the hierarchies.

Most states find a solution to this management problem by creating "managerial ideologies" with which the few who exercise authority justify the need for hierarchy and explain its use.[14] Whether the leaders are considered to be those who control the 'political system' or those who control the means of production observers have noted the explications of ideas and doctrines which aim at convincing the society that the rational organization of work in the society, although achieved through an inegalitarian power distribution, is in the best interests of all.[15]

Although management ideologies may reduce the difficulties in organizing work they do not resolve the contradiction between increasing the total output of wealth and increasing equality. Modernization academics, those who posit the need for the passing of 'traditional' society, have asserted that higher levels of both output and equality can be achieved only through an increase in institutional differentiation and an accompanying "disassociation of powers" in society.[16] The association amongst these three elements—equality, capacity, and differentiation[17]— has been widely, though by no means universally,[18] accepted amongst social scientists. The problem is however that the claimed association is a static one while the essence of the difficulty, most acutely for states with an egalitarian objective, has been in its dynamics—how does a society move towards this situation of both greater output and greater equality.

In theory and practice the tendency has been to stress output now and hope for equality later. The identification of economic development as the immediate need often follows from a view of the history of the now developed countries. The argument is that the sequence of 'crises' experienced by the states of Western Europe, for instance, national identity, legitimacy, and penetration, and then, later, distribution and participation,[19] occurred over a period of centuries and enabled them to get on with the job of constructing economically powerful nations long before they had to deal with demands for a larger say in what and how to produce. This crisis sequence was accompanied by a sequence of institutional growth in which hierarchical structures (national bureaucracies) were firmly established before the introduction of polyarchic ones (parties, election systems, assemblies).[20] Backed up by this 'theory', the practice in the underdeveloped countries has been to try to deal first with 'crises' of identity, legitimacy and pene-

14

tration through the establishment of hierarchical structures and to put off until later any serious efforts to establish popular institutions which deal with the 'crises' of distribution and participation in a forthright rather than a management ideology sort of fashion.[21] This practice has been urged or at least reinforced by the practices of aid agencies. They have based their programmes on the assumption that there will be a "catalytic flow from programs of economic aid and technical assistance to economic growth in underdeveloped countries, leading in turn to political stability . . . and the strengthening of newly created democratic institutions".[22] The practice has been further encouraged and underwritten by the insistence of the major multilateral aid agencies on monetary stability and financially solid projects.[23] The practice has not been restricted to a particular type or group of countries. Soviet development for instance has been based on a highly capacity or output oriented solution to the capacity—equality conflict.[24]

As one account of the experience of aid programmes which stress economic development first and then hope for equality later explains, "subsequent developments have failed to demonstrate the validity of this model and have called into question the cause-effect relationships implied".[25] The subsequent developments do not however seem to have altered the practice very much. The conventional wisdom has remained with its emphasis on the priority of economic productivity; the practice in most underdeveloped countries continues to be a drive for more efficient bureaucracies. The only thing which would appear to have altered is that many scholar-advisers, aware of the changing sentiment of the times, now urge a degree of subtlety in the hierarchy. Montgomery, for example, has recommended that the developing nations should look to "some of the new Western approaches, such as the 'participative' technique of management, [which] soften hierarchic distinctions without removing them".[26] Perhaps even more straightforward, seventeen scholars with a wide experience of Africa (including, Ashford, Bienen, Brokensha, Fallers, Foltz, Kilby, Kilson, W. Arthur Lewis, Norman Miller, Zolberg) concluded their 1967 conference with the following observation in their joint report: "The problem remains one of increasing the feeling of participation without necessarily increasing the local input into decision-making."[27]

The Tanzanian leaders have not subscribed completely to this "modernization" approach and its current suggestion that participative techniques should be used. They are aware that there is a "certain colonialist flavour"[28] in such advice, that the change agency remains the members of the elite in the modernizing bureaucracy, that the participative techniques refer "not to a technique of decision but to technique of persuasion".[29] Such techniques are clearly in conflict with the Tanzanian leaders' concept of development itself which gives equal weight to output and equality. Equality for them includes widespread participation in decision making; this is considered an ultimate good with an intrinsic value of its own.[30] If people are not involved in the decisions then, the argument goes, there can be no development although there might well be economic growth and change. Participation in Tanzania is thus much more than a management problem; it is intimately involved in the leaders' asserted conceptions of the good life.

The intrinsic value accorded to participation in Tanzania arises partly from perceptions of the organizational patterns of most of Tanzania's traditional societies. In the Tanzanian ideology propounded in the writings of Nyerere and the major policy statements of party and government there is a preference for the egalitarian organizational arrangements of the perceived past, for an essentially participative approach as opposed to the hierarchical (rational organization of work) one normally associated with economic growth. Not that the traditional societies are seen as having been hierarchy-free unities, or participation the only organizational principle, rather that participation is seen as having been the dominant element.[31] The intention of Tanzania's leaders is to add to this participatory society a capacity for increased production. As Nyerere has put it, development is to be built on the foundations of the past "by emphasizing certain characteristics of our traditional organization and extending them so that they can embrace the possibility of modern technology".[32]

This Tanzanian ideology is not only grounded in notions about the past in a static sense; it stems as well from an implicit 'development of underdevelopment' view of the way change occurs within and between societies.[33] Participation in this regard assumes a key instrumental value, it is necessary to ensure that 'the people' are not exploited, and involves ultimately a power equalisation[34] or non-manipulative approach. Thus the Tanzanian leaders do not, in their stated ideology, accord an initial priority to improving the bureaucracies, to making a better hierarchy. They urge participation now if both equality and greater production are to be achieved at all. This view became manifestly clear after the 1967 Arusha Declaration which was designed "not only to ensure the fair distribution of such wealth as now exists but

16

to ensure the fair division of future wealth as it is created".[35] In the agricultural sector there appeared a shift in emphasis from production to equality,[36] and at the macro-level the willingness to accept a short-run decline in economic output so as to achieve greater equality including equality of participation.[37]

We can distinguish three propositions in the Tanzanian ideology about the instrumental need for participation now. The first is that the people generally must share in the economic benefits as they are forthcoming if indeed they are to be forthcoming. Nyerere reasons thusly:

> In a country like ours, development depends primarily on the efforts and hard work of our own people, and their enthusiasm and belief that they and their country will benefit from whatever they do. How could anyone expect this enthusiasm and hard work to be forthcoming if the masses see that a few individuals in the society get very rich and live in great comfort, while the majority continue apparently forever in abject poverty.[38]

Implicit in this is the second proposition: if a hierarchy of power were to develop, those occupying its higher ranks would seek to transform power differentials into differential wealth and prestige rankings as well, thus precluding the attainment of the over-arching goal of an egalitarian society. The leadership code of the Arusha Declaration is the working out of this proposition *par excellence*. The code, which restricts the right of party and government leaders (including most salaried officials in both organizations) to have a second source of income, seeks to reconcile the need for an inequitable distribution of power (that is, for leaders) with the egalitarian goal by negating the ability of the leaders to become rich through the manipulation of their official positions.

The third ideological proposition is that for the leadership code to be effectively applied and for national programmes and projects to benefit the general citizenry, there must be mass participation in the Tanzanian political processes at all levels. This proposition was underscored by the February, 1971, TANU Guidelines (*Mwongozo*), the immediate result of the Tanzanian reaction to the January military coup in Uganda. The overthrow of Dr. Obote, who had been regarded by many Tanzanians as a popular and elected leader, raised in Tanzania the discussion of the problem of the great mass of citizens not having enough power to control their leaders or would-be leaders. Accordingly, in the Guidelines participation becomes very much a tool or an instrument: "if development is to benefit the people, the people must participate in considering, planning and implementing their development plans."[39] The Guidelines posit that the identity, legitimacy, penetration, distribution and participation crises (to use a 'modernization' concept) are linked in such a way that if they are to be met successfully they must all be satisfactorily dealt with at the same time. Redford has provided us with what is, in effect, a paraphrasing of these last two propositions on participation as the instrument with which to escape underdevelopment:

The participation idea . . . is supported on this point by historical and contemporary observation. Those who rule over others feather their own nests and make bear the nests of others. They convert their own advantages into prescriptive rights and transmit them to unborn generations as unearned privileges. They are often brutal and their positions of status humble those who are excluded. The researcher may find exceptions to these realities for limited periods, but there is no basis in experience for a belief that subjects of power can ensure their personal realization without direct or indirect participation in the power itself.[40]

Taken together the formulations of the Tanzanian ideology proclaim, as ultimately do all modern managerial ideologies, an identity of interests between the political structures organized on the basis of these propositions and the citizenry. But it also posits that should this identity not be made explicit through an egalitarian sharing in decision making and in the material aspects of progress, then the enthusiasm and hard work necessary for Tanzanian development will not be forthcoming.

In spite of this logic of the Tanzanian ideology, the existence of the consciously created and maintained hierarchies of party and government witnesses the fact that Tanzania finds it must confront successfully those basic economic and political problems common to all nations. In most underdeveloped countries the concentration of power in official bureaucracies is premised on the responsibility of government for ensuring economic development as the potential of any private sector appears small in comparison with the economic aspirations. Additionally, in the case of Tanzania, power is concentrated in these particular structures in the attempt to limit economic and social inequalities. The hope is that power will then be exercised in such a way as to minimize class and status differentials. If the arrangement is successful, the interrelatedness of the three components of social inequality—wealth, status, power—becomes dominated by the activities

18

of the state and party hierarchies and their members. It is in this sense that classes can be determined by power.[41] Yet the Tanzanian goal of human equality asserts that people should be able to participate in making "their own decisions on the things which affect them directly",[42] and consequently the concentration of power in hierarchies must be done in a way which permits of mass participation in its exercise. With their desire to concentrate power so as to facilitate economic growth and to control social inequalities and, at the same time, to have egalitarian participation in decision making the Tanzanian leadership is confronted with the contradiction: power concentration entails centralization to the few: participation requires devolution to the many.

Regardless of the neatness and internal coherence of the logical propositions of Tanzania's ideology it is one of the well-known disadvantages of any egalitarian movement that their "acquisition of power requires the development of hierarchy and discipline at some point".[43] Tanzania has not been spared this disadvantage. While the Tanganyika African National Union (TANU), as a nationalist movement in the colonial period, was able to gain independence with only sporadic reliance on hierarchical organizational methods, TANU as a government, balancing resources against objectives and, it must be remembered, attempting to maintain itself in power, has discovered that it must somehow reconcile the need for hierarchy with its development goal of participation.

The Tanzanian leadership themselves see an acceptable reconciliation being achieved in two ways. The first is a particular style of leadership which the entire range of 'leaders', including civil servants, are to adopt. Leaders are to persuade by talking (and talking) and by working with the people. Nyerere has emphasised that:

Leadership means talking and discussing with the people, explaining and persuading. It means making constructive suggestions, and working with the people to show by actions what it is you are urging them to do. It means being one of the people, and recognizing your equality with them.
But giving leadership does not mean usurping the role of the people. The people must make decisions about their own future through democratic procedures. Leadership cannot replace democracy; it must be a part of democracy.[44]

Emerging from and dependent upon each individual leader's status as 'one of the people', this style is to be based on a recognition of an equality with the people unhindered by significant disparities in mode

19

of living which might accrue to extensive wealth and prestige differentials. Nyerere, convinced that most leaders do things "according to set requirements without necessarily inner conviction",[45] sees the leadership code as establishing the basis of this approach to a hierarchy/participation reconciliation.

With the increasing concentration of the persuaders in the growing official bureaucracies the Tanzanian leaders have been made aware that it is not possible to rely solely upon a presumed socio-economic nearness of the rulers to the ruled. Thus they have tried a second way of balancing hierarchy and participation, namely the design of organizational structures which combine elements of both principles in a calculated fashion. It is the efficacy of these organizational arrangements in achieving a satisfactory mix of hierarchy and participation, output and equality, which this study examines.

That certain types of organization might be ill-suited to the attainment of certain goals is obvious. We have been reminded of the "not fully understood truism [that] certain values, ends-in-view, or ideologies carry with them implications for administrative organization that would not be relevant were the values, goals or ideologies different".[46] Both of Tanzania's objectives have led to a concentration of national power, but they carry different imperatives for the structuring of this concentration. The goal of increased production has required its concentration in government departments and parastatals organized along the "production principle"[47] — specialized branches with lines of decision-making running vertically from the field to the centre. In underdeveloped countries the dependence on the methods of production principle hierachies is partly a reflection of the notion often found in 'affluent' countries that if the poor are given the opportunity of participating in decision-making they will demand only services thus depleting limited resources without altering the basic causes of their poverty.[48] Tanzania has, as we will see, been faced with increased demand for services as participation levels have increased, but the goal of participation nonetheless requires that at various points along these governmental hierarchies opportunities be created for popular and lateral inputs to counter-balance the technical and hierarchical inputs into the decision-making process. These popular inputs are intended to be marshalled under the rubric of TANU.

The conflict between the organizational norms of production principle and participation appears at whatever level decision-making is undertaken; it is not resolved by the reallocation of administrative authority from higher to lower levels in an organizational deconcentration such as that undertaken by the Tanzanian government in 1972—1973. The following, from a recent study of participation in four small Wisconsin cities, poses Tanzania's dilemma concisely:

There is continual pressure toward bureaucratization... the expansion of agencies with specially-trained personnel entrusted with the performance of specific decisions and functions. Yet there is continual emphasis on the broadest possible public and group participation in decision-making processes... These are incompatible principles. Bureaucratization implies the insulation of decision-makers from outside influences, by definition not as competent as experts are to judge the relevant range of facts, nor to balance the objectives desired. Participation implies the right and duty of the public to intervene in the determination of decisions.[49]

This study focuses primarily on the efficacy of popular inputs into the decision-making processes of the government hierarchies at levels below the centre. More than 93 per cent of the people of Tanzania live in the rural areas,[50] the periphery. If they are to participate in making decisions about the "things which affect them directly", much of this participation must occur at the village/ward, district, and regional levels. To make this possible certain roles and organizations have been created to facilitate, *inter alia*, the participation of the rural populace in the decisions of the "production principle" hierarchies which stretch out from Dar es Salaam. In this study I have examined in Mwanza Region the activities of intendedly participatory roles and organizations which have hitherto been relatively neglected in the literature on Tanzanian development.

One of these, the village/ward development committee, is physically in the rural areas and provides a cutting edge, a locus of direct contact between the government and the people. As a vehicle of direct participation it is a point at which citizens themselves, or representatives who live in constant and intimate proximity with them, have at least the formal opportunity of affecting the activities of the government departments which penetrate into the periphery. The second participatory element which I have looked at is the role of the M.P. A parliament is usually evaluated as part of a system of "overhead democracy" in which representatives sent by the people control, as their surrogates, the national polity at its centre.[51] This aspect of the M.P.'s role in Tanzania is ceremonial and symbolic. My concern has been the effectiveness of M.P.'s as surrogate participants at the sub-centre levels. The role of the Regional and Area Commissioners is the third participatory element discussed. As coordinating, political officers in the government they have a responsibility to increase the capacity of the hierarchy to bring about change in the society and, at the same time, to ensure a degree of popular control over many of the activities of the ministerial departments. The Janus-faced quality[52] of the role of the Commissioners is also a feature of the development committees and, in Tanzania, the role of the M.P. They are expected to be agents of both hierarchy and participation. On the one hand they are to mobilize support for policies, programmes and projects of the central government whilst on the other hand they are expected to ensure that central government at its various levels acts in a way that takes account of the desires and demands of the citizenry.

The Perspective

The Tanzanian political system has historically been dominated by a single structure—the central government bureaucracy. Although within itself it has not been free of the common ills of inter-departmental conflict and the variability and ambitions of its individual members, the structure as an analytical entity has controlled the most of 'what there is to get', and, a not unrelated phenomenon, its role occupants have in many ways managed to allocate to themselves a more than goodly portion of the power, wealth and prestige that the national polity has had to allocate.

The notion of a dominant structure is fairly standard. Almond and Powell for instance mention that "we may find in some systems one or a very few structures perform all political functions. The leader of a primitive band may occupy such a dominant position."[53] In discussing 'modern' societies, 'modernization' scholars seem to rule out a dominant structure in defining a 'modern' society in terms of differentiation. We note however that their analyses of organizational structures within what are identified as more complex societies do consider their "salience" ("the relative importance of the particular structure in the performance of that function in the system") and the general tendency for most 'modern' as well as 'traditional' political structures to be "multi-functional".[54] It would seem logical that salience and multi-functionality could extend to the point that the parti-

22

cular structure was dominant in the performance of all political functions. This point is largely ignored in those otherwise useful compendiums which deal with participation mainly in terms of the response of voters and with politics in Africa mainly in terms of the tendency for one party to oust all other from the would-be institutions of parliamentary democracy.[55] To put it more crudely, descriptions of how individuals and organizations come to be, for instance, M.P.'s or the only party do not tell us *what* they do, or *how much* they do relative to others, they do not tell us who is participating in making decisions over various resources. And they can be totally misleading when the parliament or the party do not in fact have much of a say in such decisions.

The present day dominance of the central government bureaucracy in Tanzania is a colonial heritage. Although formally, after the Treaty of Versailles, a mandated territory of the League of Nations, the rule of the British in Tanganyika, and before them that of the Germans, tended to the "bureaucratic authoritarianism" common to "modern colonialism" everywhere in Africa.[56] For almost the entire duration of the colonial overrule the state structure undertook to perform all the political functions normally attributed to an entire national political system, a situation symbolized until August, 1961, by the telegraphic address—"political"—of the key "administrative" agents of the state, the Provincial and District Commissioners. Granted there are certain qualifications to be made. The colonial government was at times reacting to the African initiative or the anticipated African response; it had to come to terms with the largely encapsulated societies within and around which it operated; in the decade or so prior to independence it did make some attempt to create representative structures for the performance, at least ritualistically, of certain political functions; and in the final years the nationalist movement and others were able to successfully exert influence through the United Nations and Westminster. To the extent that there was a territorial system, however, it was clearly the imperial hierarchy which was the most effective structure politically. Policies, programmes, and projects were generated, aggregated, decided upon, and implemented in processes directed by the government bureaucracy.

It is perhaps important here to dispel notions of the neutrality of the colonial civil servant. The difficulty of separating the political from the administrative, value from fact, is a commonplace in the study of government. The following quotation from an essay by Eisenstadt

23

reveals, however, that the implications of this for the analysis of colonial rule require underscoring. Eisenstadt has written that the pre-independence bureaucracies seemed to function,

.. highly apolitically. They did not meddle in politics, and they kept up the ideal of a politically neutral civil service. They were also apolitical in that they never really participated in the indigenous political life of the country in which they served. Their very limited goals were set by the colonial powers, who were not responsible to the political groups and opinions of the countries which they ruled. They did not perform any important functions and activities among the 'colonial' population, or in the articulation and aggregation of the political interests of that population.[57]

That this view has no validity with regard to colonial rule in the area covered by this study should be evident from the discussion of pre-independence political organization in the following chapter.

More generally this view of the neutrality of the imperial civil service has been described as a "myth" rooted in the reluctance of the colonial civil servants to realize that "almost anything they did altered to some extent the distribution of goods and services and, above all, the focus of power within the community".[58]

Stressing the political dominance of the bureaucracy during the colonial period may be misleading given its limited resources and the vastness of the territory. And it should be recalled that whilst the bureaucracy was dominant in the territorial system the territorial system itself had an extremely limited capacity to penetrate the many encapsulated societies of the territory. Heuristically though the dominant structure claim is helpful in establishing an analytical baseline for this study. The egalitarian goals of independent Tanzania call for a lessening of this bureaucratic dominance in the national political system.

The recognition of this colonial heritage has formed part of the background to the continuing debate in Tanzania as to the proper role of TANU.[59] Bureaucratic dominance, referred to as the "colonial government structure", was rejected outright in the TANU Guidelines:

For people who have been slaves or have been oppressed, exploited and disregarded by colonialism or capitalism, 'development' means 'liberation'. Any action that gives them more say in determining their affairs and in running their lives is one of development, even if it does not offer them better health or more bread. Any action that reduces their say in determining their affairs or running their lives is not progressive and retards them even if the action brings better health and more bread.[60]

Organizations, however, do not relinquish a position of dominance with any less regret or struggle than individuals, groups, or classes. We are aware that the impact of inequalities is to be found in the differentials, the important thing being not how much of something one has in absolute terms, but what one has relative to others.[61] Political/administrative organizations are also involved in these zero-sum conflicts. Organizational structures have been known to survive the goals which they were created to attain, and to use "slogans" to mask the interests of their members.[62] In this study we have examined, as the Tanzanian leaders themselves have also in the past several years, the conflict between popular and production principle organizations and roles over the power to make decisions.

In the last decade or so before independence there was a heightened competition within Tanzania over the power to make national decisions including those decisions taken within the national system which would effect the people in the periphery. Some of this competition was at the instigation of the dominant imperial political/administrative structure itself, for instance the setting up of the Legislative Council and local councils. Other competitive organizations entered the conflict more on their own initiative—tribal unions, a nationalist movement, trade unions, co-operatives, *ad hoc* groups. This was permitted, almost guided in some cases, by the officials of the imperial bureaucracy in that last decade. They were projecting a future model in which the activities of civil servants would no longer be ultimately controlled by British political institutions, but by the parliament of the independent state-to-be and its appendages—special publics, a free press, politicians and political machines.

The model which the colonialists had in mind, a liberal democracy structured along the formally pluralist lines of Great Britain contradicted the "bureaucratic authoritarianism" model presented by their own behaviour. The formal model did not survive but a few years after independence. It is rejected in the strategy of the Tanzanian leaders to make TANU the only alternative structure, and, hopefully, the focal or dominant one.[63] To this end the National Assembly and other organizations (unions, co-operatives, the press, local government) were taken over by TANU and/or its government.[64] Whereas in a parliamentary model the citizen may theoretically have a number of representational structures which provide him with the opportunity for participating in decision making, in Tanzania he now relies solely upon the one party.

The swift move to attempted focalization in the form of a one-party state has been one of the universals of the politics of independent Africa. In many cases it has been followed soon thereafter by a no-party state in which popular participation falls off drastically from the levels attained in the periods immediately prior to and after independence.[65] The Ivory Coast is a case in point:

Those who have led this movement [P.D.C.I.] have taken over the bureaucratic structure against which these styles of politics were directed: not only is the structure itself perpetuated intact, but its principles are in process of extension to the party and representational structures which previously embodied value of popular expression.[66]

For Tanzania it has been argued by Bienen that the creation of a one-party state does not necessarily have to result in the implantation of bureaucratic rather than popular principles in the party, and he goes on to suggest that "we must carefully examine both the organizational ties obtaining and the norms which govern specific situations" and to observe that "in this last, the role of ideology in a political system is crucial".[67]

The propounded Tanzanian ideology provides two conflicting sets of norms to govern Bienen's "specific situations". One is hierarchy stemming from the goal of economic development and the consequent need for the rational organization of work, the other is participation in decision making stemming from the goal of equality. If the emphasis is on the former, then the bureaucracy will extend to the party its principles, while if the emphasis is on the latter then presumably the participatory principles of the party will dominate. It is important here to remember that TANU has both hierarchical and participatory principles. As Nyerere stated in 1962, TANU was to be a "two-way all weather road along which the purposes, plans and problems of Government can travel to the people at the same time as the ideas, desires and misunderstandings of the people can travel direct to the government".[68] Historically TANU developed both as a party created largely by an urbanized elite and as a movement created largely from localized rural resistance to colonial attempts to change the people's ways of doing things.[69] The TANU village/ward development committees and the M.P.'s are primarily reflections of the movement or participatory aspect of TANU. They are chosen locally and tend to represent local interests. In their "organizational ties" with the government bureaucracy they are involved implicitly in a dispute over who is eligible to

26

make which decisions and which rules or principles are to determine the process. In other words the right of theoretically rational bureaucrats to make decisions undisturbed by the irrational (by definition) public is being contested, the behavioural model bequeathed by the colonialists is being challenged.

In the case of the Regional and Area Commissioners they tend to represent the party as opposed to the movement aspect of TANU. The conflict involved in their "organizational ties" is mostly a competition in which officials of central government compete with centrally appointed officials of TANU over the power to make decisions. Should the Commissioners win this competition there is no assurance that the victory would increase participation. For the rural people it may mean nothing more than a switch of power from one hierarchy to another, neither of which is necessarily more tolerant than the other of the participation of the public in decision making. Whether the Commissioners are successful is nonetheless of importance for Tanzania's attempts to increase participation. As field extensions of the Tanzanian system of overhead democracy there is the possibility that should they be able to gain a controlling position *vis a vis* the government bureaucracy then they might be able to establish new rules for decision-making.

The broad concern of this study has been the efficacy of those roles and organizations in Mwanza Region which have been created to increase participation in the decision making of the national political system at sub-centre levels. As the government bureaucracy has been dominant historically, the study deals with the extent to which this situation has been ameliorated. As all the would-be ameliorating roles and organizations in some way have a TANU label, the study is also concerned with TANU, especially its participatory aspect.

Recent studies which have looked at the District Councils, development committees and government departments at the regional and district levels have indicated that participation, in terms of a lessening of bureaucratic control over decision making, has not increased.[70] The dominance of government officials and the predominant attention given to the co-ordination and implementation of central government programmes remains as much a feature of their activities as it did during the colonial days of the district and regional 'teams' and the Native Authorities. The present study contributes further empirical material to this growing body of information by examining other

points of contact, 'organizational ties', between hierarchy and participation in rural Tanzania. The village/ward development committees,
the M.P.'s and the Commissioners are all intended to provide the
citizenry with the opportunity to influence decision making over the
expenditure of national resources and the activities of national organizations.

Information Gathering

From September, 1968, to February, 1969, I was resident at the then
University College, Dar es Salaam. During this time I made three trips
to Mwanza Region to discuss my research with government and
TANU officials. From March, 1969, through July, 1970, I resided at
the regional centre, Mwanza town.

From April, 1969, I was given access[71] to most current government
files at the regional, district, divisional and ward levels, to District
Council and Nyanza Co-operative Union files (at Union, Zonal and
Primary Society levels), and to several TANU files at the regional,
district, and ward levels.[72] I undertook four return trips to Dar es
Salaam to follow up references in the headquarters of the economic
planning, regional administration, and agricultural ministries. I returned to Dar es Salaam and Mwanza in December, 1971 and in May,
1972 to collect further material and to discuss my conclusions with
other observers and with government and party officials.

Approximately half of my time in Mwanza Region was spent 'on
safari' in the villages and district centres. Countless meetings and discussions, formal and informal, with farmers and with government, co-
operative and party officials and employees provided the information
and the insights upon which much of this study is based. Many of the
discussions with officials were quotable in that I employed a prepared
schedule of questions, took notes in their presence, and informed them
that their responses might be referred to in later reports. In those
instances in which I was requested not to make reference by name or
position this qualification has been observed.

I undertook three surveys as part of the University's Rural Research
Project. They have been used in this study in several instances to
provide more detail for an understanding of Mwanza Region and
various organizations. They have not been used to validate arguments

through the application of tests of correlation and association. The people who were so interviewed do however form part of the basis of my perception of the Region and thus though I have not relied extensively or directly on the survey material (preferring instead to use documented material) I shall discuss briefly the sampling and field procedures.

For the Project's survey three Census enumeration areas were chosen randomly in each of Mwanza's four districts. The people in two areas in Geita District refused to participate in the Project's farm investigations and a fourth area was chosen as a replacement by the Geita Area Commissioner and Area Secretary. These thirteen areas covered the range of social, economic and political differences to be found in Mwanza Region.[73]

The Project's investigations at the farm level included four questionnaires; part of the fourth one included my peasant survey. The peasant survey was carried out between October and November, 1969. As it was undertaken during the fourth visit to the farmers by interviewers from the Project it benefited from the mutual confidence which had been established. One of the Project's three areas in Ukerewe District was not included in the peasant survey due to lack of time. In the other ten areas the questionnaire was administered to the heads of 193 households selected from stratified random samples within each of the enumeration areas. The heads of households were selected in meetings of all the TANU cell leaders of the Census area. Lists of cell leaders were taken first from the Census documents in Dar es Salaam and then completed and brought up-to-date in the field. In each area six cells were randomly selected and then four members from each of the six were chosen. This provided six clusters of four within each area. In one area in Mwanza District (Nyanza) one cell unit was mistakenly omitted from the Project surveys, and in another (Sanjo) one ten cell unit could not be located. For the peasant survey in all the areas except one a couple of farmers were not interviewed because of sickness, temporary absence, permanent movement from the area since the survey had begun, or death. Those interviewed were distributed as follows:

Table 1. *Peasant survey*

District	Division	1965—1970 M.P. Constituency	Number of Respondents
	Busega	Mwanza East	20
Mwanza	Nyanza	Mwanza West	18
	Sanjo	Mwanza East	14
Geita	Nyang'hwale	Geita South	19
	Busanda	Geita North	20
Ukerewe	Mumbuga	Ukerewe	21
	Mumulambo	Ukerewe	19
	Ibindo	Kwimba North	17
Kwimba	Inonelwa	Kwimba South	23
	Kakora	Kwimba South	22
Total			193

During April—May, 1969 I carried out a survey of TANU cell leaders. In twelve of the enumeration areas cell leaders who were not selected for the Project surveys were administered a separate questionnaire prepared by myself. 146 cell leaders were interviewed; 23 other cell leaders had been chosen for the farm surveys. The total universe of cell leaders in the enumeration areas was approximately[74] two hundred. Excluding the 23 included in the farm surveys, the cell leader questionnaire was administered to roughly 82 per cent of the eligible universe.

The enumeration areas varied greatly in population and this was reflected accordingly in the number of cell leaders in each area. At the extremes, the enumeration area in Mumulambo in Ukerewe District had 40 cell leaders whilst Ibindo in Kwimba District had five. Consequently the interviews were distributed very unevenly amongst the districts. The distribution of cell leaders interviewed is as follows:

30

Table 2. *Cell leader survey*

District	Division	1965—1970 M.P. Constituency	Number of Respondents
Mwanza	Busega	Mwanza East	10
	Nyanza	Mwanza West	9
	Sanjo	Mwanza East	13
Geita	Kasungamile	Geita East	10
	Nyang'hwale	Geita South	13
	Busanda	Geita North	18
Ukerewe	Ilangala	Ukerewe	12
	Mumbuga	Ukerewe	21
	Mumulambo	Ukerewe	23
Kwimba	Ibindo	Kwimba North	4
	Inonelwa	Kwimba South	4
	Kakora	Kwimba North	9
Total			146

A survey of 'leaders' using a questionnaire designed by myself was carried out during July and August, 1969. A total of 584 employees and officials of TANU, the government and co-operatives were interviewed in the thirteen enumeration areas of the Project. In each area two interviewers spent one week. They interviewed as many individuals as they could locate who were either employed or held a position in one of these three organizations, excluding cell leaders and Comworks personnel. One week in each area generally exhausted the possible number of interviewees.

As with the cell leaders, the disparity of population between enumeration areas tended to be reflected in an inter-area disparity in the numbers interviewed. This was largely obviated by permitting the interviewers to go outside the enumeration area to surrounding areas in cases where the actual universe was too small. There was also a tendency for disproportionately large numbers of primary school teachers and workers in clinics and dispensaries to be interviewed. This was partly a result of the fact that these categories are the bulk of government personnel, with the exceptions of Comworks, in the rural areas. This tendency was controlled by giving instructions to stop interviewing individuals in such categories after a particular number, which varied with the area, had been interviewed. The 584 interviews were distributed as follows:

Table 3. *'Leader' Survey I*

Elected Ward Branch TANU leaders	97
Committeemen (38)	
Chairmen (14)	
Delegates to District Conference (8)	
Youth League leaders (7)	
Women's (UWT) leaders (18)	
TANU elders (2)	
Paid Ward Branch TANU officials	25
Secretaries (15)	
Money Collectors (8)	
Messengers (2)	
Elected Primary Co-operative Society leaders	97
Committeemen (71)	
Chairmen (18)	
Officers other than Chairmen (8)	
Paid Primary Co-operative Society officials	84
Secretaries (30)	
Assistant Secretaries (21)	
Clerical Workers (14)	
Messengers (3)	
Labourers (4)	
Zonal employees (12)	
Government officials — I	97
Trained health personnel (29)	
Trained veterinary or agricultural extension agents (19)	
Trained rural development agents (8)	
Ward Executive Officers (14)	
Divisional Secretaries (3)	
Revenue Collectors (16)	
Others (8)	
Government Workers — II	65
Clerical (10)	
Unskilled (55)	
Teachers	124
Grade A (19)	
Grade B (8)	
Grade C (45)	
Grade unspecified (26)	
Headmasters (17)	
TAPA (1)	
TYL teacher/leaders (8)	
Others	5
District Councillors (3)	
Village Development Committee Chairman (1)	
TAPA official (1)	
Total	584

Table 4. *'Leader' Survey II*

District	Division	Constituency	Total
	Busega	Mwanza East	72
Mwanza	Nyanza	Mwanza West	42
	Sanjo	Mwanza East	56
	Kharumwa	Geita South	22
Geita	Kasungamile	Geita East	40
	Nyang'hwale	Geita South	33
	Busanda	Geita North	60
	Ilangala	Ukerewe	23
Ukerewe	Mumbuga	Ukerewe	48
	Mumulambo	Ukerewe	44
	Ibindo	Kwimba North	16
Kwimba	Inonelwa	Kwimba South	58
	Kakora	Kwimba South	70
Total			584

The peasant, cell leader and 'leader' questionnaires were all pre-tested—the first two in Shinyanga District and the third in rural areas close to Mwanza town.[75] The cell leader questionnaire was written in English and translated into Swahili by the interviewers who in their training had had group discussions on the correctness of various translations. The peasant and 'leader' questionnaires were written and administered in Swahili. I was assisted in writing the Swahili by S. K. Msuya and M. Mwambara. The phrasing of some questions was altered after the pretesting. The peasant and cell leader questionnaires were administered by Sukuma and, in the case of Ukerewe, Kerewe students of the Dar es Salaam University. The leader questionnaire was administered by students of the Nyegezi Social Training Centre selected on the basis of their knowledge of Swahili and ability to establish a good rapport with the people in the rural area.[76]

Notes

1. Ali Mazrui, "Tanzaphilia", *Transition*, 31 (1967); a letter of reply to Mazrui's article by A. Mohiddin, *Transition*, 32 (1967); C. T. Leys, "Inter-Alia—or Tanzaphilia and all that", *Transition*, 34 (1968); G. Andrew Maguire, *Towards 'Uhuru' in Tanzania: The Politics of Participation*, Cambridge: Cambridge University Press, 1969, p. xviii.

2. Maguire, *op.cit.*, pp xvii, 16; Harvey Glickman, "Dilemmas of Political Theory in an African Context: The Ideology of Julius Nyerere", in, Jeffrey Butler and A. A. Castagno (eds.), *Boston University Papers on Africa*, New York: Praeger, 1967, pp. 195—217; David Feldman, "The Economics of Ideology: Some Problems of Achieving Rural Socialism in Tanzania", in, C. T. Leys (ed.) *Politics and Change in Developing Countries: Studies in the Theory and Practice of Development*, Cambridge: Cambridge University Press, 1969, p. 86; Brian van Arkadie, "Planning in Tanzania", presented to the Crisis in Planning Conference, University of Sussex, June—July, 1969, p. 15.

3. See the Prentice-Hall series on the "modernization of traditional societies" edited by Wilbert E. Moore and Neil J. Smelser and the same publishers' series on "foundations of modern sociology" edited by Alex Inkeles.

4. Fred W. Riggs, "The Dialectics of Developmental Conflict", *Comparative Political Studies*, I, 2 (July, 1968), p. 199. See, also, Max F. Millikan, "Equity versus Productivity in Economic Development," in, Myron Weiner (ed.), *Modernization: The Dynamics of Growth*, New York: Basic Books, 1966.

5. Julius K. Nyerere, *Freedom and Unity*, Dar es Salaam: Oxford University Press, 1966, p. 7. Also, Nyerere, "Principles and Development", in his, *Freedom and Socialism*, Dar es Salaam: Oxford University Press, 1968, pp. 187—206.

6. Raymond Aron, *Progress and Disillusion: The Dialectics of Modern Society*, London: Pall Mall, 1968, p. 4.

7. S. N. Eisenstadt, *The Political System of Empires*, New York: Free Press, 1963.

8. C. J. Friedrich, *Man and His Government*, New York: McGraw-Hill, 1964, chapter 26; Victor A. Thompson, *Modern Organization*, New York: Alfred A. Knopf, 1961; B. B. Schaffer, "The Deadlock in Development Administration," in, Leys (ed.) *op.cit.*, especially pp. 190—199.

9. Barrington Moore, Jr., *Political Power and Social Theory*, Cambridge: Harvard University Press, 1958, pp. 1—11; Robert A. Dahl, *Modern Political Analysis*, Englewood Cliffs: Prentice-Hall, 1963, p. 17; on the need for hierarchical structures to meet the political problems of recently independent African states, see, Immanuel Wallerstein, *Africa: The Politics of Independence*, New York: Vintage, 1961, p. 154.

10. Amitai Etzioni, *Modern Organizations*, Englewood Cliffs: Prentice-Hall, 1964, p. 58, and more elaborately in, Etzioni, *A Comparative Analysis of Complex Organisations*, New York: Free Press, 1961, pp. 79—86.

11. *Tanzania Second Five-Year Plan, 1969—1974*, Vol. I, p. 4; Presidential Circular No. 1 of 1969, "The Development of Ujamaa Villages", 20 March 1969; Presidential Circular No. 1 of 1970, "The Establishment of Workers' Councils, Executive Boards and Boards of Directors", 10 February 1970.

12. Philip Selznick, *Leadership in Administration*, New York: Harper and Row, 1957, pp. 115—116.

13. C. Argyis, *Integrating the Individual and the Organization*, New York: Wiley, 1964.

14. Reinhard Bendix, *Work and Authority in Industry*, New York: Harper Torchbooks, 1963, p. 9.

15. Oskar Lange, *Political Economy*, New York: Macmillan, 1963, Vol. I, chapter 2; Dahl, *op.cit.*, p. 20.

16. Aron, *loc.cit.*

17. Lucian W. Pye, *Aspects of Political Development*, Boston: Little Brown, 1966, pp. 45—47. This association is of course one of the major themes of social science.

18. For some opposing views, see, C. Wright Mills, *The Power Elite*, New York: Oxford University Press, 1959; Herbert Marcuse, *One-Dimensional Man*, London: Routledge and Kegan Paul, 1964.

19. Joseph LaPalombara, "Values and Ideologies in the Administrative Evolution of Western Constitutional Systems", in, Ralph Braibanti (ed.), *Political and Administrative Development*, Durham: Duke University Press, 1969, pp. 166—219. This crisis notion of history has been extensively applied to the current experiences of the underdeveloped countries in the Princeton University Press series on political development.

20. Fred W. Riggs, *Administration in Developing Countries*, Boston: Houghton Mifflin, 1964; "The Theory of Political Development", in, James C. Charlesworth (ed.); *Contemporary Political Analysis*, New York: Free Press, 1967, pp. 317—349; "Bureaucracy and Political Development", in, Joseph LaPalombara (ed.), *Bureaucracy and Political Development*, Princeton: Princeton University Press, 1963, pp. 120—167; "The Political Context of Development Administration", *Public Administration*, XXV, 1 (1965), pp. 70—79.

21. The backing for this approach is fairly explicit in Apter's study of modernization in which he sees "potentiality" and equity as the opposing principles and nations as constrained to deal with potentiality and the establishment of authority first. David Apter, *The Politics of Modernization*, Chicago: University of Chicago Press, 1965.

22. Bert F. Hoselitz and Ann R. Willner, "Economic Development, Political Strategies, and American Aid", in, Morton A. Kaplan (ed.), *The Revolution in World Politics*, New York: John Wiley, 1962, p. 355.

23. The points is made in, Teresa Hayter, *Aid as Imperialism*, Harmondsworth: Penguin, 1971.

24. With respect to Soviet attempts to mobilize a surplus out of a traditional agricultural system with a large subsistence element, see, M. Lewin, *Russian Peasants and Soviet Power*, London; Allen and Unwin, 1968; Paul Baran, *The Political Economy of Growth*, New York: Monthly Review Press, 1960, pp. 278—279.

25. Hoselitz and Willner, *loc.cit.*

26. John D. Montgomery, "A Royal Invitation: Variations on Three Classic Themes", in, Montgomery and William J. Siffin (eds.): *Approaches to Development: Politics, Administration and Change*, New York; McGraw-Hill, 1966, p. 265.

27. "Local Development in Africa", report of a conference held at the Foreign Service Institute, Department of State, Washington, D.C. July, 1967, p. 5.

28. Martin Oppenheimer, "Participative Techniques of Social Integration", *Our Generation* (Montreal), VI, 3 (1969), pp. 106—107. A *locus classicus* of participative techniques is, Douglas McGregor, *The Human Side of Enterprise*, New York: McGraw-Hill, 1960.

29. Sidney Verba, *Small Groups and Political Behaviour*, Princeton: Princeton University Press, 1961, pp. 220—221, quoted in, W. J. M. Mackenzie, *Politics and Social Science*, Harmondsworth: Penguin, 1967, p. 185.

30. On participation as an 'ultimate' value, see, E. S. Redford, *Democracy in the Administrative State*, New York: Oxford University Press, 1968, chapter 1.

31. Redfield discusses the presence in all societies of hierarchies as well as participation thus allowing our understanding to be "advanced as a kind of dialectic of viewpoint" in which we look for the balance struck between these contradictory elements. Robert Redfield. *The Little Community*, Chicago: University of Chicago Press, 1955, pp. 132—148.

32. Nyerere, *op.cit.*, 1968, p. 2, and at p. 12: "the increased output of wealth... is the most urgent thing. But we cannot allow this need to destroy our belief in human equality and human dignity. On the contrary, we have to organize our expansion of wealth in such a way as to give the maximum possible emphasis to these other values."

33. For the 'development of underdevelopment' approach see, Andre Gundar Frank, *Latin America: Underdevelopment or Revolution*, New York: Monthly Review Press, 1969; Walter Rodney, *How Europe Underdeveloped Africa*, Dar es Salaam: Tanzania Publishing House, 1972; and E. A. Brett, *Colonialism and underdevelopment in East Africa*, London: Heineman, 1973.

34. See, Frank, *op.cit.*, pp. 248—268.

35. William Tordoff, "Development Politics and Administration", *Mawazo*, 1, 3 (June, 1968), p. 56. For discussions of Arusha and associated measures, see, Henry Bienen, *Tanzania: Party Transformation and Economic Development*, Princeton: Princeton University Press, 1970, expanded edition, chapter 13; and, Ali A. Mazrui, "Socialism as a Mode of International Protest", in Robert I. Rotberg and Mazrui (eds.), *Protest and Power in Black Africa*, New York: Oxford University Press, 1970, pp. 1139—1152.

36. Anthony Ellman, "Development of *Ujamaa* Farming", *Kroniek van Afrika*, 1971, 2, pp. 113—130.

37. This statement is based on documents available in the Ministry of Economic Affairs and Development Planning. In a draft speech which was to have been delivered by F. Byabato, a Devplan official, at a Moshi seminar in October, 1969, it was observed that the Arusha measures to increase participation did in fact lead to a fall-off in economic growth in the two subsequent years.

38. Nyerere, *op.cit.*, 1968, p. 198.

39. The Guidelines have been reprinted in full in, *The Nationalist*, 22 February 1971; *Mbioni* (Dar es Salaam), 8 (1971), pp. 4—17; and as the "Dar es Salaam Declaration" in, *Mazungumzo*, (Michigan), I, 3 (Spring, 1971), pp. 59—66.

40. Redford, *op.cit.*, p. 7.

41. P. C. Lloyd, *Africa in Social Change*, Harmondsworth: Penguin, 1967, pp. 304—330. See, also, W. G. Runciman, *Relative Deprivation and Social Justice*, London: Routledge and Kegan Paul, 1966, chapter 3.

42. Nyerere, *op.cit.*, 1968, p. 349.

43. Moore, Jr., *op.cit.*, p. 14.

44. From, Julius K. Nyerere, "Freedom and Development", *The Nationalist*, 18 October 1968. These particular admonitions are used in the TANU Youth League's leadership manual: Ingemar Sallnäs, *Youth Leadership*, Dar es Salaam; TANU Youth League publication, n.d., *circa* 1969.

45. See, report of a speech by Nyerere in, *The Standard*, 8 June 1969.

46. LaPalombara, in, Braibanti, *op.cit.*, p. 169.

47. P. J. D. Wiles, *The Political Economy of Communism*, Oxford: Blackwell, 1964, pp. 43—44.

48. Edward C. Banfield and James Q. Wilson, *City Politics*, Cambridge: Harvard University Press, 1963; Hans B. Spiegel (ed.), *Citizen Participation in Urban Development*, Washington: Institute for Applied Behavioral Science, 1968, Vol. 1, sections 2—4; Daniel P. Moynihan, *Maximum Feasible Misunderstanding*, New York: Free Press, 1969.

49. Robert R. Alford, *Bureaucracy and Participation*, Chicago: Rand McNally, 1969, p. 25; on India, see, A. H. Hanson, *The Process of Planning*, London: Oxford University Press, 1966, pp. 1—24, 394—443, 525—538.

50. "Recorded Population Changes, 1948—67, Tanzania", Dar es Salaam: Central Statistical Bureau, August, 1968, p. 6.

51. Overhead democracy is an expression used by Redford, *op.cit.*, pp. 70—71. It refers to political control at the top of government and regards official bureaucracies as neutral policy implementors.

52. The generalized nature of the problem is discussed in Harumi Befu, "The Political Relation of the Village to the State", *World Politics*, XIX, 4 (July, 1967), pp. 601—620; Max Gluckman, "Inter-hierarchical Roles", in Marc J. Swartz (ed.), *Local-level Politics*, London: University of London Press, 1969, pp. 69—93. For further discussion with reference to the colonial period, see, A. I. Richards, *East African Chiefs*, London: Faber and Faber, 1959; L. A. Fallers, *Bantu Bureaucracy*, Cambridge: Heffer, 1956; R. G. Abrahams, *The Political Organization of Unyamwezi*, Cambridge: Cambridge University Press, 1967.

53. Gabriel A. Almond and G. Bingham Powell, Jr., *Comparative Politics*, Boston: Little, Brown, 1966, p. 31. Also, David Easton, *A Systems Analysis of Political Life*, New York: Wiley, 1965, pp. 92—99, 205—211; Samuel P. Huntington, *Political Order in Changing Societies*, New Haven: Yale University Press, 1968, pp. 109 *et. seq.*

54. Almond and Powell, *op.cit.*, pp. 118, 31. Of equal importance: "some of the functions designated as characteristic of political systems are often monopolized by particular levels ..." W. H. Morris-Jones, "Political Recruitment and Political Development", in Leys (ed.), *op.cit.*, p. 115.

55. Several works on Tanzania have side-stepped this pitfall. See, Bienen, *op.cit.*; Rolf E. Vente, *Planning Processes*, Munich: Weltforum (IFO), 1970; Raymond F. Hopkins, *Political Roles in a New State*, New Haven: Yale University Press, 1971.

56. James S. Coleman and Carl G. Rosberg (eds.), *Political Parties and National Integration in Tropical Africa*, Berkeley: University of California Press, 1964, p. 659. They continue: "it is believed that in most instances the really determinative factor in the orientation of the present party elites to the political order has been their exposure to bureaucratic centralism during the colonial period. In a sense, one-party rule and 'national party' government are simply postcolonial terms for the same phenomenon. In the realm of government and administration in Africa, there is far more continuity than innovation."

57. S. N. Eisenstadt, "Problems of Emerging Bureaucracies in Developing Areas and New States", in, Wilbert E. Moore and Bert F. Hoselitz (eds.), *Industrialisation and Society*, The Hague: Mouton, 1963, p. 160. During the dyarchy Nyerere apparently put some faith in the notion of a neutral civil service. See, Chief Minister's Circular Letter No. 1 of 1960, "The Relationship between the Civil Service, Political Parties and Members of Legislative Council", October, 1960. This position was soon changed to a demand for a "politicized" civil service. See the views of former Head of the Civil Service which chart this change. J. A. Namata, "The Civil Service in Tanzania: A Selection from Speeches and Writings", Dar es Salaam: Government Printer, 1967.

58. Victor C. Ferkiss, "The Role of the Public Services in Nigeria and Ghana", in Ferrel Heady and Sybil L. Stokes (eds.), *Papers in Comparative Public Administration*, Ann Arbor: University of Michigan, 1962, pp. 174—175.

59. See, for instance, the feature articles and the letters to the editor of *The Nationalist* during May—June, 1970 and February—April, 1971.

60. "TANU Guidelines", February, 1971, in, *Mbioni*, VI, 8 (1971). Also: "We in Tanganyika would reject the creation of a rural class system even if it could be proved that this gives the largest over-all production increase. We would reject this method of securing national economic improvement because it would defeat the total purpose of change, which is the wellbeing of all our people." Nyerere, *op.cit.*, 1966, p. 237.

61. W. G. Runciman, *op.cit.*, 1966, chapter 2: Nyerere, *op.cit.*, 1968, pp. 234—236.

62. On the latter point, see, S. Ossowski, "Old Notions and New Problems", in, Andre Beteille (ed.), *Social Inequality*, Harmondsworth: Penguin, 1969, p. 86. On the idea of the bureaucracy as a political structure which attempts to maximize functional dominance over other structures in a political system, see, S. N. Eisenstadt, "Bureaucracy, Bureaucratization, and Debureaucratization", *Administrative Science Quarterly*, III, December, 1959.

63. "Since the attainment of independence, rapid political evolution has taken place in which TANU has emerged as a crucial organization dominating all sectors and institutions of society. The process wherein a single organization or institution becomes dominant shall be referred to as *focalization*." William H. Friedland, "The Evolution of Tanganyika's Political System", in Stanley Diamond and Fred G. Burke (eds.), *The Transformation of East Africa*, New York: Basic Books, 1966, p. 299. As this study

demonstrates Friedland's analysis was drastically in conflict with the reality, that is TANU did not become the focal organization. The concept itself however is useful.

64. *Ibid*, pp. 299—309; Harvey Glickman, "One-party System in Tanganyika", *The Annals of the American Academy of Political and Social Science*, March, 1965, pp. 136—149; William Tordoff, *Government and Politics in Tanzania*, Nairobi: East African Publishing House, 1967; J. P. W. B. McAuslan and Y. P. Ghai, "Constitutional Innovation and Political Stability in Tanzania", *Journal of Modern African Studies*, IV, 9 (1966); John Saul, "The Nature of Tanzania's Political System", *Journal of Commonwealth Political Studies*, X, 2 and 3, 1972. This last is interesting as Saul has adopted the hierarchy-participation contradiction as a central analytical tool.

65. Immanuel Wallerstein, "The Decline of the Party in Single-Party African States", in, Joseph LaPalombara and Myron Weiner (eds.), *Political Parties and Political Development*, Princeton: Princeton University Press, 1966, pp. 201—214.

66. Martin Staniland, "Single-Party Regimes and Political Change", in Leys (ed.), *op.cit.*, p. 135.

67. Henry Bienen, "The Party and the No Party State", *Transition*, III, 13 (March—April, 1964), p. 31.

68. Contained in Nyerere's announcement of his resignation as Prime Minister in January, 1962. Reprinted in, J. Clagett Taylor, *The Political Development of Tanganyika*, Stanford: Stanford University Press, 1963, p. 225.

69. Maguire, *op.cit.*, passim; George Bennett, "An Outline History of TANU", *Makerere Journal*, 7, 1963; Ralph A. Austen, "Notes on the Pre-history of TANU", *Makerere Journal*, 9, 1964.

70. R. G. Penner, *Financing Local Government in Tanzania*, Nairobi: East African Publishing House, 1970; Michaela von Freyhold, "The Government Staff and Ujamaa Villages: The Tanga Experience", presented to the East African Universities Social Science Conference, Dar es Salaam, 1973; G. Tschannerl, "Rural Water Supply in Tanzania", presented to the East African Universities Social Science Conference, Dar es Salaam, 1973; Paul Collins, "The Working of Tanzania's Rural Development Fund: A Problem in Decentralization", IDS Communication No. 62, University of Sussex, July, 1971.

71. Access was accorded on the basis of clearance from the Office of the Second Vice President.

72. Three students from the Nyegezi Social Training Centre outside Mwanza town, Charles Bayeka, Daudi Masija and Alois Rutaihwa, assisted me from time to time by taking notes from many of these documents on my behalf. I selected the files for them to read after a pre-reading and, where their notes were of interest, I returned to cross-check. They each also undertook formalized interviews based on schedules prepared by myself, and in all but a few cases I was able to come back at a later date to ask supplementary questions of the same officials. Mbeti Musiyi, an experienced Sukuma research assistant, also carried out interviews which I have

used in the chapter on the role of the M.P.

73. A complete description of sample selection and survey procedure can be found in, A. Larsen, "Choice of Sampling Population in Rural Sukumaland", presented to the East African Agricultural Economics Society, April, 1970, and in Arne Larsen, Tom Hankins, Robert Hulls, with James Finucane, "Preliminary Report of the Sukumaland Interdisciplinary Research Project", Research Report No. 40, Bureau of Resource Assessment and Land Use Planning, University of Dar es Salaam, 1971. Copies of the questionnaires, coding frames, and computer tapes of the coded data are in the library of the University of Dar es Salaam. R. G. Saylor participated with the members of the Project in the sample selection.

74. "Approximately" because of the impossibility of determining with any great precision the actual number of cell leaders in an enumeration area. There were substantial differences between the Census maps of the areas and the Census (1967) lists of cell leaders and, on the other hand, the situation in the field. The maps were in several instances off by a couple of miles, and it was not unusual to find the names of cell leaders who apparently never existed. The discrepancies could only be reconciled roughly as neither the TANU nor government officials at any level had updated or complete lists of cell leaders. The method used was to have the cell leaders who attended the Project's initial selection meetings participate in constructing as complete as possible a list.

75. The Project had selected three enumeration areas in Shinyanga District for the farm level investigations. Most of the pre-testing of my questionnaires was done in the areas surrounding Old Shinyanga.

76. The Centre is located five miles outside of Mwanza town. The students were doing an 18 month post-secondary, social development course. Their fieldwork and case studies were done in the neighboring villages. The nine who served as interviewers all had a minimum of Form Four education and had worked before coming to Nyegezi. Their ages ranged from 25 to 33. They were a singularly excellent groups of interviewers.

Mwanza Region

Demography, Economy and Communications[1]

Mwanza Region is located at the southeast end of Lake Victoria. Its 7,600 square miles of land area are, with the exception of Ukerewe and a number of smaller islands, rolling plains and flat stretches of scrub bush with only the occasional rock outcropping or forest of small trees to break the uniformity. It is one of the more productive agricultural areas in Tanzania with fertile soils and sufficient rainfall. Mwanza's 1.26 million people (1972) make it the most populous of Tanzania's eighteen regions with some 9 per cent of the total national population of almost 14 million. With 1.2 million of the Region's dwellers living in the rural areas, mostly in widely scattered homesteads, it is the nation's single largest unit of rural inhabitants.

Mwanza has been a Region since May, 1963, when the former Lake Region of which it had been a part was broken up. For governmental and TANU organizational purposes the Region is composed of four Districts—Mwanza, Kwimba, Geita and Ukerewe—each of which is further sub-divided into Divisions—seven, seven, six, and three, respectively—whose boundaries tend to coincide with the old chiefdom boundaries of the colonial administration. Each Division is made up of a number of wards, varying from four to eight per Division, which are the lowest administrative units of the government. For TANU purposes the wards are further sub-divided into cells of ten households each (but see below pp. 43 *et. seq.*). The population, area, and population densities of the major administrative areas of the Region, as reported in the 1967 national census, are presented on the following page.

Economically Mwanza is one of the most important regions in Tanzania. It ranks third amongst regions in contribution to Gross Domestic Product; the eighteen regions contribute 79.3 per cent of the GDP with Mwanza Region accounting for 7.5 per cent of the GDP.[3] Its cotton, which is a staple of medium length excellent for combining with synthetics and which has a good international market, produces some ten per cent of Tanzania's foreign exchange earnings and is one of the nation's major economic hopes for the future. Mwanza

Table 5. *Mwanza Region*

Population, Area, Population Densities[2]

Division	District	Population	Area (kms^2)	Density (psk)
Bugando	Geita	67,793	1,896	35.8
Bukwimba/ Kharumwa	Geita	37,683	961	39.2
Busanda	Geita	60,044	2,318	25.9
Geita (minor settlement)	Geita	3,066		
Kasungamile	Geita	80,139	1,119	71.6
Nyang'hwale	Geita	74,510	1,746	42.7
Nyakaliro	Geita	48,172	1,026	47.0
	Total	371,407	9,065	41.0
Ibindo	Kwimba	52,894	738	71.7
Inonelwa	Kwimba	42,815	782	54.8
Kahangara	Kwimba	28,875	536	53.9
Kakora	Kwimba	57,195	1,287	44.4
Mwamashimba	Kwimba	25,777	1,259	20.5
Ndagalu	Kwimba	36,501	531	68.7
Ngula	Kwimba	61,459	951	64.6
	Total	305,516	6,087	50,2
Mwanza (town)	Mwanza	34,861		
Busega	Mwanza	49,599	562	88.3
Kivukoni	Mwanza	51,469	1,334	38.6
Nkilo	Mwanza	20,478	704	29.1
Nyanza	Mwanza	40,870	593	68.9
Sanjo	Mwanza	71,531	689	103.8
	Total	268,808	3,885	60.2
Ilangala	Ukerewe	39,349	223	176.5
Nansio (town)	Ukerewe	3,607		
Mumbuga	Ukerewe	28,361	168	156.9
Mumulambo	Ukerewe	24,343	158	154.1
Ukara (separate smaller island)	Ukerewe	15,617	96	162.7
	Total	109,277	648	168.6
Mwanza Region	Total	1,055,088	19,684	53.6

town, the third largest urban area in Tanzania in population, is the major Tanzanian port on Lake Victoria and a designated industrial growth point of the Second Five Year Development Plan period (1969—74).

Although one finds some visible evidence of prosperity throughout the Region—tinned roofs, a people well-fed and clothed—available statistics indicate that, in comparison with the other regions of Tanzania, Mwanza is certainly not as well-off as its contributions to GDP and foreign exchange earnings would imply. The 1969 per capita income figure was £22 pounds sterling against a national average of £30. In 1968—70 it ranked eighth amongst the then seventeen regions[4] in doctor-to-population ration (1: 31,091), eleventh in per capita annual recurrent expenditure on health (£.40), sixteenth in primary school education (38.3 per cent of the age group in classes), and eleventh in the provision of improved water supplies.[5] During the First Plan period, 1964—69, Mwanza Region ranked sixth in per capita investment in projects of regional impact, and it ranks eighth under the current Second Plan. In a very poor country, and in spite of an important and proportionally strong contribution to the total national output, Mwanza Region has a relative prosperity standing characterisable as middling-to-poor. Given the investment patterns of the First and Second Plan periods this position will remain unchanged in the coming years.

In addition to these inter-regional disparities there are significant variations in rural farm income, rural per capita income, and access to educational facilities amongst the different areas and classes within Mwanza Region. The 'leader' survey data showed that some 75 to 80 per cent of the school age children of this group were in school,[6] a fact which with the importance of educational qualifications as primary filters in recruiting for future positions in the 'leader' group bespeaks something of the capacity of this better-off group to pass on their advantages to their children.

In our farm survey of 203 households in Mwanza, Geita, Kwimba and Shinyanga Districts[7] 50 per cent of the households were receiving only 19 per cent of the net farm income, a distribution pattern which would appear even more unequal if we had included the 16 additional households which were also earning large amounts of off-farm income. Per capita income, expressed in terms of per consumption unit income, was only slightly better with 50 per cent of the units receiving 22 per cent of the farm income and again the situation would be worse if we had included the 16 additional households. With the policy of channelling increasing amounts of economic inputs into *ujamaa* (socialist) villages the existence of these disparities and of the also very significant differences between areas—the average income in some areas was eleven times that in others—is officially ignored and hence likely to continue (see below, p. 47).

As in Tanzania generally the economy of Mwanza Region is an agricultural one. Of the Gross Regional Product for 1967, the year for which figures are available but representative of the present as well, 62.4 per cent was created in the agricultural sector, 24.2 per cent in commerce and services, and only 3.5 per cent in manufacturing.[8] Within the agricultural sector cotton is the only cash crop of any region-wide significance, and it is the largest single contributor to rural household income; it provides approximately one-third. In Ukerewe District rice is an additional cash crop and around the Lake shores fishing has in recent years been of growing importance. Food crops which are grown for consumption and sometimes for sale are cassava, maize, sorghum, millet, rice and ground-nuts, with smaller amounts of chick-peas, sweet potatoes, beans and others. Livestock, mainly cattle, are a common feature of Kwimba (more than half the households own cattle) and Geita (more than two-thirds of the households) Districts, but not so much in Mwanza (less than twenty per cent of the households) and Ukerewe (very few households) Districts. What has been reported for the Sukuma, the largest population group in Mwanza Region, is applicable for the vast majority of the Region's inhabitants: "if considered on a continuum from pure pastoralists to pure cultivators, the Sukuma occupy a position towards the cultivation end".[9]

Over the four year period 1963—67 per capita output in agriculture in Mwanza Region increased by fifteen per cent; over the same period output declined by six per cent for the nation as a whole.[10] The increased output in Mwanza Region is chiefly attributable to extensions of the amount of acreage under cultivation. As land becomes more of a factor of scarcity the emphasis must shift to more productive timing and phasing of farming operations, the use of purchased inputs such as fertilizers and insecticides, and the adoption of more sophisticated techniques. In our 1969 survey of 164 farm households in Geita, Kwimba and Mwanza Districts only five used fertilizer, none used insecticide; both were strongly recommended by the agricultural extension service.[11] The earlier study of Anthony and Uchendu in Geita District produced similar findings on the lack of acceptance of recom-

44

mended practices.[12]

The technological necessities for substantially increasing agricultural output have been recognized by the successive central government at least since the 1940's, and both the colonial and nationalist rulers have accepted that a good measure of the onus of introducing agricultural innovations rests with government. And as both governments have experienced with respect to most of the agricultural changes which they have over the years been attempting to introduce, changes are not always willingly accepted.[13] The present government rediscovered this vividly in 1965 when the Mwanza Regional Commissioner found it necessary to send the para-military unit of the police to Ukerewe to force farmers to apply fertilizers to their cotton crop.[14] With regard to animal husbandry, Rene Dumont, after visiting the Region in August, 1967, advised President Nyerere that given the non-acceptance of the husbandry methods which the government was recommending, "Tanzania has *to make compulsory* some unpopular measures, like regular dipping, respect of boundaries for each group of cattle, registration of cattle, licensing fees, soil conservation..."[15] The urgings of Dumont to the contrary, the experience of Tanzania does not support an argument defending the usefulness of bureaucratic (compulsion is bureaucracy's most extreme version) methods. Such methods, although not normally in the harsh form of a para-military unit, have composed Tanzania's approach to the agricultural sector but they have not been successful in the introduction of higher productivity methods. It may be that Tanzania's failure here has been that the particular bureaucratic arrangements which were used were the wrong ones and that a more 'rational' bureaucracy will solve the difficulties; this indeed is the premise of the major decentralization programme introduced in 1972—73. With similar logic one might argue that the ineffectiveness of compulsory methods has resulted from their not being strong or coercive enough. My own view, however, based on the history of the non-government controlled instances of increased productivity is that if the government is to be involved the most worthwhile approach would be for the bureaucracy to provide the farmers with manageable (from the quite questioning perspective of the peasant), serviceable (from the perspective of the government departments and parastatals now entrenched in the rural areas) and profitable (in relation to the peasant effort expended) crop packages or combinations, and that once these are seen to exist at an acceptable level of risk then peasants will adopt them. Coercion and lesser forms of compulsion seem to be mostly ineffectual unless the likely net benefits to the rural dwellers are attractive.[16]

Communications between the regional centre of Mwanza town and the other major centres of East Africa are good. East African Airways has almost daily connexions, often direct, to Kampala-Entebbe, Nairobi, Arusha, and Dar es Salaam. Regular boat services on Lake Victoria keep Mwanza in close touch with Bukoba, Musoma, Kisumu, and Kampala-Entebbe. Buses and trains connect Mwanza with the rest of Tanzania though heavy rains sometimes sever these links. Travelling on buses and trains however is slow; unless one can afford to fly it is presently a two day journey from Mwanza town to Dar es Salaam. Telephone communications with Dar es Salaam are good and mail services regular.

In contrast, communications within Mwanza Region are fair at best. The condition of the local roads varies with the seasons. From Mwanza town it takes two to three hours to reach the district centres of Geita, Ngudu (Kwimba) and Nansio (Ukerewe) by road, the only way to go. Some of the divisional headquarters are another two or three hours away from the district centre. If one must rely upon public transportation the journey from many of the more remote places within the Region to Mwanza town requires two to three days because of the scheduling. For government officials travelling in Land Rovers many duties are performed hastily because of their desire to begin the journey back to the amenities of a district centre by early afternoon at the latest. Telephone communications within the Region are few and, with the exception of offices located near Mwanza town, are non-existent at the sub-district level. The most reliable (short of course of a personal visit) and quickest means of communications, and the one used in many instances by officals within the Region, is the police wireless. It is quite common for information about the agenda and time of committee meetings in Mwanza and the district centres to be circulated through the police.

The daily Dar es Salaam newspapers usually arrive a couple of days late in Mwanza town (an unnecessary delay given the air services), and are four or five days old by the time they reach the district centres. Some idea of the distribution pattern of the national (Dar es Salaam) newspapers in rural Tanzania is indicated by the data of a survey I carried out in Geita District in May, 1970. The entire District was being provided with thirty-five copies of the government owned *The Standard*, three copies of the party's *The Nationalist*, and twenty-five copies of the party's Swahili daily *Uhuru*. The most widely distributed newspapers were the Swahili *Kiongozi*, a Catholic Church publication from Tabora which is produced twice a month and sold 70 copies in Geita District, and *Baraza*, a Swahili language weekly from Nairobi which sold 170 copies.[17] Books and government and party documents of any kind are especially difficult to come by. In May, 1970, the whole of Mwanza town had six copies of various writings of Nyerere and one copy of one volume of the Second Plan available for sale to the public. There has been a government Information Office in Mwanza since soon after independence. They have some old files of press releases which are not normally open to the public and during my time in Mwanza they did not distribute locally any information on current events. The 'information' officers restricted themselves to sending reports of the activities of government and partly leaders to their ministerial headquarters in Dar es Salaam, occasionally to circulating 'press releases' cleared by Dar es Salaam amongst regional and district departmental heads, and every now and then changing the pictures on the bulletin board in the market. There have been for a good while plans to open a more comprehensive information office in Mwanza. TANU has not provided a consistent information service either from its regional or district offices. *The Standard* and *The Nationalist/Uhuru* each had a full time reporter based in Mwanza. Both reporters tended to deal mainly with official statements put out by government departments or parastatals; investigative reporting was not practiced and they tended to shy away from reporting anything which could not be presented in a fairly laudatory way. Reception of Radio Tanzania is listenable if one can afford the £20 for a suitable radio. In the rural areas not many can—in our farm survey only 6 per cent of the households owned radios. The Tanganyika Library Service began operating in the Region with a well-stocked centre in Mwanza town in 1968 and is increasing its services to rural areas with a specialized mobile unit.

Political Organization

Traditional[18]
The vast majority, seventy to eighty per cent, of the people of Mwanza Region are Sukuma, the northernmost residents of Greater Unyam-

wezi and members of the Western Bantu group. More than ninety per cent of the population of Mwanza and Kwimba Districts and about three-fourths of Geita District are Sukuma. The other major population groups, the Kerewe and Kara in Ukerewe District and the Zinza in Geita are Inter-lacustrine Bantu. There are smaller related groups which are also established in the Region, and there has been considerable intra-regional migration, particularly along the Lake shores and from Mwanza and Kwimba into Geita.

One of the standard ways of distinguishing between the political organization of the Western from that of the Inter-lacustrine Bantu has been the existence of centralized rule in the latter and its relative absence in the former. This difference has been explained in evolutionary (i.e., the Inter-lacustrine being seen as having evolved from a system similar to that of the Western Bantu) and ecological (e.g., the Sukuma being identified as having "land extensive and labour intensive" and the Inter-lacustrine as having "land intensive and labour extensive" agricultural practices because of the environment, which in turn gave rise to different political forms) terms.[19] The Inter-lacustrine groups in what is now Mwanza Region were not however as centralized as most Inter-lacustrine groups, the process of shifting from hereditary to appointed or client officials not having proceeded as far and the tendency for groups to hive-off to form new entities still very evident at the time of the colonial intervention in the late nineteenth century. In this short section my description of traditional political organization refers to that of the Sukuma.

The Sukuma were organized into chiefdoms: by the midtwentieth century there were roughly fifty with a population averaging some 20,000 people each distributed amongst small villages composed of dispersed homesteads. The literature on the Sukuma emphasises the apparently autocratic position of the chief and contrasts it with the actual situation in which there were many institutional check on the exercise of power. A chief performed two broad functions: he was expected to be the impartial final judge of the chiefdom who handled cases brought to him from the villages, and he was expected to protect the general welfare of the people by providing the people with grain from his stores (built up by tribute and spoils) in time of famine and by acting as a "magico-religious facilitator"[20] in the chiefdom's dealings with the super-natural. Each cluster of villages was formally ruled by a headman who performed comparable functions at that level but with less of a role in the supernatural aspect and more involvement in the day to day affairs of his people and in the distribution of land. The power of the chiefs was restricted, a) by the chiefdom council[21] who were ultimately responsible for the advising, selecting and, when as sometimes occurred, the deposing of chiefs, b) by young men's organizations whose public demonstrations could lead to a chief's downfall, c) by the religious practitioners[22] who were consulted in the determination of the portion of responsibility which was to be allocated to the chief for wars, epidemics and famines, and d) and by the headman who though formally appointed by the chief could withdraw their support. At the village level the headman's powers were similarly restricted. The selection and activities of chiefs and headman were dependent upon the consensus of the population as articulated by members of their chiefdom and village councils, by the young men's association and by the diviners. The Sukuma appear to have regarded inter- and intra-chiefdom migration positively and both the chief and the headman were vulnerable to the sanction of dissatisfied elements changing their allegiance by shifting their residence.

The chiefs and headmen were selected from amongst members of royal lineages, but the various checks on the exercise of royal power ensured that the general citizenry were participants in the making of decisions which affected them.[23] The Sukuma outlook seems to have been the independent, egalitarian one of dispersed homesteaders balanced by a theme of association in the performance of certain agricultural, ritual, and entertainment activities. There was no tradition of penetration from the chiefdom's centre into its periphery for the extraction of any significant amounts of tribute or labour or for the regulation of behaviour.

Colonial

German expeditions reached Mwanza town in 1890.[24] From the mid-1890's when they established the rudiments of administration in the present Mwanza Region up to 1906—1907 and the reactions to the Maji Maji rebellion, the German rule in the area was one of "sub-imperialism" based on "diplomacy" and "local compromises" with the indigenous leaders.[25] The essence of it was that the Germans, with insufficient staff to rule directly, entered into agency relationships with the local chiefs in a form of indirect rule. The chiefs, sometimes opportunistically viewed German rule as a new resource to be weighed in maintaining their positions within their own chiefdoms. Iliffe has

49

summed up these early years:

The establishment of European administration at first made rather limited demands on African societies: a recognition of superior power, the provision of limited quantities of labour and building materials, an emphasis on diplomacy rather than force as a means of resolving disputes. Further, the benefits offered ... were equally limited; usually they were restricted to political and military support for those most willing to co-operate. Consequently, African societies in Tanganyika established their relations with the Germans in terms of existing political practice and without serious violence to their structures.[26]

From 1907 the German rule entered into a "more strictly administrative phase".[27] In Mwanza this was done by increasing the efforts, which had been made since 1895, to strengthen the position of the local chiefs as German agents.[28] The most onerous aspect of local administration, tax collection was made "a purely European function, so that the indigenous leaders were neither challenged by a rival African cadre nor obliged to undertake administrative tasks which might destroy their local standing and hence their utility for other German purposes".[29] German rule, which in Mwanza ended in 1916—1917 with the advance of the British, established the pattern of indirect rule —administrative penetration through cooptation of local structures.

The chiefship became everywhere an administrative as well as a ceremonial office to which patrimonial succession was the general rule. The chiefs, however, were no longer their own masters. They were the administrative agents of the Central Government and their holding office was dependent not upon their own strength but upon the new administration ... If the chiefs carried out their duties satisfactorily they were supported by the Government. If they failed to do so they were liable to be dismissed. The Germans had no reverence for traditional authorities. They ruled through the indigenous administrators simply because they did not have sufficient personnel to rule directly.[30]

From 1916 to 1926 British rule in the area was 'direct'.[31] Chiefdom boundaries were altered and the colonial civil servants selected *akidas*, often brought in from other areas, to rule on their behalf in those chiefdoms where they had deposed the local chiefs. Cameron arrived in Dar es Salaam in 1925 to take up the governorship of the territory and in the late 1920's his policy of indirect rule was put into operation.[32] From the outset it differed but little in terms of the balance between hierarchy and participation from the previous decade of direct rule. "Deliberations preceding native administration reform in Mwanza took place virtually without reference to the opinion of African leaders..."[33] The dilemma facing the "planners of Indirect Rule" in Mwanza and the "policymakers" of the central government was that,

In theory they were committed to encouraging the growth of miniature African governments, functioning spontaneously and semi-autonomously upon a traditional base. In terms of administrative practice, however, their aim had to be the creation of local subunits which could be used conveniently to produce modernization.[34]

The accounts of Maguire and Austen of indirect rule in Mwanza Region substantiate a conclusion that it was an administrative solution to administrative problems. Austen had written that though Cameron frequently asserted "the primacy of political over economic goals... an examination of his actual policies, however, suggests an effective attitude less of hostility [to economic goals] than of accommodation, with an outcome that must be blamed mainly on the circumstances with which Cameron had to deal".[35] The 'circumstances' included a shortage of private and public capital in the context of an international depression. For the process of decision making the switch from direct to indirect rule involved minimal alteration. This can be seen in Maguire's description of a particular conflict between local chiefs and a district officer during the period of indirect rule:

In 1932 the Mwanza chiefs petitioned the Chief Secretary in protest against a district officer who not only refused to consult with them before taking action in the name of the native authority, but also on occasion entered chiefs' houses without permission, abused them verbally, and assaulted them physically. The petition relates that one chief who expressed dissatisfaction with the judgement of the district officer... 'was boxed on the ears... in our presence and before our subjects over whom we reign'. Other assaults and indignities were described at considerable length...

In a memorandum to the Chief Secretary, the Secretary for Native Affairs... noted that the Provincial Commissioner 'has no doubt (the assaults) did occur... (and) definitely make the position of righteous indignation a rather difficult one to assume'. He nevertheless pointed out that the complaints had not been 'brought to the notice of the Provincial Commissioner in the proper form... (and held that) if any notice were taken of it the effect on authority would be deplorable'. He recommended that the officer continue to be posted in Mwanza.[36]

Maguire does go on to note that this early "kernel of protest" was

51

exceptional in that "physical assault . . ." was not typical of the relations between the chiefs and administrative officers.[37] In another sense however it was perhaps inevitable as the colonial administrators searched for methods which would make the chiefs into reliable instruments for the administration and implementation of colonial operations, rather than leaders responsive and responsible to citizen constituencies. Austen concluded his study of indirect rule in the Lake Victoria area with the observation that the colonialists' "conscious expressions of dedication to Indirect Rule are consistently accompanied by the strengthening of a bureaucratic apparatus which denies the possibility of autonomous local control".[38]

After World War II British colonial policy replaced what they called indirect rule with 'local government'.[39] The progression from direct rule to indirect rule to local government is analogous, and interestingly enough also parallel, in terms of time, to the progression in management theory from 'classical' to 'human relations' to 'participatory' approaches. In each instance the basic idea is of a hierarchy in which the people in the bottom ranks are to be respectively ordered, gently induced, and persuaded to follow methods and achieve goals set by those occupying the higher ranks. The resemblance of local government to indirect rule (and, to a lesser extent, to direct rule), is most explicit in the accounts of one of the more lauded attempts to soften the hierarchy. In the late 1940's and 1950's Sukumaland, which included the present Mwanza, Geita and Kwimba Districts, "became a prime experimental area for the implementation of the government's new programmes" of development through local government.[40] Maguire has described these new programmes as an attempt at "political and economic transformation". A political transformation in the colonial period could be described as such usefully only if there were an attempt to alter the dominance of the imperial bureaucracy in decision making. This was not the case with the Sukumaland experiments. The 'political transformation' was a move to increase the capacity of the bureaucracy to effect economic objectives which constituted their definition of development. Much as officials of the government of independent Tanzania the colonial administrators were convinced that they knew the broad policy requirements for the area's economic progress, and these requirements were accorded overwhelming priority over any imperatives of political progress. The impetus, rationale, and direction of the Sukumaland experiments thus came from the bureaucracy. The selection of the headquarters site and the initial plans were the product of a colonial administrator. The economies and advantages of a larger scale unit in agricultural development were emphasized by officials in 'persuading' the chiefs to accept the limited federation of financial, judiciary, and legislative functions. The chiefs were informed explicitly that any 'political aspirations' must be bent and delayed in line with the administratively determined needs of agricultural expansion.[41]

As part of the Sukumaland experiments an entire pyramid of councils at the village, sub-chiefdom, chiefdom, district and federal levels was set up. At the all-important Sukumaland Federal Council agenda items for meetings,

usually originated with European administrative or developmental officers. Chiefs infrequently suggested items of their own, but these were circulated first to District Commissioners who discussed them with chiefs at district level before approving them for general consideration. Final agenda for federation meetings were drawn up in consultation with the permanent chairman... but the administration pulled most of the weight... The chiefs found themselves acting as ratifiers of policies, programmes, rules, and orders initiated from above.[42]

The government officials used the pyramid of councils "as instruments to implement and enforce unpopular land, agricultural and animal husbandry legislation".[43] The enforcement of these regulations was, in political terms, a risky and difficult task for the chiefs and it was in the process of deciding whether or not to repeal them in 1958 (they were repealed) that the essentially powerless position of the chiefs on the Council vis a vis the officials became clear.[44] As Liebnow has argued, "the plain fact is that in many instances the term 'Native Authority' was a legal fiction meaning 'District Commissioner' while the substantive content of the rules and regulations of the councils were reminiscent of "Plato's *Laws*".[45] The experiments with 'native authority' eventually undermined the traditional authority of the chiefs not only by associating them with unpopular agricultural regulations but equally because the "emergent elite" at the time perceived that it was the administrative officials and not the chiefs who were exercising power.[46]

The excellent historical work of Maguire, specifically intended to establish a baseline for the consideration of post-independence politics and administration,[47] concentrated on the 1945—60 period. I shall remark briefly on further aspects of particular interest as part of the baseline for this study. In 1959—60 elected District Councils replaced chiefs as the local authority. Central government was by then a form of dyarchy. TANU, the pre-eminent nationalist movement, used its efforts to ensure that the people and their representatives on the District Councils conformed to the policy needs of the central government and the evolving policy and discipline requirements of the party. In the last years of colonial rule there were attempts by political forces at district level to have effective power devolved from Dar es Salaam to the districts.[48] This was resisted by TANU which by that time was stressing that the attainment of independence would increase the need for control, that it would mean work and not freedom from the obligation to obey laws and regulations. As Nyerere put it to a large gathering in Mwanza in November, 1959, the "TANU of today" was far different from the "TANU of yesterday".[49] Attempts to shift power from the centralized bureaucracy were warded off by the officials in the districts by their at least partial adoption of manipulative management methods relying upon an amalgam of 'human relations' and 'participation' techniques.[50]

The major thrust of nationalist politics in the present Mwanza Region was aimed at the take-over of the territorial rather than any district political system. The nationalists based in Mwanza were the first in Tanzania "to define the principal issue as that of national self-determination versus colonial rule *and* to build tangible support for their propositions by attempting to deal in the most concrete way possible with the complaints of people in a variety of localities",[51] urban and rural. In Mwanza's rural areas during the 1950's TANU often hit out at the agricultural regulations which were unpopular with the peasants, and although the regulations were ultimately repealed in 1958, TANU was banned in Sukumaland during 1955—58. The growing Victoria Federation of Co-operative Unions did not involve itself very much in 'politics' either during or after the ban on TANU[52] and this perhaps contributed to TANU's readiness in 1968 to have it taken over by the government. The Sukuma Union was the only tribal union which was considered dangerous to the territorial entity and banned.

As in other British[53] and French[54] colonies in Africa the nationalist movement in Tanzania directed its attention to the territorial level, to gaining power at the centre of the centralized and bureaucratized system. In the post-World War II constitutional struggle for independence they were not diverted by the efforts of colonial administrators to implement populist or 'from the bottom up' institutional strategies designed to check the educated elites and to localize conflict at sub-territorial levels.[55] In a sense the nationalists wanted nothing to do with a restructuring of the colonial system but merely desired its transfer into their hands. Tanzania's case is well summed up in Young and Fosbrooke's account of Morogoro District in 1959:

The Central Government is ... highly centralized (although the administration of policy is decentralized). The Central Government determines policies ... relating to schools, police, roads, and health. It controls educational policy ... makes policy relating to police, roads and health, with local government serving as the agent for carrying out the policy ... There appears to be no expressed dissatisfaction with the manner in which authority is divided between the Central and the local government. The goal of the Tanganyika nationalist seems to be that of putting Africans in the jobs now held by European officials, but to continue the same offices ... The nationalist seems to have no complaint about the centralized nature of government ..., they wish to control it, not to change it ...[56]

Post-independence

Changes in political organization since independence have been directed towards a monopolization of political-administrative functions by TANU and the central government bureaucracy including the parastatal organizations. With the traditional leaders and the private economic sector this process was straightforward. The chieftainships were abolished in 1963 thus removing a non-TANU leadership group. Access to the economic sector has been closely restricted and, except in instances of corruption, individuals in that sector are largely barred from the political arena in a formal sense. While not completely loophole-free this process has meant that neither entrepreneurial nor trade union elements are of any salience except as ratifiers and sometimes implementors of government and TANU decisions. The pattern of elimination of the political impact of the other major sources of possible non-TANU inputs into resource allocation decisions, in Mwanza Region— the District Councils and the Victoria Federation of Co-operative Unions—though not as linear has been no less effective.

In the early years after independence both the Councils and the co-operatives were given increased responsibilities. There was much official rhetoric about the need for 'local government' and co-operatives in the 'nation-building' operation. Their projected place in the evolving system, and the confidence with which they viewed the future, was evidenced in the construction of striking and modern office buildings for the District Councils and the VFCU. They dominated the architecture of the Region's administrative centres until December, 1971, when the new TANU regional headquarters, the successor symbol, was opened. In practice however the Councils and the VFCU had been eliminated well before 1971. The central government's notions as to the prerequisites for the rational and efficient use of resources led to the demise of the Councils and the VFCU as foci of participation during the late 1960's.

District Councils and Co-operatives

The District Councils and the central government, although both were formally controlled by the same TANU, came into steady conflict over the relative priorities to be assigned to 'service' and 'productive' projects. The Councils wanted to make large investments in education, water, and health projects, all of which entail a commitment to future recurrent expenditures, while the central government urged the concentration of resources in roads, dips, agriculture extension and assistance, and the maintenance of already existing facilities. Their different positions on primary education in particular were resolvable only through central control if the growth and structure of 'manpower development' were to conform to bureaucracy's manpower planners' projections of national needs. Manpower planning and its impact on primary education policy—enrollment figures were kept depressed through limiting the construction of new classrooms and insisting upon tuition fees—was one of the starkest cases of 'rational' bureaucrats employing their "persuasive powers" to impose their will on the political leaders at the centre, and through them and the centralized system on the people in the rural areas.[58] The general view of the bureaucrats on this issue is well represented by the views of Saul on a closely related issue: "big decisions, in a very pressing sense, cannot be left solely to politicians . . ."[59]

The inadequate revenue capacity, the increasing burden of recurrent expenditures, and the falling size, both proportionally and in absolute terms, of the capital budgets of Councils reduced the capacity of the Councils to undertake projects on their own, and hence lowered their leverage in project decisions. But this is not to say that they were completely destitute.[60] The Councils in Mwanza Region especially were doing fairly well. In 1968, the last normal year of revenue collection, the Mwanza, Geita, Ukerewe, and Kwimba Councils collected

72, 65, 83, and 85 per cent respectively of their estimated total local revenue.[61] This was despite the fact that after the April, 1968, death of thirteen local rate defaulters in a primary court cell room at Ilemela, Mwanza District, there was a "fear" on the part of the revenue collectors to be too venturesome.[62] The Councils in Mwanza Region in 1968 collected from their various local sources 18 million shillings, as compared to the 1 million shillings coming into the Region through the 'decentralized' Regional Development Fund of the central government. The realization of the Commissioners that the Councils were not too poor is reflected in their frequent calls upon them to support 'regional projects', most often facades or prestige projects, with which the Commissioners tended to identify themselves. In 1968 for instance the Councils were "ordered" by the Regional Commissioner to give 50,000 shillings each to the Gallu Settlement Scheme in Ukerewe.[63] In 1969 the Regional Commissioner instructed each Council to contribute 100,000 shillings to the TANU regional headquarters building fund which he was chairing.[64]

The Councils were brought under central control gradually but firmly through personnel regulations and financial grant procedures. More drastically the 1969 Budget speech in June announced that as of 1970 most of their functions and what was in effect 80 per cent of their revenue sources were removed from the Councils.[65] Indicative of the situation by that time the Councils did not receive an explanation of the changes until September, 1969, in discussions at a meeting of the Association of Rural Local Authorities held at Morogoro.[67] The new financial arrangements were not formally and specifically made known to the Councils until the November, 1969, issuance of Local Government Circular No. 24.[68] The central government hoped that with the 1969 changes the Councils would refrain from project politicing and devote their energies to attaining the goals which the centre considered necessary for economic development.[69] Optimally from the point of view of the centre the Councils would no longer push for service projects but would rather assist in implementing national plans through the activities of 'development corporations'. The Councils did not take readily to this idea and by the time that the Councils were abolished in 1972 only Mwanza District had set up such a corporation and it was not involved in productive projects.[70] The other Councils, and Mwanza too for the most part, lost their interest in projects when it became clear that decisions were to be bureaucratically determined. In 1972 the Councils were replaced by District Development Corporations which are intended to function in a role similar to that of the National Assembly at the centre.[71]

Beginning in the early 1950's peasant farmers, African traders, and members of the new, educated African elite created what soon developed into the largest co-operative organization in Africa, the Victoria Federation of Co-operative Unions (VFCU).[72] Centered in Mwanza town and based on the buying and ginning of cotton in the Lake Victoria area the VFCU as an expression of development 'from below' found that both the colonial and independence governments feared as well as welcomed its existence. Sometimes assisted by the colonial bureaucracy on the basis that it was useful in the development process, and sometimes hindered by the same officials who considered the political potential of a large producers' organization not firmly regulated by government,[73] the VFCU prospered on the initiative and sacrifices of its members and leaders. In driving out the Indian middlemen and providing an alternative marketing structure trusted by the growers the VFCU was instrumental in the expansion of cotton production.

Early after independence the new government began its efforts to convert the VFCU into a developmental structure capable of reliably carrying out government plans. The conversion of the central TANU leaders to the 'transformation' approach to agricultural development and their related 1963 decision to urge the mechanization of farming led to the VFCU being "reluctantly persuaded" in 1964 to support 'block farms' for large scale cotton production.[74] Forty blocks were established in Mwanza Region, members were often coerced into becoming participants, those who did join soon exhibited a 'dependency syndrome'—refusing to do many things for themselves but rather insisting that they be done by 'government'. The direct antithesis of the early self-help efforts described in Chapter 3, the blocks were financial disasters with many individuals preferring to farm the government for credit and agricultural prerequisites rather than farming the land. The losses were transferred by the government from the member farmers to the VFCU and the Lint and Seed Marketing Board. The blocks became an example of the pitfalls of over-capitalizing peasant agriculture, of the difficulties of a bureaucratic approach to site and farmer selection, and a lingering memory in the minds of many Mwanza farmers making them sceptical about other government sponsored undertakings in agriculture. For the VFCU they were the beginning of the end. Its independence had been greatly compromised, the financial losses (more than £160,000 in the first two years) weakened its organizational capacity, and in the eyes of many primary society members the VFCU was no longer their Federation.

The process was completed when in late 1967 the VFCU was taken-over ("reorganized" in official parlance) by the government, renamed the Nyanza Co-operative Union, a government appointee put in as General Manager, a third of the staff removed, and the remaining senior employees brought under the leadership code of the Arusha Declaration.[75] In 1969 there were 281 functioning primary co-operative societies in Mwanza Region; by way of comparison there were 136 TANU branches in the rural area. Though there were charges of inefficiency and corruption and the consequent need to protect the co-operative societies' members from their elected leaders and the bureaucracy of the VFCU,[76] the central government's perception of the need for central control given Tanzania's goals and resources would seem to have been the primary motivating factor. As Saul explained, "even were the membership to be successfully involved and the co-operatives' activities streamlined, there might remain problems of squaring national and local 'needs'".[77] As with the demise of the District Councils, the central government was intent upon gaining firm control over the large economic surpluses being generated by the co-operatives and using these resources and the organizational apparatus of the VFCU to penetrate the rural areas in the furtherance of the centrally decided approach to economic development.

The Government Bureaucracy

The only two organizational structures of note in Mwanza Region today are those of the central government and TANU. Since independence both structures and the relationships between them have been altered considerably. The open TANU—administration conflict of the pre-dyarchy, early 1950's was gradually eased with the removal of most of the agricultural regulations in 1958 and the co-operation between the administration and central TANU in the final years of colonialism has continued. The party and government are now closely linked at the sub-centre levels through interlocking directorates (Regional and Area Commissioners, Divisional Secretaries, cell leaders) and common membership on development committees at all levels. The appointment of the Commissioners and the simultaneous removal of most of the administrative and judicial responsibilities of their colonial predecessors, and the growth of ministerial staffs at the district and regional levels have changed the nature of government administration. The jack-of-all-trades Commissioner is a strictly historical figure; administration has become more fragmented and compartmentalized and it remains to be seen whether the 1972/73 decentralization can alter this process.

The fragmentation of administration is most obvious when considering the Regional Development Committee's steadily expanding number of member 'regional heads'.[78] In 1964 there were twenty-two regional heads on the Mwanza RDC; by 1970 this had risen fifty per cent to thirty-three regional heads, and this did not include zonal officials whose zones included Mwanza Region, officials of parastatal organizations controlling cotton marketing, banking, retail trade, transport and some manufacturing operations. The total membership of the RDC, that is regional heads and political figures, was twenty-eight in 1964; in 1970 it was forty-six. In 1962 the Ukerewe District Development Committee had fifteen members; in 1970 it had twenty-eight. The fragmentation of administration presented would-be coordinators with an increasingly challenging task. Adding to the difficulty of sub-centre coordination was the constant rearranging of ministerial organizations. A good example is Regional Administration itself. In 1963 it was in the Vice President's Office, in 1964 it was in the Second Vice President's Office (a nominal change), in 1965 it was in the President's Office, in 1966 it was in a separate Ministry of Regional Administration which included Local Government, in 1967 it was in the President's Office again, in 1968 it moved into the Ministry of Regional Administration and Rural Development. Comparable histories exist for Rural (née Community) Development and Local Government.

Prior to May, 1972, the only complementary increase in coordinative authority at sub-centre levels was the Ministry of Agriculture's 1969 setting up of Director and Coordinator positions at the regional and district levels respectively. Most of the units directly concerned with the agricultural sector thus came under the direction of a single person at these levels. Approximately fifteen percent of recurrent Agriculture expenditure authority was decentralized to the regional level providing the Regional Director with some valuable resources. The difficulty with the arrangement was that it added additional levels—the former regional heads of agriculture, veterinary, co-operatives, forestry, and game remained—and many of the subordinate units continued to look to their Dar es Salaam headquarters for guidance. There was no increase in the controlling authority of the Commissioners or other officials. Despite the experiment in Agriculture and others which are discussed in Chapter 4, and aided by the urgency accredited to national priorities by the national leaders, the flow of administration became more vertical and 'rational'. Though this and other studies (Collins, Penner, Vente) indicate that the dominance of the central government bureaucracy at sub-centre levels remained and perhaps increased, the power of the bureaucracy was spread over more units and became more specialized during the first ten years of independence.

Most surprisingly in the rural areas there has been an actual decline in the number of administrative generalists and 'mobilizers' who might have helped coordinate governmental activities. The figures for Executive Officers at the divisional, sub-divisional, ward, and village levels, TANU branch secretaries, and Rural Development workers are presented in Chapter 3, but numbers overstate the actual position. TANU secretaries were not active in coordination while Rural Development 'mobilizers' were becoming more specialized as rural construction specialists and less involved in other activities (most of their early tasks were taken up by new and expanding specialized units in health, adult education, agricultural extension, and co-operatives) or in 'mobilization' which at higher levels was being staked out as a TANU preserve.[79]

The falling number of possible coordinators has been accompanied by an increase in the number of specialist staff at these sub-district levels. The total number of trained veterinary, agricultural, forestry, game and co-operative personnel in the rural areas of Mwanza Region in June, 1964, was 155. By July, 1970, it had almost doubled to 290.[79a] The fragmentation, the small number of coordinators, the increase in specialists, combined to make the task of structuring a pattern of participatory inputs into decision-making a more complicated undertaking.

The methods and attitudes of the bureaucracy have not altered so as to offset these developments. The style swings between patronizing and compulsory with only the rare cases of less manipulative forms. Within the bureaucracy the General Orders have since the colonial period served as the rule book, and in fact much of the discussion about increasing participation after the publication of the February 19, 1971, TANU *Guidelines* or *Mwongozo* focused on the need to devise new guidelines for the civil service. Since the Arusha Declaration there have been continuing rounds of seminars and work groups for bureaucrats and TANU leaders in which it has been attempted to inculcate an approach to administration that is in accordance with the formal national ideology. However during the time of this study there was no sign that this 'political education', as it is called in Tanzania, was achieving this objective. From the innumerable actions of officials whom I observed it could be concluded that the approach of the bureaucracy was in no way different from that of the colonial officials in the 1950's.[80] The reasoning of the officials about this paradox of independence is well-stated by Oyugi in explaining his own doubts about any moves to "strengthen the hands of the local people in decision-making". The people at the local level have always exhibited "politics of ignorance—deciding how to allocate resources without knowing how it is going to be raised, etc. Like participation generally, the increased role of these institutions (councils, co-operatives, development committees) must be geared to the rate development (understanding) on the part of the people themselves."[81] To put it more bluntly, the officials should not alter their approach until the people have become more 'rational'. An academic with a wide experience of field level administration throughout East Africa, in explaining that the major advantage of a 'penetration analysis' of government and politics in East Africa is the congruence between its major theoretical assumptions and the premises of the officials, states that

... from the administrator's viewpoint, effective local involvement in decision-making about development only would add further constraints to an already constrained situation. The administrator is quite willing to challenge the assumption that people necessarily ought to be involved in managing the many services they might potentially consume.[82]

TANU

TANU has changed. Although it is certainly not a very bureaucratized party its hierarchical elements in the rural areas have increased. At the time of independence there were four central party functionaires in the present Mwanza Region. In July, 1970, TANU had sixty-three salaried branch secretaries in the rural areas and seven regional and district level administrators not including clerks, typists, messengers, and drivers. The TANU Youth League had four salaried officials at the district and regional levels who worked closely with the party administrators.[83] The representative elements have been extended down to the ten house cell, and their connexions with the central party and its hierarchical elements have been regularized through a pyramid of periodic conferences and working and executive committees at the ward, district, regional and national levels. The general trend of changes in TANU's internal arrangements in the late 1960's and early 1970's has been to increase the elected element in party units at all levels, to increase the interactions between members of the units at different levels, and to reduce the time spent in meetings.[84]

The growing apparatus of TANU, the great publicity given in the national media to the activities of its constituent bodies, and the national rhetoric of TANU supremacy conjure up the image of a viable instrument of penetration and participation. Bienen's work, based on research carried out mainly in Dar es Salaam between 1963 and 1965, underscored the reality of an organization impoverished in terms of staff and money in relation to the environment and the goals it had set for itself.[85] More recently, in a review of Bienen's book, Cliffe has cited the growing TANU budget and the setting up of a more coherent ideology as factors which since Bienen's time have given the party a more effective organization.[86] What has happened in Mwanza Region?

Table 6. *TANU Membership in Mwanza Region, 1967 and 1968*

District	Membership 1967	Membership 1968	Membership Increase
Mwanza urban	69,700	74,671	4,971
Mwanza rural	13,959	14,291	858
Geita	83,948	87,378	3,430
Kwimba	77,911	79,930	2,019
Ukerewe	13,041	13,829	788
Mwanza Region	258,559	270,099	12,066

(Source: 1968 Annual Report of the Mwanza TANU Regional Secretary.)

According to the official membership figures, of the estimated (on the basis of the 1967 Census figures) 550,000 people in 1968 eligible (eighteen years or older) for TANU membership in the Region, approximately fifty percent had joined. The membership was not, however, nearly as high as this figure suggests. The official figures include all who have joined TANU in Mwanza Region since the late 1950's. The resulting distortion is obvious—for instance, in the case of Mwanza urban, of the estimated 18,000 people in the Mwanza urban area eighteen years or older, 74,671 (*sic*) are recorded as having joined. Another indication of the usefulness of the TANU statistics: in the

1965 parliamentary election 161,792 people voted in Mwanza Region at a time when the official estimate of regional party membership was 245,000.[87] The membership figures are all the more distorted because the Mwanza rural and Ukerewe offices appear to attempt to restrict membership statistics to those joining or paying dues in any one year. All the district offices of course depend on information sent from the wards, and this is not reliable. The many ward offices I visited had *no* list of members and the figures which they could give me were rough estimates based on an estimated number of cell leaders each of whom was estimated to have ten households in unit. The mean number of cell members in a cell in our farm survey was 11.6; it was 10.9 in the cell leader survey.

Table 7. *TANU Budget, Mwanza Region, 1968*

	Revenue	Expenditure
Regional office	shs. 218,998	208,438
Mwanza (urban)	106,528	115,905
Mwanza (rural)	158,870	140,484
Geita	204,809	170,415
Kwimba	126,494	95,312
Ukerewe	34,895	21,824
Totals	shs. 850,596	752,378

(Source: 1968 Annual Report of the Mwanza TANU Regional Secretary.)

The party's capacity to raise its own revenue is an indication of and contributory factor to its organizational strength or weakness. Averaged out amongst the total (official) membership in the Region, the 850,600 shillings revenue comes to 3.15 shillings contributed per capita. In fact, a very large part of the revenue, regional officials estimated it as two-thirds, came from businessmen, many of them non-citizens. It was hoped, by the TANU National Executive Secretary, that the 1969 removal of the local rates and the increase in the number of salaried branch secretaries would lead to a rise in the amount of dues and membership payments from TANU members.[88] During the year after the removal of the rates, TANU officials and elected leaders at all levels were openly in meetings expressing their disappointment that no such increase had occured. The expansion of TANU in Mwanza—its building programme,[89] higher staffing levels, and seminars—has been financed largely from funds coming from the central party, which in turn has depended for its expansion on subventions from government and parastatals.[90]

TANU officials and leaders at all levels were aware of the party's financial problems. Another problem which they were well aware of, and which reflected on the lack of impact which the ideological articulation in Dar es Salaam had had on Mwanza Region up to 1970, was the lack of public interest in various mobilizational activities. The self-help schemes sponsored by village/ward development committees or by local TANU branches were not in 1967/70 arousing the widespread enthusiasm associated with the early years after independence. Parades and demonstrations relied for their numbers mainly on conscripted school children with smaller numbers of police, National Servicemen, and TANU workers and office-bearers. The problem was well summed up by the Regional Commissioner as he advised an adult education seminar in Mwanza on 7 April 1970 to discuss some of the difficulties of development in the Region. He said that TANU officials and all civil servants should "investigate" the following:

1) What is it that makes many people not attend public meetings and/or why is the attendance at meetings so poor? 2) Why is it that people ignore self-help projects? 3) What makes people not take an interest in educating their children, attending evening adult education classes, building good houses, taking their people to the hospital when sick, etc., and, 4) Why is it that many times TANU and government leaders when they are holding public meetings they give long speeches, very long, and you will find that speeches like these do not meet the needs of the people of that place?[91]

As an organization intended to increase popular inputs into decision-making in Mwanza Region, TANU as an entity or in the person of various TANU leaders (M.P.'s, Commissioners, Regional and District Chairmen) has been singularly unsuccessful. The trend has been towards a cooptation of the ward, district and regional party institutions by the government structures, rather than towards the exercise of control or guidance of government by TANU. It is equally the case at the very base of the TANU structure, the ten house cell.

The cells were to be the starting point of the two-way road between the people and their government. According to the official description of the "purpose of Party Cells", it was expected that "through this system of Party Cells . . . all the people will have a better opportunity to participate in the running of the day to day affairs of this Nation".[92] In practice, cell leaders in Mwanza Region (of which there were officially 14,681 in 1969)[93] have been used to gather information (how many people have latrines, children out of school, smallpox innoculations), to carry information from the government to the farmers (meeting times, agricultural advice), and to maintain the system (catching thieves, assisting in local rate collections). They have not always carried out this penetrative role very effectively and in many areas in Mwanza Region the government workers in the divisions and wards complained about the lack of co-operation from cell leaders. The penetrative nature of the role of cell leader is of course recognized by the people, and in at least several instances drunkards, lepers, and simple people have been chosen for the position.[94] More generally they have nominated obvious non-leaders who perform a middleman role limited to messenger, and who act more as buffers than as aids to communication. Many of the cell leaders themselves complain about the lack of respect which the people pay to them, though they are 'leaders', and about the time they are expected to give to meetings with no compensation.[95]

Ujamaa Villages

The lack of economic success with the block farms and other transformation approaches to agricultural development brought the realization that capital-intensive transformation was in many ways inequitable—as the VFCU observed, "never has so much been given to so few by so many"[96]—and unsuited to capital-short Tanzania.[97] The alternative chosen, which had existed in Nyerere's theory from the time of independence but which seems to have been concretized by his observation of the gradual success of the Ruvuma Development Association,[98] was the promotion of producers' co-operatives, called *ujamaa* villages, which would be self-reliant yet assisted in some respects by the government.

During 1966—68 when the *ujamaa* villages policy was being designed there was concern on the part of Nyerere that this approach should not have the degree of bureaucratization and compulsion found in the transformation attempts.[99] In this there seemed to be the promise of a new way which would break the administrative continuity existing between the colonial and independence periods. This promise has not been met in the early experience with *ujamaa* villages which I studied during 1969 and 1970 in Mwanza Region.[100]

In March, 1969, Nyerere ordered that "all government policies, and the activities and decisions of all government officials, must ... be

66

geared towards emphasizing the advantages of living together and working together for the good of all".[101] *Ujamaa* villages were to be given "priority in all our credit, servicing and extension services—at the expense of the individual producer if necessary".[102] The elite status and interests of the bureaucrats however make it very difficult in any country, and I would say impossible in the short-run without at least very strong political control, for them to change their ways of doing things; in the agricultural sector the 'progressive' farmer approach has a durability well established in the structure of elite—mass relationships and it is not easily lessened by statements pronounced in urban centers. Yet civil service officials also have an interest in their own careers and during 1969 Tanzanian officials began to realize that their bureaucratic prospects depended partly upon the extent to which they appeared to be assisting *ujamaa* villages. Quite sensibly they began to find *ujamaa* villages to assist.

The first result of the *ujamaa* programme in Mwanza Region was the report effect. In mid-1969 the Region's officials reported one *ujamaa* village, a year later they reported ten.[103] In fact seven of the villages were not villages but groups of farmers working together on a communal field for two or three days a week; another was a former settlement scheme remaining from the transformation days which managed to continue receiving much governmental attention and assistance as it was adopted by the Regional Commissioner as a 'show piece'; only two were in the nature of producers' co-operatives. It is interesting that in the two actual villages neither government officials nor the local TANU organizations played a role in their getting started. At one the priests at the local Catholic Church mobilized the people using Nyerere's writings as the legitimizing instrument; at the other, Izunya in Geita District, the setting up of the village was the result of the effort of a local farmer who was convinced that if people worked together so as to attain a larger scale of operation then they would be able to produce more than if they carried on farming individually.[104] TANU's Youth League established one of the part-time communal fields, while the other six were the product of local progressive farmers (in three cases individuals owning tractors were members), and their family and clients combing with local TANU leaders, who were eager to show that they too were promoting *ujamaa* villages. Regional officials were well aware that some progressive farmers were willing to formally establish *ujamaa* villages—*ujamaa* shells would be more apt—so as to ensure their access to credit and inputs and they were also cognizant of the difficulty of reconciling this tendency with the officially egalitarian thrust of the centre's policy of *ujamaa* villages. Nonetheless in many instances progressive farmers were able to do just that. This was possible because there was a lack of clarity as to what an *ujamaa* village was (the centre was urging, correctly in my opinion, that there be flexibility in definition); because the local TANU organizations were themselves controlled by progressive farmers and small traders; and because the bureaucrats, needing *ujamaa* villages for their reports and their careers, could not afford to be very selective and in some cases seem to have encouraged the setting up of *ujamaa* shells. Local TANU members were keen to be officially registered as *ujamaa* village members as during this period the TANU central organization was stipulating that in the future only members of such villages would be permitted to hold TANU leadership positions.[105]

The second effect of bureaucratic emphasis on *ujamaa* villages was a distortion in the allocation of governmental resources. The ten recognized villages and others in the planning stage (often in the form of neat gridiron sketches in district offices) were given a disproportionate share of resources in relation to their output or population. Though it is not possible to itemize all the costs and opportunity costs involved, an indication may be gained from the case of the agricultural extension staff in Mwanza District. In May, 1970, forty per cent of the field staff were working *only* on the District's four officially "operating" and seven "planned" *ujamaa* villages. The four had a combined total population of 155, while each of the seven was intended to have 400.[106] The rural population of the District at the time was about 260,000.

The third effect was the taking over of the officially TANU mobilization role by the specialists of the central government. TANU was to be in charge of urging the people to form *ujamaa* villages and only when they had made a decision were the specialists to be involved.[107] In practice the specialists could not wait for the length of time TANU's involvement might entail and instead set about themselves to 'recognize' *ujamaa* villages. To the people *ujamaa* villages came to appear as another one in a succession of government agricultural programmes.

The fourth effect was tension between the most firmly established village—Izunya—and government officials. Izunya's leaders desired a minimum of government assistance because as long-time residents of the area they feared 'witchcraft' (their cotton store was burned

68

down) if they antagonized their neighbors by becoming targets of disproportionate amounts of assistance, and because if they were successful with outside help then the argument which they needed to get more neighbors to join (namely that it was largeness of scale not outside help which was the key to success) would be weakened. Some government actions were clearly detrimental to the growth along the lines desired by Izunya's leaders. The increasing amount of the villagers' time (there were 34 working adult members during 1969—70) that was taken up in playing host to official visitors detracted from what had previously been meticulously planned work schedules; the chairman was insisted upon to attend TANU meetings in the District centre and to play a role in the local TANU organization (prior to the establishment of the village the chairman had held leadership positions in a number of local organizations but he had resigned all of these in 1967 to devote his time fully to the village) thus partly depriving the village of what was in fact one of their most essential resources; assistance was given to the village when it was clearly unwanted. A good example of such assistance and of the opposing interests of bureaucrats and peasant organizations in such a context is the case of the school children and the cotton harvest. The District Education Officer in Geita, in looking for ways that he could be reported as having assisted *ujamaa* villages, ordered the local primary school in May, 1969, to send their pupils to help pick cotton at Izunya. In the official books it looked like a very good move—school children had a practical *ujamaa* experience while the village had been given an extra boost. The Officer arranged a press release to ensure that his action was recognized.[108] The villagers, meanwhile, were not consulted in the decision (they were 'informed' of the children's arrival), they were not satisfied with the standard of picking by the inexperienced children and in fact claimed that overall both time and cotton were lost, and most importantly for the villagers it caused them much conflict with their neighbors (their children were picking cotton on the 'government's' *ujamaa* village rather than being at school, and if they were to be picking cotton why were they not picking it on their parents' fields were the neighbors complaints) with whom they had to continue living after the officials departed and from amongst whom they were trying to find recruits to join the village.

The prototype of the *ujamaa* village programme, the Ruvuma Development Association, was 'taken-over' by the government and TANU in September, 1969. Much as with the District Councils and the VFCU the possibility of a peasant controlled or at least local-level controlled organization not being readily amenable to government's 'rational' instructions seemed threatening to bureaucratic elements in TANU and the civil service; their response escalated from cooptation, to direction, to total control. As of late 1971 Izunya reportedly was fading as an *ujamaa* village; its membership was falling and output declining.[109] Perhaps that is to be its fate—not having the strength of the VFCU or Ruvuma it might not be able to survive a period of cooptation and directed assistance. Differences in attitudes and life styles between officials and peasants, internal bureaucratic demands upon officials, and the patronizing mentality of 'rational' officials carrying out a bureaucratic programme make the task of sustaining any instances of self-reliant development very difficult.

Concluding Remarks

Post-independence organizational changes in Mwanza, as in Tanzania as a whole, have been towards an increasingly coherent attack on the ways of life of the rural population by the central government. The strategy of this attempted "development front" is based on the

... intention to coordinate as closely and as fruitfully as possible the activities of *all* institutions with a presence in the Tanzanian countryside. Ideally this is designed to achieve the construction of an integrated phalanx of 'development agencies' over a broad front (local councils, co-operatives, government ministries) capable, in turn, of presenting a uniform set of stimuli to Tanzanian peasants, one designed to encourage their adoption of novel patterns of behaviour desired by the central government. Equally important, primary responsibility for achieving such coordination and galvanizing the related agencies into action rests, at least theoretically, with the ruling political party.[110]

In other words, the needs and goals of rural dwellers in independent Tanzania are to be determined by the central government. As during the years of 'indirect rule' of the colonial period, the need to coopt local organization is a concommitant of the low resource levels of the central government and thus the local party is to be employed in a coordinating and mobilizing role for the achievement of the centre's objectives.

Notes

1. The traditional sources of material for the background information on the Region are: D. W. Malcolm, *Sukumaland: An African People and Their Country*, London: Oxford University Press, 1953; N. V. Rounce (ed.), *The Agriculture of the Cultivation Steppe of the Lake, Western and Central Provinces,* Cape Town: Longmans, 1949. The most informative source available today is, Arne Larsen, Tom Hankins, and Robert Hulls with James Finucane, "Preliminary Report of the Sukumaland Interdisciplinary Research Project", Bureau of Resource Assessment and Land Use Planning (BRALUP), University of Dar es Salaam, 1971. This report is the locus of most of the information presented in this section. I have also used: BRALUP's "Population Density in Tanzania, 1967" and their "Regional Economic Atlas, Mainland, Tanzania", both produced in 1968; "Sample Survey of Agriculture Lake Regions", Central Statistical Bureau, Ministry of Economic Affairs and Development Planning (Devplan), 1968; Recorded Population Changes 1948—67, Central Statistical Bureau, Devplan, 1968; Devplan's internal files on Mwanza Region including Rene Dumont's notes on his visit (1967) and the draft regional plan submitted by the Mwanza Regional Economic Secretary in 1969; Lint and Seed Marketing Board, "Annual Reports", 1960 to 1969, and, *idem*, "Country Paper", 1969; and, *Tanzania Second Five Year Plan for Economic and Social Development* (1969—74), especially the third volume produced in 1970.

2. Figures are from the population Census for 1967 as reproduced in, Ian D. Thomas, "Population Density in Tanzania, 1967", Dar es Salaam: Bureau of Resource Assessment and Land Use Planning, University College, Dar es Salaam, September, 1968.

3. According to figures produced in the Second Plan's third volume, from which these and the figures below are drawn, Dar es Salaam produced 20.3 per cent of the GDP.

4. The eighteenth region was established in March, 1971, by the splitting of Mtwara Region into the present Mtwara and Lindi Regions.

5. The water supplies figure is from, G. Tschannerl, "Water Supply as a Part of Rural Development", presented to the 1971 Universities Social Sciences Conference, Makerere, Uganda, December, 1971, p. 7.

6. There were significant variations also within the leader group itself and there was some difficulty in interpreting exactly when a child was 'in' a particular family, thus a percentage range is reported rather than an exact figure.

7. Shinyanga is in Shinyanga Region and is considered part of Sukumaland. Figures for these disparities are presented in, Larsen *et al.*, *op.cit.*, pp. 81—99; and, Arne Larsen, "Variations in Income among Farming Areas in Sukumaland and Related Policy Implications", presented to the East African Agricultural Economics Society Conference, April, 1970.

8. In this paragraph the Gross Region Product figures are from the third volume of the Second Plan, while the other information comes from our farm surveys and is reported in, Larsen *et al*, *op.cit.*

9. Larsen *et al*, *op.cit.*, p. 75.

10. *Ibid*, pp. 58—59. The calculations are based on internal Ministry of Economic Affairs and Development Planning (Devplan) documents and figures.

11. See, Robert H. Hulls, "An Assessment of Agricultural Extension in Sukumaland, Western Tanzania", revised version of a paper published by the Economic Research Bureau of the University of Dar es Salaam, August, 1971.

12. K. R. M. Anthony and V. C. Uchendu, "A Field Study of Agricultural Change: Geita District, Tanzania", Stanford: Food Research Institute, February, 1969; see, also, R. G. Saylor, "Variations in Sukumaland Cotton Yields and the Extension Service", presented to the East African Agricultural Economics Conference, 1970.

13. See, Lionel Cliffe, "Nationalism and the Reaction to Enforced Agricultural Change in Tanganyika during the Colonial Period", presented to the East African Institute of Social Research Conference, Makere, Uganda, December, 1964.

14. The incident is described in, A. M. Mtesigwa, "The Politics of Agriculture in Ukerewe: the Role of Fertilizers and Cotton Production", unpublished undergraduate political science dissertation, University College, Dar es Salaam, March, 1969.

15. Rene Dumont, "Short Notes of Mwanza District", Devplan files, 1967, italics in the original.

16. *Cf.* Dean McHenry, Jr., "The Utility of Compulsion in the Implementation of Agricultural Policies: A Case Study from Tanzania", *Canadian Journal of African Studies*, 7, 2 (1973), pp. 305—318.

17. *The Standard* and *The Nationalist* were replaced by the *Daily News* in 1972. The figures presented are of those distributed commercially. There are the odd copies which people bring into Geita on returning from Mwanza or other centres.

18. For this very brief overview I have relied on the following: R. G. Abrahams, *The Peoples of Greater Unyamwezi*, London: International African Institute, 1967, and, *idem*, *The Political Organization of Unyamwezi*, Cambridge: Cambridge University Press, 1967; Ralph A. Austen, *Northwest Tanzania under German and British Rule*, New Haven: Yale University Press, 1968, and, *idem*, "Ntemiship, Trade, and State-building among the Western Bantu of Tanzania", in, Daniel F. McCall, Norman R. Bennett and Jeffrey Butler (eds.), *Eastern African History*, New York: Praeger, 1969, pp. 133—147; Hans Cory, *The Ntemi: Traditional Rites in Connection with the Burial, Election, Enthronment and Magic Powers of a Sukuma Chief*, London: Macmillan, 1951, and, *idem*, *Sukuma Law and Custom*, London: Oxford University Press, 1953, and, *idem*, *The Indigenous Political System of the Sukuma and Proposals for Political Reform*, Nairobi: Eagle Press, 1954; Audrey I. Richards (ed.), *East African Chiefs*, London: Faber and Faber, 1959, especially the introductory and concluding chapters by Richards, the chapter on the "Sukuma" by J. Gus Liebenow, and the one on the "Zinza" by J. La Fontaine; Gerald W. Hartwig, "Bukerebe, the Church Missionary Society, and East African Politics, 1877—1878", *African Historical Studies*, I, 2 (1968), pp. 211—232, and, *idem*, "A Historical

Perspective of Kerebe Sculpturing—Tanzania", *Tribus*, 18 (1969), pp. 85—
102, and, *idem*, "The Victoria Nyanza as a Trade Route in the Nineteenth
Century", *Journal of African History*, XI, 4 (1970), pp. 535—552; J. Gus
Liebenow, "Responses to Planned Political Change in a Tanganyika Tribal
Group", *American Political Science Review*, L, 2 (June, 1956), pp. 442—
461, and, "The Chief in Sukuma Local Government", *Journal of African
Administration*, XI, 2 (April, 1959), pp. 84—92; G. O. Lang and M. B.
Lang, "Problems of Social and Economic Change in Sukumaland, Tangan-
yika", *Anthropological Quarterly*, XXXV, 2 (April, 1962), pp. 86—101, and,
G. O. Lang, "Modernization in East Africa Through Cultural Continuity:
The Case of the Sukuma", unpublished manuscript, 1968; Malcolm, *op.cit.*;
Warren J. Roth, "Three Co-operatives and A Credit Union as Examples of
Cultural Change Among the Sukuma of Tanzania", unpublished doctoral
dissertation, Catholic University, 1966; C. R. Hatfield, "The Nfumu in Tradition and Change: A study of the Position of Religious Practitioneers
among the Sukuma of Tanzania, East Africa", unpublished doctoral dissertation, Catholic University, 1968; R. E. S. Tanner, "Law Enforcement by
Communal Action in Sukumaland, Tanganyika Territory", *Journal of African Administration*, VII, 4 (October, 1955), pp. 159—165; discussions
with Mbeti Musiyi, 1969—70.

19. Austen, *op.cit.*, 1968, 1969; Richards, *op.cit.*, chapters 1, 15.

20. Lang, *op.cit.*, p. 19. This paragraph is indebted to the analysis of
Lang and Hatfield.

21. The composition of the chiefdom council is not clear. The cited
writings of Liebenow identify them as royal relatives while the unpublished
paper of Lang's states that it was "composed frequently of commoners".
Liebenow has also referred to a royal guard (descendants of former slaves)
and the clan elders who advised the chief on judicial affairs. Cory seems
to allow that the council at times may have had commoner members (1954,
p. 45 *et. seq.*) but also claims that one of their functions was the judicial
one ascribed by Liebenow to the clan elders. Abrahams, *The Peoples . . .*,
p. 58, has summed up by noting that the position is "unclear".

22. On this point, see, Hatfield, *op.cit.*

23. Liebenow and Lang stress that the traditional pattern of participation was destroyed by the imposition of colonial rule. Nonetheless the traditional organization bequeathed to the present system rules for judging
whether behaviour is 'good' or 'bad' and to the extent that these rules
guide the people's consideration of present organizational arrangements
they are relevant to this study.

24. John Iliffe, *Tanganyika under German Rule 1905—1912*, Cambridge:
Cambridge University Press, 1969, p. 15.

25. *Ibid.*, especially chapter 7; Austen, *op.cit.*, 1968 and 1969; Abrahams,
The Political . . ., p. 45.

26. Iliffe, *op.cit.*, p. 146.

27. *Ibid.*, p. 163.

28. Austen, *op.cit.*, 1968, pp. 49—50.

29. Iliffe, *op.cit.*, p. 163.

30. Abrahams, *The Political . . .*, p. 46.

31. Liebenow, in, Richards (ed.), *op.cit.*, p. 239.

32. Sir Donald Cameron, *My Tanganyika Experience and Some Nigeria*, London: Allen and Unwin, 1939; Judith Listowel, *The Making of Tanganyika*, London: Chatto and Windus, 1965, chapter 8; J. Clagett Taylor, *The Political Development of Tanganyika*, Stanford: Stanford University Press, 1963, pp. 43—55.

33. Austen, *op.cit.*, 1968, p. 179.

34. *Ibid.*

35. *Ibid.*, pp. 204—205.

36. Gene Andrew Maguire, "Toward 'Uhuru' in Sukumaland": A Study of Micropolitics in Tanzania, 1945—59, doctoral dissertation, Harvard University, 1966, pp. 59—60. The officer did continue in Mwanza and in later years held a very senior post in the secretariat in Dar es Salaam. The account in the published version (1969, p. 49) is less complete.

37. Maguire, *op.cit.*, 1969, pp. 49—50.

38. Austen, op.cit., p. 254.

39. Andrew Cohen, *British Policy in Changing Africa*, London: Routledge and Kegan Paul, 1959, chapter 1; Lucy Mair, "Representative Local Government as a Problem in Social Change", *Journal of African Administration*, X, 1 (January, 1958), pp. 11—24; R. E. Robinson, "Why 'Indirect Rule' has been Replaced by 'Local Government' in the Nomenclature of British Native Administration", *Journal of African Administration*, II, 3 (July, 1950), pp. 12—13.

40. Maguire, *op.cit.*, 1969, p. 18. *Cf.*, J. V. Shaw, "The Development of African Local Government in Sukumaland", *Journal of African Administration*, VI, 4 (October, 1954), pp. 442—461; B. J. Dudbridge and J. E. S. Griffiths, "The Development of Local Government in Sukumaland", III, 3 (July, 1951), pp. 141—146. Cory's, *op.cit.*, 1954, was undertaken as part of the preparations for local government, and it also (p. III) draws our attention to other articles in the *Journal of African Administration*, C. Winnington Ingram, "Reforming Local Government in a Tanganyika District", II, 2 (April, 1950), and, C. I. Meek, "A Practical Experience in Local Government", II, 3 (July, 1950).

41. Maguire, *op.cit.*, 1969, p. 27; Liebnow, *op.cit.*, 1956, pp. 454—455.

42. Maguire, *op.cit.*, 1969, pp. 19—21.

43. *Ibid*, p. 26.

44. *Ibid.*

45. Liebnow, *op.cit.*, 1956, pp. 454—455.

46. Liebnow, *op.cit.*, 1959, p. 86.

47. Maguire, *op.cit.*, 1969, p. xxiii.

48. *Ibid*, p. 277.

49. Hugh W. Stephens, *The Political Transformation of Tanganyika*, New York: Praeger, 1968, p. 150.

50. For instance, the Geita District Commissioner who "exercised leadership by advising, rather than by directing." Maguire, *op.cit.*, 1969, pp. 293—294.

51. G. Andrew Maguire, "The Emergence of the TANU in the Lake Province", in Robert I. Rotberg and Ali A. Mazrui, *Protest and Power in*

Black Africa, New York: Oxford University Press, 1970, pp. 669—670.

52. The top leadership levels did however involve themselves in political affairs. Maguire, *op.cit.*, 1969, pp. 184—185n. For an account which suggests a more active role for the co-operatives in Mwanza in politics, see, Bennett, *op.cit.*

53. See, K. W. J. Post, "British Policy and Representative Government in West Africa", in L. H. Gann and Peter Duignan (eds.), *Colonialism in Africa 1870—1960*, Cambridge: Cambridge University Press, 1970, Vol. II, p. 55.

54. Martin Staniland, "The Rhetoric of Centre-Periphery Relations", *The Journal of Modern African Studies*, VIII, 4 (1970), pp. 617—36.

55. Martin Staniland, "Colonial Government and Populist Reform: the case of the Ivory Coast—Part I", *Journal of Administration Overseas*, X, 1 (January, 1971), p. 39.

56. Roland Young and Henry Fosbrooke, *Land and Politics among the Luguru of Tanganyika*, London: Routledge and Kegan Paul, 1960, pp. 169—170.

57. Major works on this subject are: Stanley Dryden, *Local Administration in Tanzania*, Nairobi: East African Publishing House, 1968; William Tordoff, *Government and Politics in Tanzania*, Nairobi: East African Publishing House, 1967; Henry Bienen, *Tanzania: Party Transformation and Economic Development*, Princeton: Princeton University Press, expanded edition, 1970; Lionel Cliffe and John Saul (eds.), *Socialism in Tanzania*, Dar es Salaam: East African Publishing House, Volumes I and II, 1972, 1973; Raymond Hopkins, *Political Roles in a New State*, New Haven: Yale University Press, 1971; Clyde Ingle, *From Village to State in Tanzania*, Ithaca: Cornell University Press, 1972; Göran Hydén, *Political Development in Rural Tanzania*, Nairobi: East African Publishing House, 1969.

58. See, Idrian N. Resnick, "Manpower Development in Tanzania", *Journal of Modern African Studies*, V, 1 (1967), pp. 107—123. Also, Guy Hunter, *Manpower, Employment and Education in Tanzania*, Paris: UNESCO —International Institute for Educational Planning, 1966.

59. John S. Saul, "Highlevel Manpower for Socialism", in, Cliffe and Saul (eds.), *op.cit.*, Vol. II, p. 277.

60. The position for the Councils in Tanzania as a whole is discussed in, R. G. Penner, *Financing Local Government in Tanzania*, Nairobi: East African Publishing House, 1970.

61. Figures are from the final financial statement of the Councils.

62. Annual Report of the Mwanza Regional Commissioner, 1968.

63. Letter from the Commissioner to the Executive Officer of the four Councils, 24 December, 1968, File, L.6/42/55. Gallu was later renamed an *ujamaa* village.

64. See, explanations accompanying the Kwimba District Council's Final Financial Statement of 1969.

65. *The Standard*, 20 June, 1969.

67. See, minutes of the meeting.

68. "Mabadiliko ya Mapato ya Halmashauri za Wilaya na Namna Mpya ya Utayarishaji wa Makadirio ya Mwaka ya Mapato na Matumizi."

69. *The Nationalist*, 19 March, 1971; *The Standard*, 6 August, 1971.

70. The abolition of the Councils was initially announced in January, 1972. See, *The Standard*, 27 January, 1972.

71. *Ibid*; and, Julius K. Nyerere, *Decentralization*, Dar es Salaam: Government Printer, 1972.

72. Maguire, *op.cit.*, 1969, and Roth, *op.cit.*, contain the well-documented histories of the VFCU and similar co-operative movements in the Mwanza area.

73. Both colonial and independence governments employed the tactic of coopting VFCU leaders into official positions to associate them with government policy.

74. This discussion of the block farms relies upon personal interviews with co-operative officials and members at all levels in Mwanza Region; internal Nyanza Co-operative Union files; J. D. Heijnen, "The Mechanised Block Cultivation Schemes in Mwanza Region, 1964—1969", Bureau of Resource Assessment and Land Use Planning, University of Dar es Salaam, 1969; and a publicly circulated memorandum from the VFCU to the Minister of Agriculture entitled, "A Memorandum on the Past Working and Running of the Block Farms and Proposals for the Future as seen by the Victoria Federation of Co-operative Unions Limited", Mwanza, 18 August, 1966.

75. The new name became effective 31 December, 1967. See, "Muundo Mpya wa Nyanza Co-operative Union", a pamphlet setting out the government's case which was distributed in *Ukulima wa Kisasa*, a government agricultural publication, in mid-1968. Also, Staff Circular No. 1 of 1968 of the Unified Co-operative Commission, "The Arusha Declaration: Employees of Co-operative Organisations and Leadership Conditions", Dar es Salaam, n.d.

76. In this regard see, Rene Dumont, *Socialism and Development*, London: Andre Deutsch, 1973; and, S. E. Migot-Adhola, "The Politics of a Growers' Co-operative Organization", unpublished undergraduate Political Science Dissertation, University of Dar es Salaam, March, 1969.

77. John Saul, "Marketing Co-operatives in a Developing Country: The Tanzanian Case", in, Peter Worsley (ed.), *Two Blades of Grass*, Manchester University Press, 1971, and reprinted in Cliffe and Saul (eds.), *op.cit.*, p. 150. It is interesting that in a 'development of underdevelopment' oriented discussion of co-operatives in Tanzania Saul's prescriptions coincide with those of the 'penetration' persuasion, to wit, central control now until the people have been 'educated'.

78. On the fragmentation in the agricultural sector and the difficulties in determining agricultural expenditures by the government because of the number of branches and parastatals involved, see, G. K. Helleiner, "The Composition of Agricultural Development Expenditures in Tanzania, 1963/64 to 1967/68", Dar es Salaam: Economic Research Bureau, University College, 1968.

79. See, Presidential Circular No. 1 of 1969, "The Development of *Ujamaa* Villages", 20 March, 1969.

79a. These figures are based on staff listings provided by the Mwanza

Regional Director of Agriculture in June, 1969, and, to Aloys Rutaihwa, in August, 1970. They include District Council staff and exclude unfilled positions.

80. A discussion of the resemblance of the methods of the present and colonial extension workers is in, Hulls, *op.cit.*, pp. 58—60.

81. W. Ouma Oyugi, "SRDP: An Assessment", *East Africa Journal*, IX, 3 (March, 1972), p. 38.

82. Jon Moris, "Administrative Penetration as a Tool for Development Analysis: A Structural Interpretation of Agricultural Administration in Kenya", presented to the Conference on Comparative Administration in East Africa, Arusha, Tanzania, September 1971, p. 11.

83. Aside from the central party organization and the Youth League (most of whose staff were over 35 years old) other TANU organizations were existing in skeleton form. The women's organization (Umoja wa Wanawake wa Tanganyika) had only one full-time official and she was a Rural Development officer on secondment from her Ministry which continued to pay her salary. TAPA, the parents' organization, had no full-time staff. The central trade union organization's staff in Mwanza Region numbered (probably) five—three in Mwanza, one in Geita, and one in Ukerewe. The information comes from interviews in the TANU regional and district headquarters in July, 1970. The unions figure may be wrong by one or two as no official was certain as to the number of NUTA staff in the Region!

84. The TANU structure up to 1965 has been described by Bienen, *op.cit., passim.* Up to mid-1973 the important changes since then are: the Central Committee is composed of the party's President, Vice President, five members appointed by the President, and the eighteen regional representatives elected by the party's biennial national conference; these eighteen also sit on the National Executive Committee. Formerly the Central Committee was composed of the President, Vice President and members, usually ten, appointed by the President. Members of the Central Committee now are members of the Working Committees in the regions in which they reside. The District Executive Committee now includes the branch chairman (elected) and secretaries (appointed by centre) of all ward branches as members; prior to 1971 each branch sent only one representative to the District Executive. The District Executive, however, has become somewhat unwieldy and now meets three rather than four times a year. Members of the Regional Working Committees are now members of the District Working Committee in their District, and the District and Regional Working Committees now meet once rather than twice a month. Since 1969 leaders are elected for five rather than two year terms of office. See, *Katiba ya TANU*, 1967; *Katiba ya TANU*, 1969; *The Nationalist*, September 15 and 24, 1971.

85. The first edition of Bienen's book was published in 1967.

86. Lionel Cliffe, "Tanzania Socialist Transformation and Party Development", *The African Review*, I, 1 (March, 1971), pp. 119—135.

87. This is the estimate of the TANU regional officials made in an 8 August, 1969, interview with Aloys Rutaihwa and myself. The election

figure comes from, Lionel Cliffe (ed.), *One Party Democracy*, Nairobi: East African Publishing House, 1967, appendix 1B.

88. *The Nationalist*, 25 and 26 February 1970. The Arusha Declaration (section four) has been interpreted by many people in Tanzania as a call for a vanguard party with membership limited to those possessing certain characteristics. The section reads: "the time has come for emphasis to shift away from mere size of membership on to the quality of the membership... Where it is thought unlikely that an applicant really accepts the beliefs, aims and objects of the party, he should be denied membership." In 1970 a limiting interpretation of this section was specifically rejected by the party's National Executive Secretary who said TANU was still "open to all". *The Nationalist*, 11 April 1970. As of July, 1970, TANU in Mwanza Region had apparently never excluded from membership anyone who was willing to pay with the exception, in most but not all cases, of non-citizens. Nyerere, perhaps not so concerned with the more mundane financial aspects of TANU, continues to make calls for "quality not quantity" in membership. *The Nationalist*, 9 September 1971.

89. The total cost (as of December, 1971) of the new TANU headquarters in Mwanza Region was two million shillings. One million came from "Dar es Salaam", and one million was contributed locally. Interview with the Mwanza Regional Commissioner broadcast on the National Service of Radio Tanzania, 3 December 1971. Without being able to present precise figures, it is nonetheless clear that the bulk of one million shillings raised locally came from businessmen, the government controlled Lint and Seed Marketing Board and Nyanza Co-operative Union, and from civil servants who were urged at special meetings held while I was in Mwanza to contribute to the building fund. The Regional Commissioner asked them to hold their receipts so that he could see them when visiting their offices, and reminded them that he expected civil servants to contribute in accordance with their salaries. Interviews, with several regional officers, February, 1970. The fund for the building of the TANU national headquarters has depended heavily upon parastatals, see, *The Nationalist*, 11 February and 3 April 1971.

90. Bates reported that TANU's annual budget in 1960 was 1 million shillings. Presumably the entirety of this came from TANU's own sources. Bienen reported that in 1962/63 the TANU budget was 1.5 million shillings.

TANU made public its budget, for the first time, in June, 1968. According to newspaper reports, TANU's expenditure in 1967/68 was 3.78 million shillings; in 1968/69 it was 11.37 million; in 1969/70 it was 11.29 million; for 1970/71 it was estimated at 16.7 million; and for 1971/72 it was estimated at 18.5 million shillings.

Of net revenues in 1966/67, 2.14 million shillings came from "membership payments" and 1.75 million from a government subvention. Of net revenues of 3.5 million in 1967/68, 1.91 million came from "membership payments" and 1.54 million came from a government subvention. "Membership payments" here include TANU's other sources—rents, publications, "contributions" from non-TANU individuals, mainly Asian businessmen. In other words, the largest part of the increase of TANU revenues between 1960 and 1968 came from a straight grant from government.

After the Arusha Declaration nationalization measures had been carried out, the party began to get large grants from parastatals. Of the 16.7 million shillings budgeted for 1970/71, TANU headquarters hoped that membership payments would *increase* so as to make up 3 million. Here "membership payments" means entrance fees, dues, and contributions by individual members. The remaining 14.7 million would come from contributions from non-members (read, merchants), rents, proceeds of festivals, and a government subvention. A conservative estimate would be that 13 million shillings came from a government subvention (including now the grants from the parastatals and marketing boards). For the 18.5 million shillings of the 1971/72 budget, it was stated that 10 million would come from "membership dues and other contributions". Translated, this means that 8.5 million was coming directly from the government while an unstated portion, say 5 million, was coming from parastatals and marketing boards and was listed as "contributions". In short, of the 1971/72 TANU budget, approximately 20—25 per cent comes from the party's own sources, the rest comes from the central government and parastatals. This cannot be explained simply by saying that the country is poor, or that TANU's constituency is poor. At a Saba Saba rally in Dar es Salaam in July, 1970, there was an "almost instant collection" of 300,000 shillings. This led to puzzlement amongst many TANU leaders as to why if this could be done there was such difficulty in raising money regularly.

It should also be noted that many of the TANU "functionaries" were being paid from central (Commissioners, members of party committees who were also M.P.'s) or local (district chairmen) government funds.

Sources: Margaret L. Bates, "Tanganyika", in Gwendolen M. Carter (ed.), *African one party States*, Ithaca: Cornell University Press, 1962, p. 456; Bienen, *op.cit.*, p. 193; *The Nationalist*, 13 June 1968, 12 May 1969, 25 and 26 February 1970, 11, 12 and 15 June, 1970; *The Standard*, 13 June 1968, 12 July 1970, 5 June 1971.

91. I am quoting from the mimeographed minutes of the meeting, which was also attended by the Area Commissioners for Kwimba and Mwanza Districts. The tone and content of this address (and the reality) contrast so completely with what is sometimes reported in the Dar es Salaam newspapers that perhaps one example should be given. In June, 1970, I watched the events as the Uhuru Torch, the symbol of Tanzanian independence, was brought to Mwanza on its annual tour through the nation. Its passing was observed by a small detachment of the police field force unit and National Servicemen who were accompanying it, by five members of the TANU Youth League who walked quickly with it through the streets, and by school children who had been lined up by their teachers. At the District Council a group of forty Council workers watched quietly as a prepared statement was read, and then returned to their offices. Offices and shops remained open throughout the normal hours. This is how *The Nationalist*, 22 June 1970, reported it:

"Almost the entire population of Mwanza town yesterday lined up the streets to give a colourful reception to Uhuru Torch... Revolution songs ... greeted the Uhuru Torch as it was being raced through the streets of the town. All shops and bars remained closed as the owners joined thousands of Mwanza residents to receive the torch... Peasants and workers held a colourful ceremony as the torch moved from one hand to the other. A message of loyalty was read at the Mwanza District Council during which reactionaries and saboteurs were condemned. The message also hailed President Nyerere for his efforts in building a socialist Tanzania and for dealing with reactionaries, exploiters and enemies of the country."

92. Wilbert A. Klerru, "The Systematic Creation and Operation of TANU Cells", in, *Mashina ya TANU* (TANU Cells), Dar es Salaam: Research Department of TANU Headquarters, February, 1969, pp. 11—15, reprinted in full in mimeograph form by the Department of Political Science, University College, Dar es Salaam.

93. Information Department, TANU Headquarters, "Viongozi wa TANU, 1967—69", Dar es Salaam (a small booklet), n.d.

94. *Cf. The Nationalist*, 5 August 1970, commenting on registration for the 1970 general election: "One main factor has contributed to this success: it is Tanzania's excellent political Party structure. Once again for example, the strength of our Party organisation, particularly the Party Cell System, has been proved. It was the Party Cell leaders, who went from house to house to remind people to go and register themselves. Once again, it has been amply demonstrated that Tanzanians are a highly politicised people..." With reference to Mwanza Region, such descriptions are completely misleading.

95. The information in this paragraph has been based on the interviews with 146 cell leaders which I have described in Chapter I, and upon discussions and observations with many leaders and non-leaders in the rural areas. *Cf.* J. H. Proctor (ed.), *The Cell System of the Tanganyika African National Union*, Dar es Salaam: Tanzanian Publishing House (University of Dar es Salaam. Studies in Political Science No. 1), 1971. The theoretical view is stated by Bailey: "middlemen, in the situation of encapsulation, are roles which... bridge a gap in communication between the larger and the smaller societies" (p. 167). "Middleman tend to take the form of messengers when the local community... has a high degree of autonomy and makes little use of political resources from the world outside" (p. 170). "The normative status given to the middleman is indeed an index of the degree to which the value systems concerned are... shared by the two structures. The middleman is despised in proportion to the disparity of the two cultures" (p. 171). F. G. Bailey, *Strategems and Spoils*, Oxford: Blackwell, 1969. Austen, *op. cit.*, 1968, mentions three chiefs who had been selected by their chiefdoms during the colonial period because they were weak (including alcoholic) individuals. In a move designed to increase the stature of the cell leaders and the fund raising capacity of the party, in September, 1971, the National Executive Committee decided that cell leaders will henceforth be dues collectors and will retain 20 per cent as their commission. *The Nationalist*, 15 September 1971.

96. VFCU, *op.cit.*, para. 2, a; The block farms "drew on 60 per cent of the extension personnel in the Lake area for less than 5 per cent of the cot-

ton crop, and thereby... resulted in an opportunity cost of £250,000". Lionel Cliffe and Griffiths Cunningham, "Ideology, Organization, and the Settlement Experience in Tanzania", Rural Development Research Committee Paper No. 3, University College, Dar es Salaam, 1968, p. 3.

97. See, Antony Ellman, "The Introduction of Agricultural Innovations Through Co-operative Farming: A Brief Outline of Tanzania's Policies", *East African Journal of Rural Development*, III, 1 (1971), pp. 1—15; and, *idem*: "Development of *Ujamaa* Farming", *Kroniek van Afrika*, 1971, 2, pp. 113—130.

98. On Ruvuma see, Dumont, *op.cit.*, 1972; R. Ibbott, "Ruvuma Development Association", *Mbioni*, III, 2 (July, 1966); and, *idem*, "The Disbanding of the Ruvuma Development Association", a privately circulated mimeographed report from London, n.d.

99. Julius Nyerere, "Freedom and Development", *The Nationalist*, 18 October, 1968.

100. I visited all of Mwanza's *ujamaa* villages in 1969—70 and the somewhat viable ones I returned to periodically. On the four villages which were most established I prepared detailed reports of their organizational, social and production histories which were circulated locally.

101. Presidential Circular No. 1 of 1969, *op.cit.*, para. 2.

102. *Ibid*, para. 6.

103. See the statements of the Minister of Regional Administration and Rural Development, *The Standard*, 15 July, 1969; *The Nationalist*, 29 July, 1970.

104. The man, Lusasu Mibako, had worked on clove estates in Zanzibar during 1955—60. He had experience in cotton growing, and was convinced that the block farms which had failed in the area (Kharumwa) had failed because of ineffective management. He tried certain communal fields and work sharing approaches during 1961—1966, and in 1967 convinced some neighbors to combine their fields to start Izunya *Ujamaa* Village.

105. Within the villages the distinction was made between members of the 'farm' (working members who to some extent actually lived and worked together) and members of the 'village' (political officials living away from the physical village or fields who did not participate in the work). Incredibly some of the latter had not once managed to pay a visit to 'their village'.

106. Interview with Mwanza District Agricultural Coordinator, 8 May, 1970.

107. The most important committee was at the district level consisting of the Area Commissioner, the TANU chairman, the area secretary, the District Council executive officer, and the district officer of Agriculture and Rural Development. They decided who was to receive intensive governmental assistance as '*ujamaa* villages'—some groups would receive such assistance before qualifying as a village—and a reading of their minutes indicates that it was the specialist officials on the committee along with some of their colleagues at the district level—particularly the education and water and irrigation officials—who were pleading for quick recognition to be given to would-be *ujamaa* villages.

108. See, *Sunday News* (Dar es Salaam), 25 May, 1969, wherein it is reported that "more than 200 teachers and school children ... have volunteered to help cotton farmers at Izunya *ujamaa* village to harvest their crop".

109. This 1971 information comes from December, 1971, interviews with regional officials.

110. Lionel Cliffe and John Saul, "The District Development Front in Tanzania", Dar es Salaam, mimeograph, 1969, p. 1; also contained in Cliffe and Saul (eds.), *op.cit.*, Vol. I.

Village Development Committees

Background

The Village Development Committees (VDC's) officially launched in May, 1962, by Prime Minister Kawawa,[1] were charged with advancing economic and social improvement in the rural areas. They were to be the grassroots of a national network of development committees extending through the district and regional levels to the national Economic Development Commission—"a chain of command providing the essential two-way flow of ideas between government and the people".[2] Their establishment has been described as following from the government's awareness of the need to build the nation "as much 'from below' as from 'above'", and the necessity, if this were to be achieved, for a "better link with the people in the rural areas".[3] The setting up of the VDC's was, in the opinion of Hydén, "the most important [step]... taken by government to improve the responsiveness to local demands".[4]

The experiment with the VDC's lasted seven years. In July, 1969, they were dissolved and replaced by Ward Development Committees. In this chapter I consider the activities of the VDC's in Mwanza Region and their success in contributing to a "two-way flow".

The idea for the village development committees reportedly originated in the discussions of Nyerere and other TANU leaders during 1957—58. They concluded that the "old parish councils should be refurnished as development committees when independence was attained".[5] After some experimentation in Musoma, the TANU executive committee in early 1962 worked out "the format of the VDC's. The parish council and the self-help ideas were combined".[6]

The VDC's in Mwanza Region were in many instances developments which paralleled the discussions of TANU's national executive.[7] The committees were well established in Ukerewe by May, 1962, (prior to Kawawa's announcement or the statement by the Minister in the Assembly) with the District Development Committee (DDC) already dealing with requests from eight VDC's for assistance in the construction of four dispensaries and eight bridges.[8] By July, 1962, when the Regional Commissioner, acting on instructions from Dar es Salaam,

83

was ordering that VDC's were to be set up to prepare proposals for assistance which the DDC's might consider, the Ukerewe DDC was processing requests concerning an additional ten dispensaries and three schools.[9] In Mwanza, Geita and Kwimba Districts the monthly reports of the Divisional Executive Officers to the Executive Officers of their respective District Councils record that the Community Development and District Council officials who toured the rural areas over the period July, 1962—March, 1963, ostensibly to establish VDC's, in a good number of cases met committees in existence upon their arrival.[10]

As organized by the touring civil servants, each VDC initially covered a *gunguli*, a Village Executive Officer's administrative area. The number of households in each *gunguli* varied from about 1,800 to 160, distributed amongst a dozen or so villages.[11] [12] The selection of committee members was done in mass open meetings by voice voting with the members subsequently choosing their own chairman. In a rough way selections were distributed on a *kijiji* basis to ensure a somewhat comprehensive areal representation. The selections were made, however, not by the residents of the *kijiji* concerned, but by all those who attended the mass meeting. The secretary and executive officer of the VDC was the local Village Executive Officer.

As the VDC's at the outset were the product of local initiatives which preceeded the concern of the TANU government manifested by the touring officials, the size of the committees and the relationships between committee leaders and local TANU leaders were determined by the local situation. In some cases this led to arrangements which the central government found unacceptable and soon moved to reduce. In July, 1964, the Area Commissioners in Mwanza Region, acting on instructions issued by the Ministry of Local Government, ordered that all local branch chairmen of TANU were to become *ex officio* chairmen of the VDC's in their areas.[13] [14] In 1966 a Government Paper designated the membership of the VDC as all the cell leaders in a "ward".[15] These moves to give an appearance of conformity to the composition of the committees were intended to obviate the political competition which had on occasion occurred between the leaderships of the VDC's and the local TANU branches.[16] [17]

The use of the term "ward" in the Government Paper was surprising. A "ward" in 1964—66 was not an administrative area, it was a District Council electoral constituency which often overlapped several VDC areas. With most TANU branches in Mwanza Region organized on a ward basis, it was not uncommon for one branch to have within its boundaries two or three village development committees. There was some doubt on the part of both the villagers and the officials as to whether the TANU chairman, under the 1964 instruction, was to be chairman of all the VDC's in his branch area (ward), or of only the VDC in whose area he resided. This was not an altogether intractable problem even without further central clarification—the number of functioning VDC's was less than the official reports indicated, and in many instances TANU had locally established sub-branches which provided additional chairmen for filling VDC positions.

Despite the 1964 order there appears to have been no firm pattern to the selection of VDC chairmen in Mwanza Region in subsequent years. The practice varied from an immediate compliance with the central instruction to persistent intransigence. In some areas the VDC chairman became the *ex officio* chairman of the TANU branch, the reverse of the ordered procedure yet one which had the same effect in reducing blatant VDC—Tanu competition. In the majority of cases it seems that the VDC's continued to elect their own chairmen from amongst themselves. While this often led to the election of the local TANU chairman, in certain instances it resulted in the defeat of the TANU chairmen and the reinforcement of a bitter split between the TANU and VDC leaderships.[18] There was no co-ordinated or consistent attempt to impose TANU chairmen on the VDC's, and for this reason there was no significant conflict on this matter between the VDC's and the government and party officials at the district level.

Village Development Committees and The National Political System

The lack of a uniform response to the 1964 attempt to meld the VDC and TANU chairmanships was a minor difficulty. It added, however, to the uncertainty which was already existing at that time over the structure and activities of the VDC's. There was confusion regarding the position and role of the officials on the VDC's, the relationships between the VDC's and the government and party institutions at the district level, and the role of the VDC's themselves.[19]

Official representation of the VDC's was to comprise all the various extension workers posted on the VDC's area (e.g., health, community development, agriculture, veterinary), teachers from the local primary schools, and any other officials who happened to be in the vicinity at the time of the meeting. These, along with the VDC's secretary, the Village Executive Officer, would all be non-voting members. In practice the extension workers adopted the position that they would attend meetings only when they had something specific to discuss, while the Assistant Divisional Executive Officer, who was more often concerned with the collection of local rates than with the giving of extension advice, was the most frequent visiting official. As late as 1969 VDC minutes contain queries on the lack of any consistent official attendance and requests that the Area Commissioner or the Executive Officer of the District Council clarify the matter.

The relationship of the VDC's to the political and administrative institutions at the district level evidenced a disparity between government and party rhetoric and the reality. Officially, up to 1966, the VDC's functioned informally; from that point on they were to "function in direct conjunction with and under the supervision of the District Development and Planning Committee (DDPC)".[20] On the ground they remained as they were from the beginning, part of what the Ministry of Local Government Officials referred to as "floating government".[21]

Minutes of VDC meetings when forwarded (in most cases they do not seem to have been forwarded at all) were sent to the offices of the Area Commissioner and the District Council's Executive Officer. The former had no continuing dealings with the VDC's except in using them as the organizational framework for addressing villagers on tours, and when brought in by the local TANU leaders or the Rural Development staff to provide a show of legitimacy in enforcing regulations. The Area Commissioners received the minutes as a formality and none of the four Commissioners interviewed in 1969 were aware that their offices did receive the VDC minutes.[22]

The connexion between the District Council and the VDC's was fairly strong. They were tied to the DDPC, a committee of the Council, through their formal responsibility for preparing development plans. More importantly the VDC's secretary, the Village Executive Officer, was responsible to the Council's Executive Officer through a direct line of command of Divisional and Assistant Divisional Executive Officers. In some instances the VDC's acted in effect as the Council's agents, for example in granting remission from school fees[23] and local rates, and in approving *pombe* club locations. The Councils did not, however, and nor did they try to, establish themselves in a controlling position *vis a vis* the VDC's.

The District Rural Development Officer was responsible for the spending of the self-help funds which the DDPC allocated, and in this capacity he was at times closely involved with the VDC's. The DDPC usually requested that he select those projects which merited assistance from amongst the proposals which had been sent from the VDC's by the Villiage Executive Officers or by the Rural Development Assistants.[24] The district office of the Rural Development Division, as did the other central government agencies, used the VDC's as a framework within which to campaign for their programmes (adult education, nutrition, child care, and others) but they most often came into contact with the village committees in the process of ascertaining whether the money, materials, and skills which had been allocated for the self-help projects were correctly expended.

The scarcity of Rural Development Assistants in the field ensured that any departmental involvement with the running of the VDC's would be limited. Geita District, for instance, had twenty-two RDA's in the field in 1968 and twenty-one in 1969 to cater for an official total of seventy-four VDC's. Nine of these field staff of Rural Development worked mainly with women's groups, and most of them resided in divisional headquarters. Some of those who did live in the villages were posted in pairs which further reduced the coverage possible.

The RDA's in the field had the task of explaining to the VDC's the procedures with which they were to operate, but they seem to have been little regarded in this by some VDC's and Village Executive Officers. Although most of the RDA's from the outset adopted a live-and-let-live position on the tendency for the VDC's to be *ad hoc* in their procedures, some attempted to dissolve recalcitrant bodies and replace them through new elections.[25] Such hierarchical solutions to rural resistance occurred in the early years of the VDC's when the RDA's were very much involved in mobilizing the people for self-help projects. In the later years the RDA's continued to complain in their reports to their district officers about the lack of regularity in the VDC's, but hierarchical methods were eschewed.

TANU had a general interest in mobilizing the masses for development. One of the frameworks in which this mobilization, especially for nation building through self-help, was to take place was the VDC[26] and thus the party was interested in the organization and operation of these bodies. The party, however, was as sketchily staffed at the village level as the Rural Development Division (Geita District in 1968 had eleven salaried branch secretaries and in 1969 sixteen) and this coupled with the local rather than central nature of TANU in the rural areas meant that the party's relationships with the VDC's varied with local factors.

In the majority of areas where there was a fair coincidence between the VDC and TANU leaderships, it would have been difficult to distinguish between the two, particularly, as often happened in the early years of self-help, the TANU rubric was used as the legitimizer of the VDC calls for the people to participate in communal tasks.[27] Some VDC's were so closely intertwined with the local TANU branch that TANU business was discussed and decided upon in the VDC meetings. In the final years of the VDC's the main institutional link, aside from the sometimes common chairmen and other leaders, was the practice of the members of the local TANU Youth League to act as the enforcement agency and messengers of the VDC.[28] The TANU secretaries and money collectors were usually present at the VDC meetings, in some instances as 'invited' members or cell leaders who participated in all the proceedings; in other instances they came strictly to collect TANU dues and contributions, and to urge the cell leaders to urge their members to pay their TANU dues and to contribute to TANU fund raising campaigns.

Government and party institutions which needed something done in the rural areas all felt competent to use the VDC's to inform, instruct, and to collect money. With no single institution assuming complete responsibility for the VDC's, conflicting instructions from the different institutions were sometimes issued.[29] More characteristically, the relationships between the other institutions and the VDC's were sporadic, with the VDC's being left alone to organize and operate as they would. From the district centres, the VDC's appeared to officials to be unreliable: village development plans were not produced,[30] assistance which was sent for self-help projects was sometimes not properly accounted for, VDC constitutions were not adhered to, and many seemed to be composed of a majority of lazy individuals. To be sure, some committees in the estimation of district officials were competently helping to bring development to their areas especially by providing the necessary forum where government and party officials could put messages across to the rural population. But the general consensus at the district centres was moderately expressed in the report of the Geita Rural Development Officer written five months before the seven year experiment with the VDC's was abandoned: "the truth is that many committees do not understand what is required to be done to bring a revolution of rural development to their areas".[31]

What was to be done by the committees was never reconciled in any congruence between the ideal and the reality. LeMarchand's description is an idealized version of the optimal expectations of district party and government officials:

Their functions are manifold, ranging from the elaboration of development plans and the assessment of costs to the allocation of responsibilities to various departments, the communication of 'progress reports' to area commissioners, and the hiring of district specialists.[32]

Except in some cases for the elaboration of plans the VDC's in Mwanza Region did not perform these functions. The development plans which did come from the VDC's were not plans as such but rather compilations of items for which the VDC's were seeking funding. They differed little from the normal requests for self-help money and it was perhaps indicative of their origin that many of those which were sent in came from areas in which a Rural Development Assistant was resident or had recently visited. These plans were neither costed nor descriptive of the economic benefits which might be expected to accrue.[33] The plans which were produced were too late to influence allocative processes. In Ukerewe, where the VDC's were most successful in producing plans, the DDPC received them in September, 1965, at least two years late if they were to be considered in a national process of planning, and dealt with them as they dealt with all requests for assistance from the villages: some were referred to other Council committees, some to the Regional Development Committee, and some (those which might actually have a valid claim to self-help funds) to the District Rural Development Officer. There was no consideration of the pluses and minuses of the plans as coherent outlines for development.

In the early years of the VDC's there was a wide rural participation in self-help projects.[34] This was mainly directed towards the increase of services (e.g., schools, clinics) and not towards other more productive projects which were more in line with national policies and which entailed less of a recurrent financial burden for the local and central governments (e.g., feeder roads). This tendency was perhaps inevitable given the dominance of local political factors in the VDC's. As the government progressively attempted to direct VDC activities towards productive projects through its allocation policies for the self-help funds, and as the amount of self-help funds available was reduced (15,000 shillings per district in 1968—69), the interest on the part of the VDC's declined. This position was not altered by the initiation of the Regional Development Fund in 1967. Up to June, 1969, the Rural Development Assistants who were working with VDC's continued explaining that they should undertake development projects, while the committees themselves were reluctant if the projects were not of a 'service' nature.

The lowered willingness of the VDC's to participate put a responsibility on officials to define more specifically what individual committees might do, and it was at this point that dismay and uncertainty over the role of the VDC's was manifested. In Geita[35] from 1964 onwards and in Ukerewe[36] from 1965 onwards the District Development Committees were not receiving enough requests for assistance to cover those funds which were available. In July, 1967, district and regional officials were expressing confusion as to what the VDC's should be doing.[37] What the village committees were doing, and how they were linking the villagers with the national political system will be clearer after a close look at the committees in one District.

A Closer Look: The Number and Activities of VDC's in Geita

The first difficulty for the researcher looking at the VDC's in Mwanza Region is discovering how many there were. The Village Executive Officers were not consistent in sending minutes of VDC meetings or reports on their activities to the Area Commissioner or the District Council. Nor was there any great concern on the part of district level officials as to what was happening to the reports and minutes which were supposed to be coming in. The DDPC's and the District Councils refused VDC requests for the provision of minutes books taking the position that minutes of VDC meetings were the responsibility of the VDC's.[38] It was thus not possible to extract from VDC records at the district level the number of VDC's.

Interviews with District Rural Development Officers and the Executive Officers for the four districts yielded another difficulty in the form of conflicting official accounts of the number of VDC's—Kwimba, one-hundred ten and one-hundred fifteen; Mwanza, sixty-three and eighty-nine; Ukerewe, twenty-three and twenty-five; Geita, seventy-four and forty-three. Adding to the enumerative problem, some of the VDC's covered areas which had formerly been under several different VDC's. This was particularly true in Ukerewe (and to a lesser extent in Mwanza and Geita) where in 1967, forty-nine VDC's were formally amalgamated into twenty-five and later to twenty. In 1969 some of these amalgamated VDC's had within their areas other VDC's which had not in practice accepted the new arrangement. These other VDC's, although not quite official, continued to have officials attending their meetings and to send intermittent correspondence to the District Council.

In this situation a calculation of the number of committees actually functioning could only be attempted by going to the villages. I did this in Geita District, interviewing on this point party and local government officials at the village/ward and divisional level over the period March—June, 1969, and by reading VDC files and minutes books at divisional and ward levels over the period June, 1969—July, 1970. Taking as the one criterion of functioning the holding of at least one meeting after July, 1967, probably between thirty and thirty-three committees, less than half the reported number, were actually in existence during the last two years of the VDC experiment.[39] Officials at the district level were of course aware in a general way of this situation. The Geita Rural Development Officer in fact had noted that the former seventy-four VDC's had slowly been reduced to forty-three early in 1969 in preparation for the setting up of the Ward Development Committees. He was not informed on how far or how early this process of reduction had proceeded.

The difference between the official figures and the reality, if it is assumed that there was a total of seventy-four at some point, was due to the failure of official knowledge to keep pace with the organizational changes in the rural areas. The number of VDC's was reduced in relation to two factors. First, during 1967 the Geita District Council in an economy move gradually reduced the number of Village Executive Officers from seventy-one (actual positions filled) to forty, and increased the number of rural Revenue Collectors from thirty-one to fifty-eight. The remaining VEO's, as secretaries to the VDC's, would have had to either serve more than one committee, or allow some of the committees to go without official secretaries. The latter alternative was the one chosen.

Few of the committees which were neglected by the smaller corps of

VEO's took up the organizational slack. This failure of most of the neglected committees to continue under local initiative is related to the second factor in the decline of the VDC's; in their connexions with the larger political system the VDC's had become increasingly penetrative—forums for exhortation, tax and TANU dues collection, and the downward flow of information. Spontaneous demands for local projects, usually 'service' projects, was a type of participation too uncontrolled to be able to comply with the goals and policies of the national structures. The more penetrative function of the VDC's was represented most immediately by the increased number of Revenue Collectors and the likelihood of the committees to be used as the focal point of rate collection campaigns, a fact borne out by the recurrence of rate collection items in the VDC's agenda over their last two years.

Of the thirty some VDC's in Geita, I analysed the activities of three as indicated by their files, minute books, and discussions with local leaders and officials. Two of these VDC's, Nyanchenchen and Mayuya, were in areas randomly selected for the interdisciplinary studies of the University College, although one, Mayuya, was in an area in which the people had refused to participate in the team's farm surveys. The other area in Geita selected on a random basis, near Kharumwa, was also one in which the people had decided not to participate in the farm surveys, but unlike Mayuya it had no functioning VDC in 1968—69. The third VDC which I examined was in Butundwe, an area selected by the Area Commissioner and the Area Secretary as a replacement for the non-cooperating Mayuya and Nyanchenchen.

The Butundwe VDC was considered by district officials as one of the better ones in Geita District, while Nyanchenchen was thought to be neither progressive nor particularly troublesome. The Mayuya VDC was not well regarded by government and party officials, which was not surprising as it was consistently resistant to central control over either its leadership or its activities. In its last twelve months it was credited with cleaning one well, its non-TANU chairman won reelection by defeating the local TANU chairman in a straight contest,[40] its non-TANU chairman was deposed on the Area Commissioner's instructions in a meeting boycotted by half the *vijiji* within its area, and the TANU chairman himself was later jailed for allegedly selling the land which was intended to form the beginnings of a communal plot.

I classified the activities of these three committees from July, 1968 to June, 1969, as indicated by the minutes of their meetings. To widen

the scope I also classified all the minutes of rural[41] VDC meetings held
during the period January—June, 1969, which had been sent to the
Geita District Council or to the office of the Geita Area Commissioner. These, grouped in the category of 'others', comprise the minutes
of eleven committees and fourteen meetings (three of the committees
having sent in the minutes of two meetings).[42]

In looking at the activities of these VDC's I was interested in their
performance as a channel for a "two-way flow of ideas between government and the people".[43] The first point considered was the attendance of officials at meetings on the premise that their presence
would be one way of creating the physical possibility of a government
—people dialogue. Other observers have written that nearly half of
the committee membership was made up of officials.[44] The figures set
out below tell of a very different situation for the VDC's in Geita.

Table 8 a. *Officials' Attendances at VDC Meetings*

Committee	Number of meetings	Average No.[b] attending including officials	Average No. of officials attending	Officials as percentage of total attending
Butundwe	27	27	3.5	12.9 %
Mayuya	15	36	2.9	8.1 %
Nyanchenchen	14	53	3.4	6.4 %
Others	14	35	2.6	7.4 %

Table 8 b. *Distribution of Officials' Attendances* (expressed as the
percentage of meetings attended by a representative from a particular
agency)

	TANU[a]	Health	Rural Devl.	Agri-culture	Admin-istra-tion[c]	Educa-tion	None[d]
Butundwe	22	56	33	45	45	11	22
Mayuya	67	0	0	13	33	80	20
Nyanchenchen	57	07	0	14	43	36	0
Others	36	07	07	21	14	36	29

a Includes TANU branch secretaries and money collectors. None of the
meetings considered were attended by TANU district officials.

b Rounded off because of the difficulty in precisely determining total
number present in a good number of cases.

c Local council administrative personnel *excluding* the VEO's.

d This column is the percentage of meetings attended by no officials
other than the Village Executive Officer.

This presentation of the figures tends to overstate the rate of official attendance.[45] Officials of agencies other than TANU, local administration, and the local primary school attended meetings for specific purposes and departed when their business was completed. The common practice was to have the officials of agencies such as health and agriculture give their speeches, often related to a 'campaign', in the beginning of the meeting so that they could leave early, an arrangement which seemed to satisfy the officials. The TANU attendances recorded are those of branch secretaries and money collectors, all of whom were local individuals chosen by the local TANU branch secretary.

The most senior official who attended and who stayed for the length of the meetings was the Assistant Divisional Executive Officer, the immediate superior of the VEO. The ADEO's seem to have been the most reliable institutional link with the larger political system. The attendance of the local primary school teachers varied widely, but when they did come to the meetings they participated in all the proceedings thus adding a modernizing element to the discussions which, while not always heeded by the VDC's, was greatly valued by the VDC leaders and apparently by the teachers themselves.[46] The poor attendance of the Rural Development Division is of course largely accounted for by their low number of field staff. Overall the most striking figure is that in Butundwe, Mayuya, and the 'others', 20—29 percent of the VDC meetings were held with no official present other than the local Village Executive Officer. There are notations in several sets of minutes that certain officials had been invited to the meeting but failed to attend or to send their apologies; this would seem to imply that the VDC's did not entirely accept this low level of official attendance.

The activities of the committees supply another measure of their effectiveness as a link between the government and the citizenry. I have classified the agenda of these selected committees into activities which resulted in communications from the VDC's upwards to higher levels in the political system, those which involved communications to the VDC from these higher levels, and those which were localized being discussed without reference to the larger political system. Communications upwards were requests for assistance, queries on government activities, and complaints; communications downwards reflected the entire spectrum of governmental and party programmes, such as tax collection drives, self-help exhortations, agricultural advice and regulations, calls to build proper latrines, and so on. Activities of a

94

local nature were extensive, including land allocation, the setting of market times and locations, arrangements for catching thieves, and discussion of self-help fines.

I have also classified the activities as to whether they are concerned with development or with care and maintenance. Even more so than with the classification by information flow, classification by whether some activity is developmental or of a care and maintenance nature is arbitrary.[47] Development in this context involves the process of changing attitudes and ways of life; care and maintenance on the other hand has to do with the continuance of present norms and arrangements. Land allocation in Mwanza Region is clearly a care and maintenance activity; adult education classes are clearly developmental. Others, for instance discussions of the application of self-help fines (classified as developmental) and the excusing of individuals from paying school fees and local rates (classified as care and maintenance), are not as clear cut. I would not want to argue too strongly for the distinction itself, but it does seem to have an analytical usefulness in providing an insight into the activities of the VDC's.

Table 9 a. *Village Development Committees' Activities.* Agenda classified by direction of information flow (percentages in brackets)

Committee	No. of Meet- ings	Upwards	Downwards	Localized	Total
Butundwe	27	6 (8.1 %)	12 (17.6 %)	56 (75.7 %)	74
Mayuya	15	9 (9.2 %)	29 (29.6 %)	60 (61.2 %)	98
Nyanchenchen	14	4 (8.5 %)	8 (17.0 %)	35 (74.5 %)	47
Others	14	12 (14.0 %)	16 (18.6 %)	58 (67.4 %)	86

Table 9 b. *Village Development Committees' Activities.* Agenda classified by 'development' or 'care and maintenance' nature of activity (percentage in brackets)

Committee	No. of Meetings	Development	Care and Maintenance	Total
Butundwe	27	31 (42.0 %)	43 (58.0 %)	74
Mayuya	15	43 (43.9 %)	55 (56.1 %)	98
Nyanchenchen	14	19 (40.4 %)	28 (59.6 %)	47
Others	14	28 (32.6 %)	58 (67.4 %)	86

Table 9 c. *Village Development Committees' Activities*. Agenda classified by direction of information flow and by 'development' or 'care and maintenance' nature of activity (percentage in brackets)

Committee	Upwards		Downwards	
	Development	Care and Maintenance	Development	Care and Maintenance
Butundwe	3 (4.0 %)	3 (4.0 %)	8 (11.7 %)	4 (5.9 %)
Mayuya	6 (6.1 %)	3 (3.1 %)	14 (14.3 %)	15 (15.3 %)
Nyanchenchen	2 (4.3 %)	2 (4.3 %)	7 (14.9 %)	1 (2.1 %)
Others	4 (4.6 %)	8 (9.3 %)	8 (9.3 %)	8 (9.3 %)

Committee	Localized	
	Development	Care and Maintenance
Butundwe	20 (27.0 %)	36 (48.7 %)
Mayuya	23 (23.5 %)	37 (37.7 %)
Nyanchenchen	10 (21.3 %)	25 (53.2 %)
Others	16 (18.6 %)	42 (48.8 %)

As with the classification of official attendances, the presentation of the tables 9 a—c, as sets of figures probably distorts certain aspects of VDC activity. There was no way of determining how much time was spent on most items, but some of the localized care and maintenance items were big time consumers. For instance, entire meetings were at times devoted to a single item such as land allocation. On the other hand, developmental and care and maintenance communications downwards, such as agricultural advice and warnings on the observing of brewing laws, were more in the nature of announcements requiring little time. These factors gave the classification scheme a bias in the form of overstating the proportion of activities undertaken which linked the larger political system in a downwards or penetrative fashion with the VDC's.

Withstanding this penetrative bias of the agenda analysis, it is clear from their activities in the last two years (six months in the case of the 'others') of their existence that the VDC's were more localized in their operations than the notion of a "two-way flow" would imply. A clear majority of the items (61—75 percent) were discussed without reference to any of the national structures which are intended to link Tanzania with her villages. Those activities which did involve a flow between the villages and the nation were by a more than two to one margin penetrative (downwards) rather than participative (upwards).[48]

In their localized activities the VDC's were concerned with many aspects of village government. At the same time, they were to some extent the final link in the national chain of development committees. It is thus relevant to this enquiry into participation to know who it was that was participating in these village authorities. The sets of figures in tables 8 a and b indicated that the number of officials who attended the VDC meetings was not normally very many. As for the villagers themselves, the attendance figures below indicate that members absented themselves from many meetings.

Table 10. *Attendance of members at Village Development Committee Meetings*

Committee	Total Membership[a]	Average No. of Members present	Average percentage present
Butundwe	98	23.5	24.0 %
Mayuya	61	33.1	54.2 %
Nyanchenchen	189	49.6	26.2 %

[a] The total membership varied over the July, 1967—June, 1969 period to which these figures refer. The figure which I have used is necessarily an average.

The membership of the VDC was all the cell leaders in the area. It was clear from the minutes that certain cell leaders were regular while others were extremely lax in their attendance. There were two factors of recognizable impact at play in this regard—'progressiveness' and proximity.

VDC and TANU leaders were in agreement that those cell leaders who were more 'progressive', which usually meant having some degree of literacy or being a farmer who followed modern techniques, tended to attend meetings more regularly. These 'progressive' characteristics are often associated with a better-off economic status. Assuming that there is a tendency amongst peasant leaders, as amongst people generally, to work in their own interests when possible, the predominantly 'progressive' character of those attending may have enabled the VDC's to operate in such a way as to heighten the economic distinctions amongst people in the rural areas. This has of course been a problem elsewhere,[49] but given the Tanzanian government's stated

97

objective of building an egalitarian society it is interesting that with the VDC's certain governmental and party practices were such as to increase rather than alleviate the possibility of this problem at the village level.[50] Both party money collectors and local council revenue collectors regularly gathered at VDC meetings to make their collections. There were frequent calls from these officials that only those cell leaders who had paid their TANU dues and their local rates should be permitted to participate in the meetings. The size of this problem should not be underestimated; the Geita District Council reported that in 1968 a *majority* of the farmers were not able to pay their local rates.[51]

Local leaders also thought that proximity was a factor. In Nyanchenchen in particular the more distant cell leaders, residing six or seven miles from the meeting place, found it difficult to attend. Meetings held during the rains when the roads are often not passable were very poorly attended in Nyanchenchen—average attendance during February—April was twenty-five, while for the rest of the year it was fifty-six. For Mayuya, where the roads are better and the distances shorter than in Nyanchenchen, the *vijiji* which were not represented by at least one cell leader were noted in the minutes of the meetings. Excluding the trading centre where the meetings were held, Mayuya had eighteen *vijiji* in its VDC area. Of these, ten missed only one or two of the fifteen meetings held over the 1967—69 period; five *vijiji*, however, missed five or more of the meetings, with one missing eight. In discussing this point, the local TANU leaders maintained that the five *vijiji* with the poor attendance records were the most distant ones. While other factors may have been involved as well, it would appear that proximity was an important variable.

Ward Development Committees: Some Concluding Remarks

In July, 1969, Ward Development Committees (WDC's) officially replaced the village committees.[52] Today it is the WDC's which form the final link in the development committee chain. The areal basis of each of the new committees is the ward, thus coinciding with the District Council electoral constituency, the TANU branch organizational unit, and the administrative area covered by the new Ward Executive

Officers who, also in July, 1969, replaced the former Village Executive Officers. The WEO, as was the VEO with respect to the village committees, is the secretary of the WDC, while the TANU branch chairman holds the WDC chairmanship *ex officio.*

The ward committees were set up during July—November, 1969, at meetings to which all the cell leaders in a ward were invited.[53] Addresses by the Ward Executive Officer and, usually, the Divisional Secretary explained the change-over to the WDC. Most of these inaugural meetings were actually meetings of the old VDC's which had continued functioning until the end of their seven year period. In Geita and Mwanza Districts the change brought about an increase in the number of committees actually operating in the rural areas (in Geita where I can be fairly specific the increase was from about thirty-three to forty), while in Ukerewe and Kwimba Districts there was a slight decline brought about through the amalgamation of some of the existing VDC's. The change to ward committees ended the existence of committees which had maintained the practice of electing their own chairmen, and hence in some areas, Mayuya for instance, removed VDC leaderships which were distinct from the local TANU leadership.

The membership of the WDC's was to be different from that of the VDC's. On the cell leader side there was to be a reduction. Each group of nine or ten cell leaders, or as was often specified by the WEO or the Divisional Secretary the cell leaders from each *kijiji*, were to select one from amongst themselves to represent their people at the meetings. There were no suggestions as to the process to be used in selecting the one representative, and there were no subsequent attempts during the year that I observed the committees to regularize representation. Indeed, those committees in Geita which I studied closely—Mayuya, Nyanchenchen and Butundwe—had the same people attending the meetings as had previously been attending the VDC meetings. In the latter two committees the numbers attending the WDC meetings were about the same; in Mayuya, some of whose area was hived off to form part of a new ward, the number attending was reduced. More importantly perhaps, the same elements as before continued to be underrepresented—those who were more distant and those who were poorer.

On the official side, the WEO's and Divisional Secretaries explained, the teachers would not be members of the new committees. They were to be allowed to attend to discuss specific items after which they would depart. The rationale put forward was that too much time was being lost from the classrooms. However, during the first year of the new committees, the teachers continued as before to attend and to contribute a consistent 'modernizing' voice to the proceedings. The Ward Executive Officers did not question their attendance and in interviews stated that they welcomed their presence.

Although it is much too early to give a rounded evaluation of the ward committees, the most striking aspect of their first year was how little they differed from the old village committees. The low number of officials who attended meetings, the localized nature of most of the activities, the predominance of a penetrative or downwards linkage in their connexions with the national political system, the poor attendance of cell leaders at meetings, and the tendency for the economically better-off cell leaders to attend while their poorer associates stayed home—these were the aspects of the VDC's which made them ineffective in performing as a channel for a "two-way flow of ideas between government and the people". They did not seem to have been very much, if at all, altered by the setting up of the WDC's.

The 1969 removal of the local rates made it less hazardous for the poorer cell leaders to attend, although there remained, with perhaps more vigour, the call for the payment of TANU dues and the various TANU fund raising drives.[54] The number of connexions between the Region's rural areas and the larger political system remained about the same or increased slightly in terms of development committees,[55] but the links through the administrative generalists—the Village Executive, the Assistant Divisional, and the Divisional Executive Officers and, under the new arrangements, the Ward Executive Officers and the Divisional Secretaries have declined.[56]

Table 11. *Administrative Generalists in the Rural Areas of Mwanza Region, 1967—1970*

District	July, 1967[a]	July, 1968[a]	July, 1969[b]	July, 1970[b]
Geita	79	53	46	46
Ukerewe	52	38	23[c]	18[c]
Mwanza	110	77	42	42
Kwimba	139	125	47	47
Mwanza Region	380	293	158	153

[a] Village Executive, Assistant Divisional Executive, and Divisional Executive Officers

[b] Ward Executive Officers and Divisional Secretaries

[c] The number of wards in Ukerewe was reduced from twenty to fifteen in February, 1970.

The ranks of the mobilizational generalists were not sufficiently increased to make up the decline. The number of rural development workers in the rural areas remained at between seventy and eighty between July, 1967 and July, 1970.[57] TANU gradually increased its cadre of salaried branch secretaries to a point in July, 1970 where sixty-three of the 131 wards had secretaries, an increase of twenty-one from the July, 1968 number of forty-two. The other branches remained with money collectors in-charge working for a 20 percent commission on the dues collected. Where the change from money collector to secretary was made, it was usually contractual with the former collector becoming the new secretary.[58]

TANU staff at the regional and district level discouraged branch secretaries from applying for the post of Ward Executive Officer, not wishing to lose the few trained people they had in the rural areas. Money collectors in-charge were, however, often urged to apply for the new posts. Of the 116 Ward Executive Officers in the three districts (Mwanza, Geita, Ukerewe) where I was able to get fairly complete figures, thirty-three were former money collectors in-charge and three were ex-branch secretaries. Fifty-one had been Village Executive Officers immediately prior to their appointment, four were ex-revenue collectors, nine were TANU branch chairmen (who continued to hold their chairmanships though posted outside their wards) and one was a District chairman of the TANU Youth League. Overall, the change was primarily one of retrenchment rather than a bringing in of new staff.[59]

The new arrangements should not be appraised in terms of the number or quality[60] of staff and committees without reference to the changes taking place at levels above the village/ward which are altering the intended balance in the relationship between the committees in the rural areas and the national political system. The removal of the main revenue sources and most of the major functions of the District Councils made it less likely than before that demands from the villages, where there is still a great desire for services, would be well received. Unless they complemented the increasingly specific and centrally promulgated guidelines for the allocation of the Regional Development Fund ward demands moving upwards in 1969/70 had no place to go. The central government, faced with a chronic shortage of funds, no more felt it could permit of local demands for services than it did in the mid-1960's. In this context village level operations of development committees were necessarily ancillary to the implementation of central policies. They did not lead to participation through some chain in the formulation of these policies, in the design of programmes, or in the selection of projects.

Notes

1. Henry Bienen, *Tanzania: Party Transformation and Economic Development*, Princeton: Princeton University Press, expanded edition 1970, p. 336. In June, 1962, the Minister for Co-operative and Community Development stated that it was "now" time for the VDC's to become involved in development activity. *Tanganyika Hansard*, First Meeting (Second Session), 25 June 1962, col. 886.

2. Bienen, *op.cit.*, p. 349, quoting from a 1963 address by Vice President Kawawa to Regional Commissioners. Kawawa had made a similar statement in the parliament the previous September. *Tanganyika Hansard*, First Meeting (Third Session), 25 September 1962, col. 29.

3. Göran Hydén, *Political Development in Rural Tanzania*, Nairobi: East African Publishing House, 1969, p. 135.

4. *Ibid.*, p. 139.

5. Normal Miller, "Village Leadership and Modernization in Tanzania: Rural Politics among the Nyamwezi People of Tabora Region", unpublished Indiana University doctoral dissertation, 1966, p. 68, quoting an interview with Selemani Juma Kitundu.

6. *Ibid.*

7. Miller, *loc.cit.*, writes that the first VDC's were those organized in Morogoro Region in 1962 by the Morogoro Regional Commissioner, Selemani Juma Kitundu. The VDC's in Mwanza Region began at least as early.

8. Minutes, Ukerewe District Development Committee meeting, 19 May 1962.

9. Minutes, Ukerewe District Development Committee meeting, 23 July 1962.

10. Divisional Reports, Mwanza, Geita and Kwimba Districts, 1962 and 1963. Presumably these were remnants of the Sukumaland Federation experiments.

11. This approximation is based on the numbers of VDC members after membership was regularized to cell leaders in 1964—66. The assumption is that on average each cell contained 10 households.

12. The use of the word village here follows the usage (1969—70) in Mwanza Region. In the Sukuma areas a village or *kijiji* (also referred to by the Sukuma word, *kibanda*) is sometimes strictly an administrative designation. *Cf.*, Heijnen's discussion of Bukumbi subdivision in Mwanza District: "Each *gunguli* is made up of a number of *nzengo*. The *nzengo* can be defined as the smallest residential unit larger than the homestead and is, in the sociological sense, the equivalent for a village ... For administrative purposes often a number of the smaller *nzengo* have been combined

to form one *kibanda* ... But these combinations have merely administrative significance, in other parts of Sukumaland this construction is unknown." J. D. Heijnen, *Development and Education in Mwanza District, Tanzania: A Case Study of Migration and Peasant Farming*, Rotterdam: Bronder Offset, 1968, p. 32. A further discussion of some of these points can be found in, Hans Cory, *The Indigenous Political System of the Sukuma*, Nairobi: Eagle Press, 1954, pp. 49—51. A *gunguli* in the colonial period was sometimes referred to as a "parish", and a *kibanda* as a "sub-parish".

13. In Geita District the Area Commissioner went a step further and ordered that where there was a TANU committee, the TANU committee was to become the VDC. Minutes, Geita District Development Committee meeting, 21 July 1964.

14. Constitutionally this move was interesting as it came before the establishment of the one party state.

15. Tanzania Government, "Government Paper No. 1—1966, Proposals of the Tanzania Government on Local Government Councils", Dar es Salaam, Government Printer, 1966, p. 3.

16. The change-over to cell leaders as the VDC membership had actually occurred in most areas in Mwanza Region with the establishment of the cells in 1964—65.

17. Miller, *op.cit.*, pp. 69—70.

18. This was the case with one of the VDC's which I examined fairly closely, Mayuya in Geita District. The TANU chairman was narrowly defeated in a VDC chairmanship election at a meeting on 17 October 1968. In May, 1969, another election was held. The Area Commissioner, when questioned on this point, observed that the second election was held on his suggestion to give the people another opportunity to choose a TANU chairman. The local leaders interpreted this suggestion as an order. The TANU chairman was duly elected to the VDC post, but the cell leaders from nine of the Mayuya VDC's eighteen *vijiji* refused to attend the election meeting. The Area Commissioner's intervention was unusual and was carried out as part of the preparation for the establishhent of the Ward Development Committees in July, 1969.

19. The discussion is based upon the Divisional Reports for Mwanza, Geita, and Kwimba Districts, 1962—1967. Also upon interviews with the Area Commissioners and the District Officers in charge of Rural Development in Mwanza and Ukerewe Districts, and with the Executive Officers of the Mwanza and Ukerewe District Councils, carried out by myself in August, 1969. Interviews with their counterparts were carried out in Kwimba District by Aloys Rutaihwa in May, 1969, and in Geita District by Charles Bayeka in August, 1969.

20. Tanzanian Government, "Government Paper No. 1—1966 ...", p. 3.

21. Miller, *op.cit.*, p. 68.

22. Interviews, see note no. 19, above.

23. Dubbeldam notes that parents' committees performed this function in Mwanza District, and in his discussion makes no mention of the VDC's role in this. The practice varied from district to district; the Geita VDC's spent a good bit of time on school fees. L. F. B. Dubbeldam, *The Primary*

School and the Community in Mwanza District, Tanzania, Gronigen: Wolters-Noordhoff, 1970, pp. 49—50, 141.

24. Proposals were as well sent directly to the DDPC by primary schools, co-operative societies, and *ad hoc* groups. These were referred back to the local VDC for consideration.

25. The Community (after the Arusha Declaration changed to Rural) Development worker in Kome in Geita District in January, 1964, dissolved the VDC's of Buhama and Rugata and organized a new election. The people refused to attend the meetings called by the CD worker to elect the new committee. The Area Commissioner went to Kome in February, dissolved a new committee which had been appointed by the CD worker, and ordered the citizens to hold another election. He also sent a directive throughout the District instructing CD workers not to act in this fashion. Minutes, Geita District Development Committee meeting, 18—19 February 1964. The minutes of the development committees of Mwanza and Ukerewe Districts contain several references in the 1964—66 period of Area Commissioners reminding Rural Development and Village Executive Officers that VDC's are not to be ordered or forced to undertake projects or follow specific procedures, rather they were to be persuaded.

26. Rene LeMarchand, "Village-by-Village Nation Building in Tanzania", *Africa Report,* X, 2, (Feb. 1965), pp. 11—13.

27. This was true of the Nyanchenchen VDC which was one of the committees whose activities I studied.

28. This enforcement role lessened with the decline (because of the central emphasis on 'productive' projects) of the self-help projects, and with the closing down of most of the village Youth League branches and the setting up of new ones in the schools under the control of teachers. In August, 1969, the Geita District Executive Secretary of the TANU Youth League informed me that all Youth League branches in the district were then in schools. This was a change which necessarily altered the Youth League's former 'special constable' role. *Cf.*, the decision of the Geita District Development Committee in March, 1964, that the Youth League was to assist in apprehending illegal brewers.

29. The same observation was made for Tabora District by Miller, *op. cit.,* pp. 197—198.

30. Many of the plans which were produced were produced by district officials for the villages. For instance, the Geita Executive Officer in October, 1967, instructed his officials (in his letter to Divisional Executive Officers, A/3/1/ vol. IV/56) that each village plan would be made by an elected Crops Committee which would ensure that each farmer had two acres of cotton and two and a half acres of food crops, and that each village would have a 20 acre communal plot to be used for demonstrating modern farming methods.

31. Report from the Geita Rural Development Officer to the Regional Rural Development Officer, Mwanza, RDR. 9/65, 6 February 1969.

32. LeMarchand, *loc.cit.*

33. These failings have been cited elsewhere with regard to district level as well as village level project planning in Tanzania. P. Raikes *et al.,* "Re-

gional Planning in Tanzania: An Economic View from the Field", Economic Research Bureau (Restricted) Paper 68.8, University College, Dar es Salaam, 1968, p. 3.

34. A journalist's account of this is, Alexander MacDonald, *Tanzania: Young Nation in a Hurry*, New York: Hawthorn, 1966.

35. See, minutes of the Geita District Development Committee meetings of 14 January and 25 August 1964.

¯36. See, Minutes, Ukerewe District Development Committee meeting, 8 April 1965.

37. Minutes, Ukerewe District Development and Planning Committee meeting, 27 April 1967.

38. See, for instance, the minutes of the meeting of the Geita District Development and Planning Committee of 18 May 1965 and those of the meeting of the Geita District Council's Finance Committee of 19—20 May 1965.

39. Bienen, *op.cit.*, p. 350, refers to a "purported 7,500 VDC's for Tanzania as a whole", but goes on to mention that "some of these may be formed only in theory".

40. Report from Geita Rural Development Officer to Regional Rural Development Officer, 16 February 1970, Geita file RDR. 9/73; and, note no. 18, above.

41. Minutes from the meetings of the Geita minor settlement committee were excluded because of its location at the district administrative centre.

42. Three of the eleven could not be identified as they omitted to put their name on their minutes. The other eight were: Mwingiro, Nyamazugo, Bukolwa, Lubanda, Shibumba, Sengerema, Mhana, and Nyangenda.

43. The phrasing is Kawawa's. See note no. 2, above.

44. See, W. Tordoff, *Government and Politics in Tanzania*: Nairobi: East African Publishing House, 1967, p. 120, who refers to Stanley Dryden, "Local Government in Tanzania", draft thesis for the M. A. degree, University of East Africa, chapter 3. It appears that Dryden included co-operative society officials in making his estimate. No co-operative society officials attended any of the seventy meetings which I studied in their capacity as co-operative society leaders.

45. It should be noted that figures for official attendance when expressed as the aggregate percentage of the total number attending, as I have set out in Table 8 (a) or as in the statement of Tordoff referred to above, can be somewhat misleading since official attendances tend to be clustered with campaign style administrative techniques bringing a fairly large number (as many as nine) to some meetings and none to others.

46. Dubbeldam, *op.cit.*, p. 86, reports that of 294 teachers in eighteen selected primary schools in Mwanza District, 209 or 71 percent agreed that "the headteacher of a village school should always be consulted before a decision is made in an important village affair".

47. Hydén, *op.cit.*, pp. 174—175, classified the agenda of 145 meetings of five VDC's in West Lake according to problem type—identity, legitimacy, penetration, allocation, and participation. My own initial attempts at classification attempted to follow a pattern similar to Hydén's. However,

I found that the tendency for agenda to be classifiable under more than one "problem type" and the consequent arbitrariness of the final classifications was even more of a difficulty than with the scheme I have used here.

48. Hydén, op.cit., p. 178, after looking at selected VDC's in West Lake, writes that an "interesting feature in the minutes is that, there are few references to actual requests for government assistance in various local development projects. There is less traffic of demands 'upwards' than 'downwards'."

49. For instance, with respect to India, see, Charles Bettelhiem, *India Independent*, New York: Monthly Review Press, 1969, pp. 214—220, 329, 360; A. H. Hansen, *The Process of Planning*, London: Oxford University Press, 1966, p. 426.

50. This was all the more striking because of the occasional rhetoric in Dar es Salaam newspapers about the need to beware of "rich peasants". *Cf.*, the conscious attempts in the Soviet Union in the late 1920's to increase the number of poor peasants on village level authorities. See, M. Lewin, *Russian Peasants and Soviet Power*, London: Allen and Unwin, 1968.

51. Geita District Council, "Memorandum to Accompany Estimates 1969 (complete)", p. 2. Penner, dealing with 1965 data, estimated that one-quarter to one-third of the rural adult males escaped paying the local rate. R. G. Penner, *Financing Local Government in Tanzania*, Nairobi: East African Publishing House, 1970, p. 39.

52. Act No. 6 of 1969. Presidential Circular No. 2 of 1968, "Self-help Schemes", 24 August 1968, gave the VDC's in their final days the authority to impose certain types of traditional sanctions so as "to ensure that the masses of the people shall never have any reason to lose their enthusiasm through the feeling that they are being exploited by a few who do not want to work but do want to benefit". This authority was retained by the new WDC's. I found no indication in Mwanza Region that the decline in enthusiasm in VDC's and their self-help projects was in any way related to a 'feeling' of exploitation.

53. I was present at the initial meetings in Mayuya, Butundwe, Nyanchenchen and Nyamatongo, and was able to read the minutes of the initial WDC meetings in Nyakasungwa, Nyangenda, Vigemba, and Nyagundwa—all in Geita District. I also read the minutes of fifteen other first meetings in Ukerewe, Mwanza and Kwimba Districts.

54. In their first year of operation the WDC's were normally used, *inter alia*, as a forum for the solicitation of money for various TANU purposes. In each of the twenty-three initial meetings which I either attended or read the minutes of, at least one TANU financial plea was made. One, an unusual case, decided that all those who were allocated land by the WDC must contribute ten shillings to the local TANU building fund. See, the minutes of the Igokero WDC meeting, 17 October 1969, in Mwanza District Council file C. 40/64/4. All WDC's seem to have been employed in the fund raising drive for the construction of the TANU regional headquarters.

55. Some observers have seen the "demise" of the VDC's and the VEO's

as the losing of an "essential link between the Ward/Branch and the Cell", because in most cases the official number of WDC's is considerably less than the figure formerly given out for VDC's. See, Bureau of Resource Assessment and Land Use Planning, "North-East Nzega Planning Project: Report No. 2", University College, Dar es Salaam, September, 1969 (revised copy), p. 18n. The point that I am making here is that one should not accept the official figures on the VDC's or WDC's without village level checking, and that on the basis of thorough checking in Geita District and, only slightly less comprehensively for the rest of Mwanza Region, there was no decline in the overall number of functioning committees and in some districts there was an actual increase.

56. Figures for the following table and the subsequent discussion come from the records of the District Councils and the Rural Development Division offices in the four districts, and from discussions with TANU, District Council and Rural Development staff. The figures refer to actual positions filled.

57. This figure includes trainees and staff paid with District Council funds, but it excludes staff at the district and regional headquarters.

58. The normal progression is for a youth to move from money collector, to money collector in-charge, to (if he has completed seven-years of schooling) the post of secretary. Money collectors are appointed by the secretary or the money collector in-charge. They receive a commission the size of which is negotiable. The general practice is to appoint more collectors during the cotton harvest, in fact some secretaries informed me that the number of collectors that should be appointed is determined by the number of cotton buying posts or co-operative societies in the ward. The salary of a secretary in July, 1969, started at about 184 shillings per month (at every level and in almost every office I was given a different explanation of how much TANU branch secretaries were paid), while that of a Ward Executive Officer began at 198 shillings per month. Several times during my stay in the Region, TANU District offices advertised for branch secretaries. The response was, according to District staff, disappointing and in the case of Geita not enough applied to fill the five positions vacant. Three branch secretaries persistently requested me to find them jobs in Mwanza town.

59. See pp. 124—5 of the next chapter for a discussion of the position and background of the Divisional Secretaries.

60. Over the decade since independence the quality of staff has of course greatly improved. In the early 1960's there were many complaints that the headmen (later, Village Executive Officers) were illiterate and 'not modern'. The Ward Executive Officers are literate (minimum of seven years of education) and have basic training in agriculture and 'political education'.

Regional and Area Commissioners

Introduction

One of the first post-colonial changes of the Tanganyika Government was the replacement of Provincial and District Commissioners with politically appointed Regional and Area Commissioners beginning in early 1962.[1] Such was the urgency that the government appointed ten Area Commissioners prior to the enactment of the relevant legislation in June, 1962.[2] The new appointees were not given all the responsibilities of their predecessors. In the National Assembly the Minister for Local Government and Administration explained that there had been a separation of the magisterial (to the judiciary) and supervision of local government (to civil service Local Government Officers) functions from those "miscellaneous tasks" which would remain directly under the Commissioners and their executive staff—"things like the organization of famine relief, elections, processing of village development schemes, coordination of the Central Government effort, and that vague, but very important function of dealing with the 'shauris', and 'shidas' of the general public".[3]

As political officials at the top of the government hierarchies in their areas, the Commissioners in coordinating the efforts of the ministries and in serving as a channel for the flow of complaints and demands were to be agents of participation who would exercise popular TANU control over the bureaucracy. The new Commissioners also became the secretaries of the TANU organization at their respective territorial level, a move intended to increase the control of the TANU centre over its constituent branches in the periphery.[4] *Vis a vis* these local party organizations, participatory elements in the national system which historically had been loosely tied to the centre, the Commissioners were to be agents of the central TANU hierarchy.

Complicating an explanation of the nature of the Commissioners' government/party role as approximating a participation/hierarchy duality is the existence of what might be termed minor strains. In his governmental capacity, which is essentially one of increasing participation, a Commissioner was also expected to mobilize the people for development along policy and programme lines which have been centrally established and in this he was to stand as a representative of hierarchy.[5] In his TANU capacity, which is essentially one of hierarchy, a Commissioner was also expected to represent the local party to the TANU centre and to transmit the demands of the people to the "higher echelons".[6]

The colonial role of Commissioner was within the "major territorial-imperial hierarchy",[7] and though some colonial Commissioners did come to play a participatory role as they represented and protected the interests of their district, the chief impact of the colonial Commissioners was a hierarchical one of penetration. The Commissioners of independent Tanzania, while retaining a hierarchical function as mobilizers, have been charged with the political control of the bureaucracy as well, and thus with ensuring that their role is equally, and perhaps even primarily, a participatory one.

This chapter is a discussion of the activities of the Commissioners in Mwanza Region which concentrates on what they were doing in 1969—70 in relation to the conflicting pressures upon a role which is intended to be both hierarchical and participatory in its impact. As a preface I make a few observations on the recruitment and tenure of the commissioners.

With the exception of some of the initial appointments,[8] the recruitment of Regional and Area Commissioners has not followed a specific pattern other than they be from outside the Region.[9] Of the four[10] Regional Commissioners, two were manifestly politicians[11] prior to their appointment while the other two were civil servants.[12] The Area Commissioners have more often been on the politician side of the civil servant—politician dichotomy, but the appointment of one traditional leader and one salesman weakens the insights to be gained from such a dichotomy. In most cases the Area Commissioners have been younger and have had fewer years of formal education than the Regional Commissioners.

Over the period October, 1963 to October, 1971, the fifteen Area Commissioners for the four districts averaged 25 months in office, while the Regional Commissioners over the same period averaged 24 months. Two of the Area Commissioners, Msonge of Ukerewe District and Kaseko of Kwimba District, were each in office for five and a half years during this eight year period, a fact which distorts the average and somewhat belies the tendency for Area Commissioners to serve a slightly shorter term (eighteen months if Msonge and Kaseko are excluded) than the Regional Commissioners.[13]

The structural similarities in their roles have led me to consider the roles of Regional and Area Commissioner together, albeit the frame of reference does shift at many points. It should be emphasized, however, that the individuals have been of quite different stature politically: the Regional Commissioners have been national figures, of recognizable achievement prior to their appointments, known personally by the President and *ex-officio* members of TANU's National Executive Committee; the Area Commissioners have been much lesser figures, men of promise, not necessarily known by the President,[14] and mostly relegated to activities in the periphery both before and after their appointments. Indicative of the lesser importance of the Area Commissionership, the commissionerships of Kwimba and Mwanza District were each vacant for more than four months during 1969 awaiting the appointment of new officers to replace the transferred former occupants. The pressure on and the functions of the Commissioners are similar, but the differences in the stature of the roles and the individuals who have filled them are considerable.

The Commissioners and The Local TANU Organizations

At their respective territorial levels the Commissioners are members of the conference and the executive and working committees of TANU; the Area Commissioner is a member of the regional conference and executive committee and the Regional Commissioner is at times a guest at the meetings at the district level. In the meetings of these TANU bodies and generally in his relations with local party leaders, the primary goal of a Commissioner is to gain local support for national policies and programmes and to have the local party take initiatives in the directions desired by the centre. In his efforts a Commissioner relies on his persuasive abilities as supported by three types of sanction or resource[15]—force, material allocations, and influence upon the considerations of higher level leaders—and it is in the context of these sanctions that we can understand the relationship between the local party and the Commissioner.

The ability of a Commissioner to use force, the ultimate expression of a hierarchical approach to development, relies upon his residual responsibility for the maintenance of law and order. A Commissioner is not a Justice of the Peace unless specifically appointed. He does have the authority to detain individuals for 48 hours and, although the chain of command in such activities is often unclear even to the participants,[16] to order the police to take actions varying from the closing of bars and banning of types of dress and music[17] to using the paramilitary field force unit to enforce agricultural regulations.[18] Such measures are, however, seldom brought into play. The use of force is severely circumscribed by a national ethic of persuasion,[19] by an awareness of its often detrimental effect on popular support for leaders and policies,[20] and by the lack of a developed coercive apparatus.

Force as an expression of a personal aberration or quarrel of an individual Commissioner, as occurred in a celebrated case in Ukerewe in 1969,[21] is always a possibility, but the system, with its courts, the Permanent Commission of Enquiry, and the President's admonitions, most often works to discourage its use as a policy instrument.[22] Unless a local leader contemplates an open attack upon a national policy or a Commissioner's method of implementing it, the threat of force is not effective. In the event of local leaders not actively supporting particular policies, insofar as they refrain from public disavowals[23] the possibility of coercive action is remote.

Material allocations, the second type of sanction available to a Commissioner, can be looked at in terms of those controlled mainly by the government, party, and co-operatives. As becomes clear in the discussion of the Commissioners' relations with the government bureaucracy in the following section, the capacity of Commissioners to affect government allocations is (pre-1972) greatly restricted by the making of almost all allocations in Dar es Salaam rather than at the district or regional levels. It is chiefly the Regional Development Fund and some local government funds which are somewhat at their disposal but which they have tended to allow effective control over, with the notable exception of several prestige projects, to remain with the representatives of the ministries.[24]

A Commissioner's control over party allocations is not very significant. As the party has grown administratively it has accumulated more rules and regulations concerning the expending of its resources, and these are enforced by TANU's Executive Secretaries (sometimes referred to as Deputy Secretaries) at the regional and district levels. A Commissioner who attempts to use the party machine in gaining leverage over the local leaders discovers that it is not, as it has been described by some observers, an "instrumentality directly available to the Commissioner".[25] The sorts of resources which constitute the machine—information, money, men—are scarce commodities the expenditure of which is increasingly controlled through centrally issued instructions. The discretionary uses of the Commissioners are limited with the expending of allowances, transport, files, and offices following procedures which make the Executive Secretary the warrant officer. In several instances in 1969 at which I was present Executive Secretaries without hesitation rejected written instructions from Commissioners as not being 'proper' and refused to comply without specific orders from TANU headquarters in Dar es Salaam.[26]

Though a Commissioner's influence in government and TANU allocative processes is weak because of the now established procedures in both hierarchies, this is not so with the allocations of the Nyanza Co-operative Union, the name of the former Victoria Federation of Co-operative Unions which was taken over by the government in late 1967.[27] During my time in Mwanza Region there were many allegations of Commissioners 'ordering' the NCU or one of its zonal offices to take specific actions. Most of these were obviously intended to achieve a higher cotton production, to increase the number of and quality of services to *ujamaa* villages, and to encourage support for other national goals. Some other orders, however, were more likely to have been fairly direct attempts by Commissioners to sanction particular local leaders, and it is these which are of interest in the present context. After hearing of one such case I interviewed those concerned. The summary notes which follow are, I think, largely self-explanatory.[28]

October, 1968. Tractor MZ 9999 sold by a Zonal Liason Officer, an NCU official, to Madaha (not his real name), a local TANU chairman. Liason Officer estimated the value of tractor as shs. 5,000 of which Madaha pays shs. 2,300, receiving an official receipt.

February, 1969. Liason Officer transferred from Region.

June, 1969. Madaha presents new Liason Officer with balance due; money is refused and Madaha informed that former Liason Officer acted without authority, that the tractor is to be taken back, and that it is not known when Madaha's shs. 2,300 would be returned.

August, 1969. Area Commissioner who has been in office for three years, say Madaha was aware at the time that the Liason Officer had no authority, but that Madaha persuaded him and, with the implication clear, reminds me that four former NCU liason officers are currently being prosecuted for corruption. He says that part of his job is to ensure that the NCU abides by national policies; the tractor is needed for an *ujamaa* village. He describes Madaha as "troublesome" and responsible for the lack of any *ujamaa* villages in his ward.

August, 1969. Former Liason Officer says he was ordered by the Area Commissioner to sell the tractor to Madaha in the first instance, and offers the opinion that Madaha and the Area Commissioner are two former friends who are having a quarrel.

August, 1969. New Liason Officer says his predecessor was too afraid of politicians. Also explains that if 'orders' from Area Commissioners are not complied with, instructions to do so are soon forthcoming from the NCU's general manager, a government appointee, and thus it serves little purpose to refuse to comply. Area Commissioners threaten NCU staff with dismissal, and this is much more effective than a bribe. As for the tractor sales, meetings are held of all the zonal delegates (elected from the constituent societies) with the Area Commissioners and the Area Secretary to determine the credit-worthiness of prospective buyers. In these meetings, he says, the two government officials are overpowering. MZ 9999 is needed at a ginnery and not at an *ujamaa* village. Asked why it was this particular tractor which was needed, he replies that I should inquire from the Area Commissioner.

September 1969. Mahada, a prosperous farmer, self-educated, and elected councillor who sits on the District Council's Finance Committee, describes the Commissioner as having no respect and as an outsider who does not understand the true needs of the people of the District. Says the Commissioner is quarreling with him for personal reasons and is using his official position in trying to destroy him. Mahada vows to warn against bad leaders in TANU meetings and in the Council.

October—November, 1969. NCU sends six letters instructing Madaha to return tractor to zonal office. Madaha does not reply. Informs friends that if they want to discuss the matter the co-operative officials must come to his farm.

December, 1969. Area Commissioner is transferred out of the Region.

July, 1970. Madaha still has tractor. New Commissioner says he knows nothing of the affair. NCU's officer in charge of tractors at Mwanza headquarters says he will soon go to Madaha's to appraise tractor and fix the balance which Madaha must pay. Says the tractor should not have been sold, but too much time has now passed and it is best that Mahada keeps it, that the matter be closed, and efforts devoted to development.

This case is not to be interpreted as an indication of a generalized inclination of Commissioners to try to use co-operative resources to sanction local leaders, yet it does indicate the ability of a Commis-

113

sioner to have an impact on such allocations if he so chooses. Whether this is a function of the newness and uninstitutionalized nature of the relationships between the co-operatives and the Commissioners will emerge after more time has passed and other studies are made. For the present study, the conclusion would seem to be that as recently as 1969 the co-operative was an important source of resources available to a Commissioner.[29] That in the end Madaha retained the tractor in spite of the efforts of the Area Commissioner is a reminder that the local leaders can also manipulate this resource.

The third type of sanction available to a Commissioner is the discrediting of local leaders (or their projects) in the estimation of national leaders. Local leaders are aware that as a member of the National Executive Committee the Regional Commissioner participates in discussions leading to the rejection and expulsion of leaders, and that the opinion of Area and Regional Commissioners will be considered in evaluating nominees for elected positions and for appointment to salaried posts in the party and government.

The national standing of a Commissioner is, however, a resource difficult to measure and of changing value. Though others have drawn attention to the direct access of Regional Commissioners to the President,[30] only matters of the most urgent nature can be taken to the President irregularly, otherwise a Commissioner must wait until meeting the President in a scheduled meeting, which for an Area Commissioner may be limited to those occasions when the President visits his District (and there are 61 Districts). Regional Commissioners, with their duties in Dar es Salaam,[31] meet the President quite often; one estimated it was ten or twelve times a year at least. These meetings between the President and a Regional Commissioner have been helpful in adding to a Commissioner's prestige and they have been useful in freeing funds for "regional projects" such as the Mwanza Development Scheme, yet local leaders understand the reality that those who have such access are also vulnerable to central disfavour. One Commissioner, after a private meeting with Nyerere in Dar es Salaam, spoke upon his return to the Region of the assurance he had been given that he would be in the Region for a long time so as to get certain projects well underway. Shortly afterwards he was transferred out of the Region, being informed of the move by police radio thirty minutes before it was publicly announced on the mid-day news broadcast. This experience was widely known and discussed amongst political leaders in the Region at the time.

114

The ability of a Commissioner to bring about the rejection of local leaders by national leaders, while well deserving of calculation, is a delayed sanction. In the short run the few aspects of this resource which a Commissioner can manipulate, such as the excluding of local leaders from tours and the displaying of a disapproving deportment toward them, are not in themselves central disfavour but merely imply it, and depend for their effectiveness on the national and local political standing of the Commissioner relative to that of local leader within his own organization and, sometimes, nationally.[32] Politically it is a difficult situation, especially for the Commissioners at the district level. They most often lack any clearly recognized claim to national stature and District TANU leaders normally have a political base with which the Commissioners are unfamiliar. The expenditure of the unmeasurable and fluid political resources which accrue from national or local political status involves risk to all the parties involved.

The difficulty which Commissioners have in accurately estimating the political risk of a conflict with local leaders and the bringing of their resources into play arises from their stance outside the intricacies of local politics, a problem stemming only partly from the policy of appointing Commissioners to areas other than their own.[33] In conversations Commissioners were generally unable to recall the names of elected and appointed TANU officials at the ward level, and in several instances were unfamiliar with Regional and District personalities other than those holding the more prominent positions.

A Commissioner's knowledge of the personalities and issues of local politics would be enhanced from a pattern of personal contacts with local TANU leaders, but the shortcomings in this respect in 1969—70 were apparent. One Commissioner described his position as "isolated", an isolation which he could not very well move to reduce as it might threaten the prestige of the "personal representative of the President" (himself), and in a more immediate way, might be construed as conferring favour upon certain local leaders, disfavour upon others (the Commissioner used the analogy of an ambassador), and have repercussions unpredictable to one with an insufficient knowledge of the personalities and other factors. This is not the feeling of all Commissioners. Two Area Commissioners, both young and somewhat expansive, undertook to meet and engage in informal conversation as many local personalities as possible. The outstanding example of a concerted effort to broaden contacts was one Commissioner's practice of regularly inviting local leaders and others to his home for extended evenings of casual discussion on regional and national problems.[34]

More formal contacts between the Commissioners and the party leaders—in development committee meetings (although absenteeism on both sides is high), at party and District Council meetings—in most months totalled about three or four times for an Area Commissioner and two or three times for a Regional Commissioner who is more often out of the Region. In meetings other than the party meetings the agenda were put together by civil servants and there was not normally any advance coordination of positions between Commissioners and the other TANU leaders. Tours, a constant activity mostly at the district level, were sometimes taken in unison reminiscent of the early years after independence. More commonly, one TANU leader from the district or regional level seemed to be considered sufficient legitimation for encouraging support for a local project, and while everybody was often travelling at the same time, they were quite regularly headed in different directions. Commissioners appeared to spend more time touring with civil servants than with TANU leaders. This was reinforced by the district TANU chairman's *ex officio* chairmanship of the District Council which gave him a series of responsibilities unrelated to the exhortative and mobilizational activities of the Area Commissioners and their tours. The Chairmen spent most of their time in their District Council offices (although in Mwanza the TANU district office since late 1969 has been in the District Council office building), and Commissioners spent most of their time at the District administrative centres, and the TANU offices were left in the care of the District Executive Secretaries.[35] If a Commissioner wanted another TANU personality along on a tour, or at times as a stand-in for the Commissioner himself, it was the District Executive Secretary who was often chosen. Other TANU leaders in the districts usually lived outside the administrative centre and as non-paid office-holders had other interests which required their attention. Tours themselves have had a declining capacity to assist in the creation of personal links. With the improved roads tours are increasingly less arduous and officials rarely stay overnight outside the district or regional centres.

Symbolizing the position of the Commissioners in their contacts with the local leaders, the Regional Commissioner's official residence is situated on a promontory jutting over, yet removed from the life of Mwanza town. Except for the RDC's sub-committee of which the TANU Regional Chairman is a member, local party representatives as such sit on no allocative bodies of significance in the Region. The local party itself mainly allocates positions within its own organization and thus party discussions are often of the type in which a Commissioner's lack of a local grounding places him in the position of an outsider. As a mobilizer for development in his area a Commissioner is concerned with exhortations to support centrally decided policies and programmes, and those projects which appear to conform with the central policies. Ostensible support is rarely withheld by TANU leaders and they faithfully, if not always very urgently, exhort the peasants to work harder and follow national policies. For the Commissioners to require more, for instance for them to insist that the local exhorters do as they are exhorting others to do,[36] would raise the possibility of a conflict which, as noted above, involves risk to the Commissioners. In this context "'party discipline' is replaced by 'intra-party diplomacy'".[37]

The Commissioners and The Bureaucracy

The relationship between a Commissioner and the officials of the various government departments is the critical one if he is to increase participation in the political system. As the political head of his area he must ensure that the civil servants implement policies in a way consonant with broad national goals, and at the same time ensure their responsiveness to the demands of the local people. These two aspects are of course at times contradictory, but before a Commissioner can be in the position of choosing between conflicting national and local political pressures, he must be able to control the activities of the bureaucracy.

The term 'control' as used here is more encompassing than co-ordination. Co-ordination of governmental activities at the regional district levels in Tanzania has been recognized as a problem which is intensifying with the growth of governmental staffs and activities. The improvements in communications between the centre and the periphery have re-enforced the tendency for regional officials to make referrals back to their Dar es Salaam headquarters rather than relying upon the arbitration or guidance of a Commissioner to resolve differences amongst themselves. The tension between co-ordination, which is seen as a primary function of a Commissioner,[38] and a department's goal of technically correct and independent decision making has elsewhere been viewed as a conflict between areal and functional criteria of administration,[39] or between generalists and specialists.[40] In Tanzania it has been seen as a conflict between overarching national policies and the more narrow programmes and interests of the individual government departments.[41] This tension was acknowledged in the key document outlining the official strategy for the rural development programme of *ujamaa* villages:

United action from all Government Ministries and public organizations concerned with the rural areas is vital to the whole success of the new approach for the promotion of *Ujamaa* Villages, and the co-operative production units which we hope will be stages on the way to full *Ujamaa* Villages. It is essential that all Ministries put their services, and that of their field staffs, to the promotion of these policies to the maximum extent possible. The fact that this requires co-operation with Maendeleo in Dar es Salaam and with Regional and Area Commissioners at lower level does not imply a loss of control by the technical Ministries; it simply means that there will be a coordinated attack for the furtherance of our *Ujamaa* Policies and the transformation of our rural economy. For this policy and this responsibility is not just of, and for, Maendeleo; it is a Government policy and responsibility.[42]

The problem of governmental co-ordination in the regions has been seriously addressed in recent years. The 1968 appointment of Regional Economic Secretaries, and the 1969 appointment of Regional Directors of Agriculture[43] and Regional *Ujamaa* Village Officers were attempts to produce a more effective co-ordination in the periphery. The December, 1971, announcement of a deconcentration of departmental authority to the regions would seem to be a further step in this direction of a better meshing of the administration.[44] But the need for co-ordination, if it is successfully met, may make more crucial the necessity of political control. As better co-ordination of governmental activities is achieved, the penetrative capacity of the governmental hierarchy will be increased (*ceteris paribus*). A Commissioner, in his participatory role, is charged with ensuring that these co-ordinated activities are directed in particular, politically chosen, directions; in other words, he must not only facilitate co-ordination, he must control it as well.[45] The Commissioners are of central importance in this process because in many respects it is they alone who are to judge the political acceptability of governmental actions in the periphery: there are no elected representative bodies at the regional level and the District Councils since 1969 have little power; and neither the national nor local TANU organization has other representatives in authoritative positions in the government hierarchy outside of Dar es Salaam.[46]

The instruments available to a Commissioner are few, given the historical dominance of the bureaucracy. Force is not a realistic alternative. Civil servants are at least superficially malleable to the legitimate demands of a Commissioner for time, information and deference, and they do not indulge in controversial public statements. The material allocations which affect the civil servants personally are either centrally controlled by their own ministries (promotions and, usually, leave), or by civil servants at the district and regional levels (housing, travel and subsistence allowances). Central regard for a civil servant, manifested in letters in a personal file, transfers, and promotions, whose career is normally to be within his own department, relies upon the approval or disapproval of other civil servants in his ministry or, occasionally, of the Administrative Secretary. In fact, to the extent that control has been exercised over the activities of the technical departments and their civil servants by individuals not within their own ministries, it has been the Regional Administrative Secretaries, and not their Commissioners, who have been the most effective.[47]

The Administrative and Area Secretaries are considered the most senior civil servants in their areas, and all governmental communications to, and most often from, the Commissioners pass through their offices.[48] As chairman of the housing committees at their respective levels, the Secretaries have been adamant in refusing to allow the Commissioners influence in the allocation of official accomodation; with the severe chronic shortage of housing, especially at the regional centre, and consequent jockeying amongst departments and officials for accomodation, this is a considerable power.[49] The Secretaries also can, and do, write confidential letters for inclusion in an officer's personal file and this undoubtedly has a bearing on his relationships with the other civil servants. Perhaps the most potent instrument open to the Administrative Secretary, and through him the Area Secretaries, is the authority to communicate directly with an officer's Principal Secretary to complain about an individual's performance. Such communications have had the effect of immediately producing explanations and apologies from the officer concerned.[50]

Within the administrative process at the regional level the position of the Administrative Secretary is enhanced by his role as the effective executive officer of the Regional Development Committee's sub-committee.[51] This is the primary co-ordinating body, and it is also the focus for decision-making on the expenditure of the Regional Development Fund, that is, the bulk of the development funds allocated at sub-national level. The Administrative Secretary in Mwanza has been able to issue decisions as to who should sit on the committee and on the acceptability of agenda proposed by other regional heads. He also sits as the chairman of the Regional Development Committee in the absence of the Regional Commissioner, a task which garners recognition and deference from the other regional officers.[52] Symbolically, he is the only civil servant with a private washroom and its 'executive key'.

In one sense, an Area or Administrative Secretary is indeed helpful to a Commissioner—he sees to it that actions and expenditures are legally proper, he is almost always in the office thus providing a continuity which an often absent Commissioner cannot,[53] and he prepares and carries out much of the work of correspondence, agenda preparation, and miscellaneous tasks, including deputizing for the Commissioner at official functions and listening to grievances of the public, in which Commissioners have not been able or inclined to involve themselves. Theoretically this allows the Commissioners time to deal with TANU and to inspire and enthuse the masses. For a Commissioner's goal of controlling the officials, however, this position of the Secretary can present an added difficulty in that he becomes the sole link between the Commissioner and the civil servants. He is aware of (and often present at) meetings of other officials with the Commissioner and is informed in a general way of what transpires.

To the extent that a Commissioner is a line superior of the officers in his area, the Administrative or Area Secretary is the link through which this authority is exercised.[54] The Secretary is, however, more than just a communications linkage. He is at the same time the only adviser to the Commissioner. Since independence the Secretaries have served as the sole staff officer of the Commissioners and they have retained a monopoly of the provision of general advice[55] to the Commissioners.[56] This is most apparent when it is done in confidential letters to the Commissioner from his Secretary in which evaluations are made of the proposals of the advisers and technical officers, letters which the specialists do not normally see and which can, at times, contradict their advice.[57]

The establishment of two positions in 1968—69 was partly intended to strengthen the position of the Regional Commissioner by creating in his office a 'kitchen cabinet' of civil servants who would be his personal advisers concerned with issues which overlapped the interests of single departments. If successful these moves would have limited the Administrative Secretary's role as the Commissioner's hitherto general adviser. One was the appointment in early 1969 of the first Regional *Ujamaa* Village Officer, a former Kwimba District Co-operative Officer, to assist the Commissioner in the co-ordination of the various programmes of the several ministries which were to be working towards the setting up and support of *ujamaa* villages. He was to "work directly under, and to, the Regional Commissioner".[58]

In his first year in the position, however, the *Ujamaa* Village Officer did not work at all closely with the Regional Commissioner. In practice he worked strictly through the Administrative Secretary who vetoed his requests, very important in the context, for transport, his use of travel and subsistence allowances, and the reports which he forwarded to the Regional Commissioner, appointments with whom were made through the Administrative Secretary, and he did not become an adviser to the Commissioner on *ujamaa* village affairs.[59]

The other appointment intended to strengthen the position of the Regional Commissioner was the posting in late 1968 of a Regional Economic Secretary to Mwanza. The decision to appoint Economic Secretaries to the Regions evolved from several strains of thought of which it will be helpful to distinguish two. The first was a desire to increase the effectiveness of central planning,[60] initially by improving the information gathering process in the periphery and later, and this was not achieved, by producing regional and district plans which were implementable and which were within the framework of a national plan. This line of thought was essentially a product of the professional and technical desires of the Ministry of Economic Affairs and Development Planning (Devplan).[61]

The second strain, and of particular interest here, was the desire on the part of the President and other political leaders to increase popular participation in the planning process. The first Plan's regional documents (not that they were necessarily taken into account when the national Plan was being put together) from Mwanza had come almost entirely from civil servants.[62] The appointment of Economic Secretaries to the Regions was initially and primarily intended to alter this lack of popular inputs at the regional and district levels by strengthening the position of the Regional Commissioner.[63] The Minister of Economic Affairs and Development Planning, after a consultation with the President on 19 April 1968, reported in a memorandum to his Ministry the reasoning and instructions of the President:

121

It is essential to involve the masses in future planning and implementation of development projects. To this end you are required to re-examine the present machinery for planning and implementation of projects with a view to decentralizing authority. As an immediate step you are asked to provide a Planning Officer to each Regional Commissioner.[64]

At a further meeting with the President on 24 April 1969, the Devplan Minister, accompanied by seven of his senior officials, was instructed to post to the Regions, "economic advisers to the Regional Commissioners".[65] Shortly afterwards the first group of Regional Economic Secretaries was selected, trained, and posted to the regions.[66] The Mwanza Regional Economic Secretary took up his post on 18 November 1968, seven months after the initial Presidential instruction.[67]

During this seven month interim the Presidential emphasis on increasing the involvement of the "masses" in the planning process was superseded by Devplan's continuing desire to strengthen *central* planning through full-time, regional planning officers. In fact the training programme for the new Secretaries was itself used as an information gathering process by the central planners who needed project data from regional officials. The timing of the posting was such that there was only one month in which to produce the regional plan for consideration in the national process,[68] an impossible task, and when it was produced in June, 1969,[69] the final version of the Second Five Year Plan had already been completed.[70]

It was not, however, only the timing which made any effective regional contribution unlikely. The Secretaries' "terms of reference" had specified that the preparation of regional and district plans was to have priority.[71] And the Cabinet had in 1967 decided that as it was impossible to devise lower level plans unless the broad national economic directions were specified, the planning ministry was to produce "guidelines" for the District Development and Planning Committees.[72] In spite of these indications, Devplan officials took the position, which they were able to maintain throughout the planning process, that if regional and district level investment intentions were divulged, it "would be embarrassing if later cuts were made or projects rephased".[73] Consequently the Regional Economic Secretaries were not given the information which would have made possible lower level planning. Their role in the planning process then became one of investigating and reporting to the central planners on implementation, a role which somewhat duplicated the reporting procedures of the other departments. With a shortage of travel funds, with a very limited access to other departments' files, and lengthy absences from the Region on official duties of an *ad hoc* nature, the Mwanza Regional Economic Secretary up until my departure in July, 1970, had not been able to take up this reportorial role very extensively. It is interesting in this regard that when the Regional Commissioner appointed a three man team to report on the progress of all projects funded with Regional Development Fund Monies, in April, 1970, the Economic Secretary was not amongst them.

That the Economic Secretary's contribution to the planning process was negligible need not have obviated his intended role as an "economic adviser to the Regional Commissioner". Indeed, there was a need for the Commissioner to have broad analyses undertaken of the ongoing and suggested projects of the various ministries and to thus have an independent source of economic advice to counter-balance the 'localism' of the departments.[74] As it happened though, the Economic Secretary was put in the position of reporting to the Commissioner and to Devplan through the Administrative Secretary. This was something more than the normal 'through' procedure; as the Administrative Secretary explained to the senior regional officials prior to the economist's arrival, the Regional Economic Secretary was "under the Administrative Secretary".[75] In practice this meant that the economist's advice to the Commissioner was evaluated by the Administrative Secretary,[76] before being passed on, and thus the Commissioner remained with only one adviser—the Administrative Secretary. The notion that the economist might be a general adviser to the Commissioner on economic affairs, thus increasing the Commissioner's capacity to judge and hence control the technical departments seemed to be disregarded by the Commissioners, who treated the Economic Secretary as a fairly junior line civil servant under the Administrative Secretary, and by the Economic Secretaries themselves who thought that it was better not to get involved and who, appreciating the authority of the Administrative Secretary, thought it well advised not to compete with him.

The claim that I am making here that an Administrative or Area Secretary is in a position more powerful than his Commissioner *vis a vis* the civil servants should not be put too dogmatically. Aside from the fact that my focus has been limited to Mwanza Region, during the two years that I was either visiting or living in the Region for purposes of the study there was only one Administrative Secretary.[77] And

123

although I did have the opportunity of observing his relationships with two different Commissioners (Namata and Muhaji), I would hedge on any conclusions until I have seen more pairs in action.[78]

To argue too strongly on this point would also divert from an understanding of the more general structuring of the political administrative process within which a Commissioner operates, namely that most funds are allocated centrally and no officials, political or civil servant, at the Regional level have any great impact at stages other than implementation. The only exceptions to this which have been of some importance are the District Council funds (and since 1969 these have depended largely on central government subventions)[79] and the four percent of development expenditure which is allocated to the Regional Development Fund (RDF).[80]

The RDF has provided some leverage for the Commissioners. In Mwanza Region, however, they have devoted their attention to "regional projects" such as the Mwanza Development Scheme and the Gallu Settlement Scheme (latterly, *ujamaa* village) and Motel. Commissioners have been successful in diverting RDF funds to these large projects, and sometimes in raising central government funds as well—for instance, the Saa Nane Island game reserve and the TANU regional headquarters building—and each one of Mwanza's four Commissioners has spent a large part of his time on one or two of these "regional projects", all of which qualify for the label 'prestige project' or 'façade'. Consequently they have not become decisively involved with the allocation of the bulk of the RDF monies which has been left, in effect, to the civil servants sitting on the RDC sub-committee.[81]

The attempts to increase the participatory capacity of the Regional Commissioner through the development of a staff of personal advisers has been, in the case of Mwanza Region, ineffectual. Other attempts have been made to increase this capacity by strengthening the Commissioners as heads of a line ministry in their own right. The Presidential Circular on *ujamaa* villages emphasized that the Commissioners were Maendeleo (Rural Development) officials.[82] Then, in July, 1969, the Divisional Executive Officers throughout the Region were replaced by Divisional Secretaries.[83] The Divisional Executive Officers had been District Council employees reporting directly to the Council's Executive Officer. The new Divisional Secretaries were to be in positions similar to that of the Commissioners (in fact in some of the preliminary discussions the references were to 'Divisional Commissioners'), that is they were to be the Divisional Secretaries of TANU and political heads of government in their areas. They were to be responsible directly to the Area Commissioner. The change was seen as bolstering the Commissioners who had hitherto been regarded as having no line officials under them in the rural areas.[84]

During their first year in the field, the Divisional Secretaries found their positions to be almost anamolous. With TANU not organized on a divisional basis, with few governmental resources to expend, and no development funds to allocate at their level, the Divisional Secretaries were largely restricted to exhortative tours. They themselves and TANU and government officials at the District level expressed puzzlement over their role and their relationship with the Area Commissioner and the District Council.[85] There was confusion even as to the Divisional Secretaries' place in the Administration, with most considering themselves as much under the District Council and its Executive Officer, as under the Area Commissioner, both of whom they addressed letters to directly (and it was more often the Executive Officer) depending upon the issue. They were not, in their first year, operating as intended as line officials directly responsible to and supportive of the initiative of the Commissioners.

Some Concluding Remarks

The Commissioners in Mwanza Region were not able to significantly lessen the dominance of the bureaucracy in favour of increased political participation in economic and political decision-making at the district and regional levels.[86] Their official positions as TANU secretaries served mainly to make this phenomenon more difficult to perceive. Partly this was because they did not come to be a part of the local TANU organizations to the point of being a possible focus for the input of popular demands. More generally, however, the weakness of the role of a Commissioner was a result of, a) the highly centralized process of resource allocation tending to sectoral and departmental rather than areal inputs, and national rather than local priorities, and, b) the Commissioners' lack of a sufficient stock of sanctions which they might wield with respect to the civil servants who are nominally under them. The civil servants were also under their own departments and it was to these departments which they looked for guidance and career advancement; with respect to the Commissioners, the civil servants were chiefly induced not to give the appearance of being unco-operative or obstreperous.

What did the Commissioners do during 1969—70? In Mwanza Region they devoted most of their time and energies to exhortative tours in support of central policies and programmes, and to the supervision of prestige projects in search of central approbation. There was tremendous pressure from the central government and party for them to have their areas produce politically acceptable achievements and this was undoubtedly a key factor in their opting, in those instances where they had some allocative power such as the Regional Development Fund, for these large scale, visible projects rather than for a maze of small projects none of which might be found worthy of central recognition.[87] The Commissioners also listened to complaints and grievances, but certainly not as much as would seem to have been intended by the initial parliamentary descriptions of their functions. Nor were they the most important 'Bwana Shauris' in the rural areas; the Administrative and Area Secretaries, and the Executive Officer of the District Council each spent much more time in dealing with individual citizens and groups and their problems.[88]

The Commissioners for the most part then were agents of the hierarchy, especially of the government hierarchy, attempting to mobilize the people to follow central directions. Only marginally, if at all, did they increase participation either by exerting TANU control over the bureaucracy or by representing the interests of the people of their area in the national allocative processes. Vente's view from the centre as to what the Commissioners are doing coincides with my view from Mwanza Region:

... the Regional or Area Commissioner is to be supervisory, that is to say, to deal with the promotion of the implementation of decisions already taken, but that his influence upon the concrete working out of the decision not to mention upon the actual decision itself is limited.[89]

Organizationally one of the more interesting features of the role of the Commissioners was the attempt in the late 1960's to create a staff of personal advisers to the Regional Commissioner. The conflict between area and function, generalists and specialist, or, in Tanzanian terms, between co-ordination for the attainment of national goals and "ministerial interests and jealousies",[90] was attacked, *inter alia*, by posting Regional *Ujamaa* Village Officers and Regional Economic Secretaries to the regional centres with the intention of their becoming

126

something along the lines of a Regional Commissioner's office or department. The rationale behind the establishment of these posts, most explicitly in the case of the economists, was to increase the participation of the masses in the planning and implementation of development projects by strengthening the position of the Regional Commissioner.

The setting up of these posts was not an innovation in the wider sense, that is, other governments[91] have employed, at times with good results, the principle of using 'expert' staff members to support the capacity of a political official to control the 'localism' of the civil servants in the regular departments. In Mwanza Region, however, the experiment was not during my time there proving successful. The Regional Commissioners were not provided with a staff which was as free as possible from loyalty to specific departmental interests and programmes, and which instead was loyal to a Commissioner's goal of achieving broad national objectives and able to advise him competently on the relationship between departmental programmes and projects and the national goals and policies. Rather, the Commissioners remained as they had since independence with a single adviser, the Administrative Secretary.[92] Advice to the Commissioner from the *Ujamaa* Village Officer and the Economic Secretary was channelled, as were most communications between department heads and the Commissioner, through the Administrative Secretary who appended his own evaluation, sometimes in confidential letters to the Commissioner which the intended 'adviser' was not permitted to read.

Notes

1. Stanley Dryden, *Local Administration in Tanzania*, Nairobi: East African Publishing House, 1968, pp. 22—41, discusses the changes in Regional Administration after independence.

2. This was pointed out in the Assembly debates. *Hansard*, First Session (Second Meeting), 6 June 1962, col. 75. See, also, William Tordoff, *Government and Politics in Tanzania*, Nairobi: East African Publishing House, 1967, p. 100.

3. *Hansard*, First Session (Second Meeting), 15 June 1962, cols. 514—515. The formal responsibilities of the Commissioners are listed in Henry Bienen, *Tanzania: Party Transformation and Economic Development*, Princeton: Princeton University Press, expanded edition 1970, pp. 313—317.

4. Bienen, *op.cit.*, pp. 119—120.

5. The dual nature of a Commissioner's role is well recognized by Tan-

zanian leaders. Nyerere, in a 2 February 1962, press conference, described them as "representatives of Government as well as being representatives of the people". Referred to in, *Hansard*, First Session (First Meeting), 17 February 1962, col. 288. The Parliamentary Secretary in the Ministry of local Government and Administration noted that the job of the Commissioners was to "keep the pressure on (the civil servants) and keep the people's enthusiasm up". *Hansard*, First Session (Second Meeting), 12 June 1962, cols. 313—314.

6. The official Tanzania government paper presented to the Fourth Social Welfare Seminar held in East and Central Africa in Dar-es-Salaam, 27 December 1970 to 6 January 1971, stated: ". . . at all levels it is the aim of TANU to provide party functionaries or cadres who are expected to 'take down' people's demands to the higher echelons. This transmission line has become very important today after the birth of the Arusha Declaration . . ." The report of the seminar, including the Tanzanian paper, have been published by The Tanzania National Council on Social Welfare and the German National Committee of the International Council on Social Welfare as, *The Role of Social Welfare Services in East and Central Africa*, Nairobi: Afropress, 1971.

7. Max Gluckman, "Inter-hierarchical Roles: Professional and Party Ethics in Tribal Areas in South and Central Africa", in Marc J. Swartz (ed), *Local-Level Politics: Social and Cultural Perspectives*, London: University of London Press, 1969, p. 71. This essay by Gluckman is a discussion and review of the anthropological literature on these conflicting pressures focused on the colonial administrators and chiefs. An equally stimulating consideration of a related topic is the essay, in the same volume, by Hugh Tinker, "Local Government and Politics and Political and Social Theory in India", pp. 217—226.

8. See, G. Andrew Maguire, *Toward 'Uhuru' in Tanzania: the Politics of Participation*, Cambridge: Cambridge University Press, 1969, pp. 325—328.

9. This is the general practice in Tanzania.

10. In March, 1962, Richard Wambura was appointed the first Regional Commissioner of the Lake Region which included the present Mwanza Region. He was replaced by John Malecela in March, 1963. In May, 1963, Mwanza Region was formed with Malecela becoming its first Regional Commissioner.

11. Joseph Nyerere, Regional Commissioner from November, 1964, to July, 1967, the President's brother and, when appointed and subsequently, the Secretary-General of the Youth League; and, Alhaj O. A. Muhaji, Regional Commissioner from April, 1969, to February, 1972, a nominated M.P. and Junior Minister of National Education when appointed, sometime Secretary-General of the East African Muslim Society, national leader in TAPA, and reportedly (this background information on Muhaji comes from the *Nationalist* reporter in Mwanza), an ANC leader in Singida in 1960—62. Muhaji was also a teacher in primary and middle schools and eventually became a district education officer after independence.

12. John Malecela, Regional Commissioner from March, 1963, to No-

vember, 1964, and Joseph Namata, July, 1967, to April, 1969. Both were district officers in the final colonial days and both did courses at Cambridge. Malecela was at the time of his appointment a foreign service officer and Namata the Head of the Civil Service and Secretary to the Cabinet.

13. *Bienen, op.cit.*, pp. 119—152, discusses at length many aspects of recruitment, including the appointment of civil servants, and tenure.

14. While serving as chairman of the 1969 TANU national conference, the President identified R. R. Mbilinyi as the Ruvuma Area Commissioner. Mr. Mbilinyi corrected him by replying that he was a Divisional Executive Officer. *Majadiliano ya Mkutano Mkuu wa TANU: Taarifa Rasmi* (the official verbatim report of the conference), 29 May 1969, col. 109. Area Commissioners are appointed by the President but are normally sworn in at the Regional headquarters by the Regional Commissioner.

15. Etzioni distinguishes three types of power—coercive, remunerative and normative. These categories coincide with the types of sanction I discuss here, with the exception that offices, promotions, etc., are not considered as normative symbols, but rather as valued goods by themselves. The notion of normative power is analogous to Schurmann's conception of the Chinese using ideology to guide organizational activities. Although great efforts are being made, ideology did not appear to have had much effect on the behaviour of individuals during my time in Mwanza Region. Amitai Etzioni, *A Comparative Analysis of Complex Organizations*, New York: Free Press, 1961, chapter 1; Franz Schurmann, *Ideology and Organization in Communist China*, Berkeley: University of California Press, second edition 1968, *passim*.

16. The Reports of the Permanent Commission of Enquiry contain notes on cases in which the Regional Administration took action involving the Police with subsequent lack of certainty as to who ordered the action. See, Annual Reports of the Commission for the years, 1966/67, 1967/68, 1968/69, published by the Government Printer, Dar es Salaam.

17. In August, 1968, the Mwanza Regional Commissioner ordered all the bars closed after accusing the people of not producing enough cotton because of drunkness. Within five days all the bars were open again, a fact which the Regional Commissioner thought it "best not to take note of". Interview, Regional Commissioner, 6 March 1969. Referring to bans in general promulgated by Area and Regional Commissioners, and in particular to those on the Masai mode of dress and 'soul' music, the Chief Justice of Tanzania labeled them "vestigal exercises of chiefly power" which have "absolutely no legal standing" and which "should not be taken too seriously. They are just personal opinions dressed up in TANU banners." Public address, Nyegezi Social Training Centre, 6 February, 1970.

18. In December, 1965, the Field Force was sent to Ukerewe to force farmers to use fertilizer and to plant cotton. A discussion of the incident and its background is, A. M. Mtesigwa, "The Politics of Agriculture in Ukerewe", unpublished undergraduate Political Science dissertation, University College, Dar es Salaam, 1969.

19. *Cf.*, Clyde R. Ingle, "Compulsion and Rural Development in Tanzania", *Canadian Journal of African Studies*, IV, 1 (Winter, 1970), pp. 77—100.

20. The 1965 Ukerewe case referred to in note no. 18, above, adversely affected popular support for a wide range of development projects and for Regional and Area Commissioners personally. The successor Regional Commissioner, in a 6 March 1969 interview, stated that the lesson of Ukerewe was that force was not effective in rural development and that were a similar situation to arise again he would not permit its use.

21. In April, 1969, the Ukerewe Area Commissioner ordered the police to detain a taxi driver who was drinking with the Commissioner's estranged wife. The order was preceeded by a fistfight between the two men. Soon after the incident the Commissioner was replaced by a new appointee and later he was appointed Area Commissioner for Kiomboi. The case was tried in February, 1970, by a Mwanza Resident Magistrate who found the Commissioner guilty of wrongfully confining the taxi driver and sentenced him to five months imprisonment and shs. 700. In the appeal to the High Court in May, 1970, the verdict was upheld and the sentence changed to six months imprisonment *or* 3,000 shillings. During the trial the Commissioner described Ukerewe District as "a place full of political intrigues". The police officer leading the prosecution stated that he had been ordered by Dar es Salaam to prosecute another public official in Mwanza Region for a similar offence also committed in 1969, but there were no subsequent prosecutions. Newspaper accounts of the case are in the *Sunday News,* 15 February 1970; *The Nationalist,* 24 February and 14 May, 1970.

22. But, see Ingle, *loc.cit.*

23. The public nature of the opposition of the two West Lake M.P.'s to the Regional Commissioner's way of implementing the *ujamaa* village programme was probably a key factor in their subsequent expulsion from TANU in 1968. The affair is considered in H. U. E. Thoden van Velsen and J. J. Sterkenburg, "The Party Supreme", *Kroniek van Africa,* 1969, 1; also, "Report of the West Lake Commission Enquiry", *Sunday News,* 13 October 1968.

24. This is clear from my own research and from, Paul Collins, "The Working of Tanzania's Rural Development Fund: A Problem in Decentralisation", IDS Communication No. 62, University of Sussex, July, 1971.

25. Lionel Cliffe and John S. Saul, "The District Development Front in Tanzania", (mimeo.), Dar es Salaam, October, 1969, p. 12.

26. The general observations in this paragraph depend on interviews with Commissioners and Executive Secretaries in all Mwanza's Districts. Two of the incidents which I witnessed involved written requests from Area Commissioners to District Executive Secretaries—one, to provide temporary office space for a university student working with the Rural Research Project of the University College, Dar es Salaam; the other, to assist in accomodating another student from the same project. The third was a request from the Regional Commissioner for cell leader lists to be provided the Project to facilitate the choosing of a random sample for a farm survey. In all three cases, the requests were rejected: in the first one the Secretary claimed the request to use TANU offices was "not proper", in the second the claim was that the Secretary had not been "properly informed" of the project, and in the third, that cell leader lists were confidential and the

Regional Commissioner had no authority to disclose such information. The national lists are, in fact, available to the public at the offices of the Census bureau in Dar es Salaam; I later discovered that the Regional and District offices of TANU in Mwanza had only out-dated and incomplete lists of cell leaders. Since 1968 the District Executive Secretaries have normally been presidentially nominated members of the District Councils and members of the Council's Finance Committees. If funerals are indicative of the status of an individual, see the report of the funeral of the Kilimanjaro Regional Executive Secretary, *The Nationalist*, 1 September 1970.

27. The *Report of the Presidential Special Committee into the Co-operative Movement and Marketing Boards*, Dar es Salaam: Government Printer, 1966, paragraphs 278 and 279, referring to Regional and Area Commissioners and other politicians, records the finding of the Committee that, "while political interference in the co-operative movement has plainly been excessive ... in almost all cases the pressures were exerted under the (however mistaken) notion that it was for the good of the country". The not quite clear position of the Commissioners is reflected in Government's response to this report, in which they made a distinction between "interference and necessary intervention; and also between unauthorized politicians on one hand and on the other hand the Minister, Regional and Area Commissioners whose duty may require their intervention. The reference to 'political' interference, however, is unfortunate; a better and more appropriate reference could probably have been intervention, by persons in authority, through their incursions into matter which judging strictly by financial results they are not qualified to deal with." *Proposals of the Tanzania Government on the Recommendation of the Special Presidential Committee of Enquiry into the Co-operative Movement and Marketing Boards*, Dar es Salaam: Government Printer 1966, p. 17. *Cf.*, John S. Saul, "An Introduction and Commentary on Co-operatives", *Mbioni*, III, 8 (December, 1966), pp. 2—8.

28. This account relies upon interviews and a reading of the relevant files in the NCU's Zonal office and Mwanza Headquarters.

29. Governmental control over the co-operatives can of course lead to an over-all lessening of participation. I have not considered the co-operatives specifically in this study, but it is relevant to note in passing the conclusions of the Nordic advisers on co-operatives in Tanzania. They refer to the "alienation of the farmer" from the co-operative, a tendency "among farmers to view the co-operatives as less under their control and more as simple instruments of government". They saw this as happening in the cotton co-operatives because of the Lint and Seed Marketing Board's more rigid conditions for the sale of seed cotton, and "the actions by government in recent years to assume management of all societies and the unions ... just to correct operations by relatively few societies ..." From the mimeographed report of the discussions of the Nordic Advisers (Co-operatives), Dar es Salaam, 28—31 July 1969, on, "Problems at Society and Union Levels".

30. Cliffe and Saul, *op.cit.*, p. 4.

31. Along with being on the NEC, the Regional Commissioners are *ex*

officio members of the National Assembly and usually sit on at least one governmental or parastatal board or commission, and are also sometimes on the national committee of one of TANU's affiliated bodies—TAPA, TYL, NUTA, and CUT.

32. The Regional Chairman sits as a voting member of the National Executive Committee, and the regional representative (usually referred to as M. N. E.—Member of the National Executive) elected by the National conference sits as a voting member of both the National Executive and Central Committee.

33. One case, in some ways I think instructive, which I observed in May, 1969, was the election of the branch chairman of the Mayuya branch in Geita. The Area Commissioner opened the meeting with a few words on the importance of the popular election of leaders and then departed. Three weeks later in an interview he observed that he did not yet know who had won the election. Mayuya, which has been as administratively and politically resistant as any in Geita to directions from above, I had thought would be an area in which the Commissioner, who has an overall responsibility for mobilization, would have followed closely changes in the local TANU leadership.

34. The opinion of the Commissioners that their contacts are insufficient is reflected in a decidedly structured approach to a solution. It is the practice that the evenings before a regional or district executive committee meeting the leaders spend the time together in an organized, semi-private party. I attended one such party, prior to the meeting of the Regional Executive Committee held in Ukerewe, 3—4 April 1969. The conversation was jocular, but, with all sitting in a large circle, distinctly removed from specific issues or personalities. Through several hours the conversation was dominated by local leaders, who often used Sukuma, a language not spoken by the Commissioners. The Regional Commissioner was particularly quiet, speaking only to the Area Commissioner and Area Secretary, while the Ukerewe Area Commissioner spent almost the entire time making dinner arrangements, ensuring that accomodation was satisfactory, supervising the use of the one Land Rover, and informing sundry arrivals that the bar was closed as a TANU meeting was in progress. The two other Area Commissioners who were present participated in the general discussions, but the use of Sukuma often meant they (as well as I) missed the punch line of many of the humourous stories.

35. The frequency with which Commissioners and local TANU leaders consulted and coordinated with each other was also indicated by the extent to which they visited each other's offices. In Geita and Ukerewe the offices of the Area Commissioner and TANU are about a half-mile apart, and the arrival of an Area Commissioner at the TANU office is an important event. Messengers and clerks in the government offices and in the TANU offices, in response to questions, thought that the Commissioners visited the TANU premises about once a fortnight either for meetings or to hold a political surgery for the hearing of people's complaints and grievances. The District Executive Secretaries said that the Commissioners came two or three times a week; and the Commissioners informed me that they made a point of

visiting the TANU office at least once a day. My own impression, given that the commissioners were out of the district centres ten or twelve working days a month on tours or visits to the Regional Centre, and excluding visits which were strictly for the passing of salutations, was the Commissioners went to the TANU district offices four or five times a month. The Regional Commissioner's office and the Regional TANU office were adjacent making contact between the two difficult to estimate. The Regional Chairman of TANU did accompany the Regional Commissioner on his tours and on public days, more so than was the case with their District counterparts, and in fact tours by the Regional Commissioner were the events which consistently brought leaders at ward, district, and regional levels together. In this sense it was unfortunate that the Regional Commissioners spent as much time out of the Region as in it. The national party's 1970 annual report admonished the Commissioners for not spending a few hours every month or fortnight at the TANU offices at the district and regional centres. *The Nationalist*, 8 June 1971.

36. The lack of urgency accompanying the leaders' support of the *ujamaa* village policy was the recurrent example. In discussions in homes and backrooms of bars they spoke of the need for 50 or 60 years to pass before their efforts at persuasion will have borne fruit, while in public meetings it was heavily emphasized that nobody would be forced to join a village. Of the seventeen regions Mwanza ranked seventeenth in 1969 and sixteenth in 1970 in the officially reported number of *ujamaa* villages.

37. Cliffe and Saul, *op.cit.*, p. 16.

38. Cabinet Paper No. 70 of 1967, "The Promotion and Implementation of Rural Development", submitted by the Minister for Local Government and Rural Development and accepted on 8 November, 1967, was the authoritative statement on the administrative arrangements for most of the rural development strategy. It stated: "the Area Commissioner's chief role should be that of political inspiration and explanation, and co-ordination of the activities of the Ministerial representatives. Only if he fails in his co-ordination efforts should the matter need to be referred to this Ministry" (for submission to a standing committee of Principal Secretaries, see note no. 41, below).

39. *Cf.*, James W. Fesler, *Area and Administration*, University, Alabama: University of Alabama Press, 1964.

40. *Cf.*, V. Subramaniam, "Specialists in British and Australian Government: A Study in Contrast", *Public Administration*, Autumn, 1963, pp. 357—373. F. F. Ridley, *Specialists and Generalists*, London, Allen and Unwin, 1968.

41. Cabinet Paper No. 70 of 1967, *op.cit.*, led to the setting up of a Standing Committee on Rural Development Policy, consisting mostly of Principal Secretaries, to "solve any difficulties as they arise [so as] ... to ensure that the co-ordinating role of the District Development and Planning Committee is not disrupted by Ministerial interests and jealousies". One of the working papers which led to the Cabinet decision claimed that one of the "obvious weaknesses of the development system [in Tanzania is] ... the lack of effective joint interests. In most instances members of

the District Development Committee are only interested in their own programmes. Also, they operate to the advantage of the Ministries rather than to the advantage of the people who are faced with the problems." A memorandum originally prepared by the Ministry of Community Development and National Culture, dated 12 April 1967, and sent to the Principal Secretary of Devplan by the Principal Secretary of Local Government and Rural Development on 15 August, 1967, with the reference no. LGRD /C/P.2, in Devplan file MDPC/L.60/4/5.

42. Presidential Circular No. 1 of 1969, "The Development of *Ujamaa* Villages", 20 March, 1969, para. 19.

43. The Regional Directors of Agriculture were to have increased authority over local expenditures. This has been reported as being 15 percent of recurrent expenditures contained in votes such as upkeep of station, travel allowances, etc., D. B. Jones, "Rural and Regional Planning in Tanzania", presented to the Conference on Comparative Administration in East Africa, Arusha, Tanzania, September, 1971, p. 16

44. *The Nationalist*, 11 December 1971; *The Standard*, 28 January 1972 See the Appendix.

45. E.g., a Commissioner who was successful in co-ordinating governmental activities with a resultant increase in cotton production could not, given Tanzania's over-arching goals, be regarded as successful unless he also ensured that the increase was generated and the benefits distributed in a politically acceptable fashion.

46. Cabinet Paper No. 70 of 1967 (see note no. 38, above) stated that plans should be "people's" plans and not "officials'" plans, and that it was the task of the Regional and Area Commissioners to ensure that they were "people's" plans "where the impetus for this is lacking at the local level". Recently there have been some arguments made in favour of a regionally elected representative body. See, A. Rweyemanu, "The Preconditions for Regional Planning: the Case for a Viable Institutional Framework", presented to the Conference on Comparative Administration in East Africa, Arusha, Tanzania, September, 1971.

47. The relations between the Commissioners and these Secretaries, and even more so their relative positions *vis a vis* the civil servants, has been one of the more neglected areas of Tanzanian administration. Bienen devoted several pages to it but they are largely descriptive and concerned with formal structuring. The more analytical piece by Cliffe and Saul devotes one line to this topic. See, Bienen, *op.cit.*, pp. 317—320; Cliffe and Saul, *op.cit.*, p. 4.

48. This communication procedure was formally agreed to by the Cabinet in May, 1966. It is referred to in a letter from the Principal Secretary of State House to all Principal Secretaries, Heads of Independent Divisions, and Regional Commissioners, dated 6 May 1968, with the State House file reference as SHC/N.80/20/15, a copy of which is in the Devplan file MDPC/D.10/35. Also, it made clear that all communications from the centre to the region would pass through the Administrative Secretary: "All instructions from headquarters to Regional heads (are to) be sent to the officer concerned, but copies to State House, Utawala and the Ad-

ministrative Secretary of the Region for the Regional Commissioner's attention."

49. The Administrative Secretary in Mwanza sat often as a one man housing committee. In several instances he was able to prevent or delay officers who had been specifically requested by the Regional Commissioner from coming to the Region by taking the stand that no housing was available.

50. Some of the explanations and apologies, and references to the letters which the Administrative Secretary has written to various principal secretaries, can be found in the Mwanza Regional Administration files on the Regional Development Committee's subcommittee.

51. At the district level this role is shared between the Area Secretary and the Executive Officer of the District Council who is the secretary of the District Development and Planning Committee.

52. Various series of letters in the Mwanza Regional Administration file C/5/83 bear this out. One of the most interesting was a letter from a newly appointed Regional Agricultural Officer on 31 March 1969 to the Administrative Secretary reprimanding him for his handling of a Regional Development Committee meeting in a way that put the Agricultural Officer in a bad light. The RAO's letter concluded: "I hope this will never happen again for the good of us all." The Administrative Secretary replied with a sternly worded letter demanding a "better explanation", warning the RAO "not to try to blame me", and concluded: "Unless I receive a more satisfactory and less pretentious explanation, I intend to make a full report of the incident to your Ministry." Two days later the RAO sent a letter of apology and undertook not to have a similar incident arise again. The letters, pointedly, were copied to all other regional heads—the deference order was being openly challenged and defended.

53. The Regional Commissioners who are often out of the Region are aware that this leads to perhaps a too great dependence on the Administrative Secretary, Regional Commissioner, interview, 6 March, 1969.

54. In certain cases the Administrative Secretary was able to disregard the orders of the Regional Commissioner. One instance in particular is instructive in a study concerned with increasing participation. On several occasions the Administrative Secretary informed me of his opinion that the Regional Development Committee was "too political", with the politicians giving sometimes "embarrassing speeches" about things which they "knew nothing". Later, he informed a government official (who remarked to me on the matter immediately afterwards) that there were only two "socialists" in the Region, naming two individuals. The following month, one of the two socialists was asked by the Regional Commissioner if he would sit on the Regional Development Committee. The socialist agreed, and the Commissioner instructed the Administrative Secretary to put his name on the list. The Administrative Secretary delayed and finally refused, telling me later, in response to a question, that he had decided that the committee was already too large and that it was better not to add another participant. The Regional Commissioner did not pursue the matter further. Interviews, Regional Administrative Secretary, 10 September 1969, 16

March 1970. This is an exceptional case. More generally the Administrative Secretary is an intermediary with varying, but more difficult to estimate amounts of influence.

55. Another group of officials who are potentially general advisers to a Commissioner are those from Rural Development (Maendeleo). In practice however, they work under the Administrative Secretary. This also holds true for the Rural Development Officer (Local Government) in his role as secretary of the RDC subcommittee and adviser to the Regional Commissioner on Council affairs.

56. The Kwimba Area Commissioner, in describing the job of his Area Secretary, distinguished between administration (and he listed the specific duties of the Secretary) and "advising me on all the things which my office handles". Interview, 20 March 1970. Bienen, *op.cit.*, p. 318, writes that the Administrative and Area Secretaries "are supposed to advise and assist the commissioners in their statutory, administrative, and political duties".

57. See, for instance, note no. 76, below, on the Administrative Secretary's advice on the Mwanza Development Scheme.

58. Presidential Circular No. 1 of 1969, "The Development of *Ujamaa* Villages", 20 March 1969, para. 20.

59. I did not read all of the files of the *Ujamaa* Village Officer, but I was able to observe his activities quite frequently during his first year and to have frequent discussions with him about the various aspects of his position.

60. This decisional strain has a longer history than the second, popular participation, strain. Most importantly for Mwanza Region, the first strain had earlier brought Devplan officials to the Region. In June, 1965, during a state visit to France, the President requested experts for Devplan. In February, 1966, two agricultural specialists from SATEC, a French aid agency, arrived and were assigned to Economic Zone 6 (consisting of Mwanza, Shinyanga, Mara, and West Lake Regions) with instructions to draw up a plan for Mwanza Region. They decided to concentrate on Geita District and in July, 1966 produced a plan for the District. It was largely a compilation of information and was not taken into account during the national planning process. Devplan file MDPC/D.10/46. Robert Chambers has classified this Geita plan as an example (along with the Mwanza Region Plan for the Second national plan) of "planning without implementation". See, his, "Planning for Rural Areas in East Africa: Experience and Prescriptions", presented to the Conference on Comparative Administration in East Africa, Arusha, Tanzania, September, 1971.

61. During 1968 there were several attempts by Devplan officials to define regional planning. Although no formulation was authoritatively accepted, the apparently least controversial one within Devplan itself indicates their emphasis on the technical strain: a regional plan was to identify "the various localized development efforts which in view of the available resources will more productively contribute to the realization of the national development objectives". Devplan file MDPC/C.60/4.

62. For instance, the following was the description on one section of the 'plan' submitted by Mwanza Region, as described by the Administrative

Secretary, the Regional Community Development Officer, and the Deputy Regional Secretary of TANU in a 22 November 1963, letter to the Director of Planning: "the plan as presented below gives what can be done by the Water Development and Irrigation Division rather than what is wanted by the people. The programme could be later fitted to the requirements of the people as these develop, without much affecting it." Devplan file MDPC 36/12/5. See, also, Gary Karmiloff, "Regional Plan Implementation: Tanzania's Experiment", *East African Economics Review*, I, 2 (June, 1965); and, R. C. Pratt, "The Administration of Economic Planning in a Newly Independent State: the Tanzanian Experience 1963—66", *Journal of Commonwealth Political Studies*, (March, 1967), pp. 30—59.

63. The 1967 setting up of the Rural Development Fund was also devised to increase participation, although this was somewhat obviated at first by the need for central approval of all projects over 50,000 shillings, and later fairly well disregarded with the deconcentration of decision-making to the RDC subcommittee (which is in effect the regional team) and the central promulgation of very specific guidelines on the sorts of projects eligible for funds.

64. The Minister's report of this consultation is in the Devplan file MDPC/C.60/4.

65. *Ibid.*

66. P. Raikes, P. Lawrence, D. Warner, and G. Saylor, "Regional Planning in Tanzania: An Economic View from the Field", E. R. B. (Restricted) Paper 68.8, Economic Research Bureau, University College, Dar es Salaam, January, 1969, contains some notes on the training and establishing of the Regional Economic posts. The training included a trip to the Regions which was variously described as being to "assist the Regional Development Committees work out regional plans", "extensions of the two-week orientation course", and "'stocktaking' exercises". The Devplan Minister was very sensitive about criticisms from Area and Regional Commissioners that Devplan was formulating another 'official's' plan and he had earlier ordered his Principal Secretary to take steps to "correct this impression". See his minute of 31 August 1968 in Devplan file MDPC/L.60/4.

67. The first Economic Secretary in Mwanza was J. Kinyunyu, with degrees from Addis Ababa and Paris (the latter taken during the time of the students riots). In mid-1969 he was posted to Rural Development's *ujamaa* village section in Dar es Salaam and replaced by C. Rwechungura, who had a Master's in agricultural economics from America. Rwechungura still held the position as of December, 1971, although since September, 1971, he was at the Hague on study leave.

68. Devplan had ordered that all regional plans were to be submitted by the end of December, 1968. Letter of 9 October 1968 from the Principal Secretary to all Regional and Area Commissioners, Devplan file MDPC /L.60/4.

69. By which time it was styled a "report on regional planning—Mwanza Region" and was, in the Economic Secretary's words, a listing of "some of the projects submitted by the Districts for implementation during the second Five-year Plan", which, with "a careful look" one would realize did

not contain information "detailed enough for a clear project evaluation". Mwanza Regional Administration file D.3/144/3, 21 June 1969.

70. Late in May, 1969, the Plan had been "explained" to the TANU national conference, and it came into effect on 1 July 1969. See, the speech by the President to the conference which is reproduced in Vol. I of the Plan. The time-table was completely outlined in a letter of 10 February 1969 from the Devplan Principal Secretary to all other Principal Secretaries, Devplan file MDPC/D.10/74.

71. The initial discussions within Devplan on the "terms of reference for Regional Economic Secretaries", in Devplan file MDPC/L.60/4, emphasized that the drafting of regional and district plans was urgent. The other functions, broadly referred to as "orientation" and "appraisal and review" were considered of secondary importance. The final terms of reference are contained in a letter from the Principle Secretary, Ministry of Regional Administration and Rural Development, to all Regional Commissioners, 2 October 1968, LGC.48/010. The official statement on the priority of the Secretaries' task of drawing up plans was made in the Devplan letter of 9 October 1969, referred to in note no. 68, above.

72. Devplan file MDPC/C.60/4, contains the accounts of the November, 1967, Cabinet discussion which led to this decision.

73. This position was formally taken in a 15 January 1968 meeting held at Devplan headquarters of officials from six ministries on the implementation of the Cabinet decision. Minutes of the meeting are in Devplan file MDPC/C.60/4. For the 1971/72 Annual Plan the situation was apparently the same with Regional officials learning of regional allocations only *ex post*. See, Bevan Waide, "Trends in Annual Planning Procedures in Tanzania", presented to the Conference on Comparative Administration in East Africa, Arusha, Tanzania, September, 1971.

74. The problem of 'localism' or departmental loyalties has been recognized in China as necessitating organizational arrangements which will off-set its detrimental effects. One of their approaches has been to issue broad guidelines to lower level units of government and production, and to then have committees at these levels, comprised of 'red' as well as the various 'expert' elements, make the detailed decisions involved in policy implementation. The Chinese have not completely done away with the problem, primary because many tasks require specialization. Barnett concluded a study of Chinese organization with the observation, "the problem of generalists versus specialists (which the Chinese Communists, with their penchant for slogans, label the 'red and expert' problem) is a basic one and is likely, in fact, to become increasingly important as time goes on". Doak A. Barnett, *Cadres, Bureaucracy, and Political Power in Communist China*, New York: Columbia University Press, 1967, pp. 431—433. The Tanzanian experiment with Regional *Ujamaa* Village Officers and Economic Secretaries is a different approach to the problem of 'localism'. See, note no. 91, below.

75. This was stated in Paper no. RDSC/1 of 25 October 1968, which was circulated to Mwanza Regional heads by the Administrative Secretary, Mwanza Regional Administration file, C/5/83. It was interesting that many

in Devplan considered the Economic Secretary a line official of their Ministry.

76. The effects of an Administrative Secretary's advice on technical matters was often decisive. For instance, the first assignment given the new Regional Economic Secretary in Mwanza in July, 1969, by the Regional Commissioner was to appraise the viability of the Mwanza Development Scheme (a government financed farm and trades training workshop) and to recommend whether or not a bridging loan for which they were applying should be granted. After a month's work the Economic Secretary, in a lengthy report, supported the scheme's application. In a confidential letter which the Economic Secretary was not informed of, the Administrative Secretary briefly advised the Regional Commissioner not to grant the loan (it would have come from the RDF monies and thus the Regional Commissioner was the decision maker) on the basis that the scheme was uneconomic with no further explanation being given. For reasons largely involved with the Administrative Secretary's personal quarrels with the manager of the Scheme, he had long been opposed to its various proposals for expansion. The Regional Commissioner, who had taken up his post in April, 1969, decided not to support the loan application. This information comes from several discussions with the Administrative and Economic Secretaries in August and September, 1969.

77. The Administrative Secretary had completed Secondary School in 1952, attended a technical college in 1953, passed the Administrative Law Examination in 1961, and did a nine month course at an American university in 1966—67. He was an Assistant District Officer during 1959 and 1960, a District Commissioner/Magistrate during 1961 and 1962, and Administrative Secretary during 1963 and 1964, a Principal Assistant Secretary for Defence and National Service from 1965 to mid-1968, when he was appointed Mwanza Administrative Secretary, the post which he currently (December, 1971) holds. He is, in short, a highly qualified and experienced civil servant.

78. Between October, 1963, and October, 1971, there were four Administrative Secretaries for Mwanza Region and four Regional Commissioners. Over the same period, for Ukerewe, Kwimba, and Geita Districts there have been fourteen Area Secretaries and ten Area Commissioners. (I exclude Mwanza District as since mid-1969 it has normally had two Area Secretaries.)

79. Well before the 1969 Budget speech which announced the removal of some 80 percent of the revenue sources of the District Councils, there was a realization on the part of the Commissioners that the Councils' days as a source of development funds which might be influenced were limited. A Devplan official's minute of 19 February 1968 noted that one Regional Commissioner thought the Government had decided "to bury the District Councils" or at least to have them dealing with only recurrent expenditure. Devplan file MDPC/D.10/35. A Regional Commissioner as the "proper officer" of the Councils was in some ways able to influence their activities (there were in Mwanza Region, for instance, continuing rumours that this or that sacking was done on the "order" of the Regional Commissioner).

but in Mwanza the Commissioners used their influence over the Councils mainly to get them to contribute to schemes which were classified as "regional projects".

80. Jones, *op.cit.*, p. 18.

81. This is clear from a reading of the extensive report on the expenditure of RDF monies in Mwanza Region for 1968/69 and 1969/70 which was compiled by a three man committee appointed by the Regional Commissioner. It was produced in April, 1970, and is located in the Mwanza Regional Administration files C5/83 and C5/69. The RDF has been competently analysed by Paul Collins. See, especially, the discussion paper he prepared to introduce his paper to the Comparative Administration in East Africa Conference, Arusha, Tanzania, September, 1971, "The Working of Tanzania's Regional Development Fund: Its Implications for Policy Making, Planning and Local Administration for Development".

82. "It is the responsibility of Maendeleo, working through the Regional Commissioners' and Area Commissioners' offices..."; "the officers of Maendeleo, including Regional and Area Commissioners..."; "the role of Maendeleo—which of course includes the Regional Commissioners and Area Commissioners...". Presidential Circular No. 1 of 1969, "The Development of *Ujamaa* Villages", 20 March 1969, para. 12.

83. I interviewed two of Ukerewe's three Divisional Secretaries on 31 March 1970, and five of Mwanza District's six Division Secretaries over the period 6—10 April 1970. One was in his late 20's, one in his early 40's and the five others were in their 30's. All had at least 8 years of education, two had been TANU branch secretaries and more recently Divisional Executive Officers prior to their appointment, three had been teachers, one an Assistant Divisional Executive Officer, and the other had worked in both government and private public relations and personnel positions. All were from the general area to which they were assigned. Before taking up their posts they had been trained for nine months at a National Service camp, at Kivukoni College, and at an Agricultural Training Institute. My impression was that they all considered themselves to be good administrators with modern ideas and, to a lesser extent, politicized. They seemed to combine elements of both 'red' and 'expert', with the accent on the latter.

84. *Cf.*, Cliffe and Saul, *op.cit.*, p. 6. Personal ambitions and protocol dilute the line relationship between Regional and Area Commissioners. The following case is instructive: The Administrative Secretary was asked by a regional officer if the Regional Commissioner would officiate at an opening ceremony while touring Nassa (Mwanza District) on 25 February 1970. After checking with the Regional Commissioner the Administrative Secretary confirmed the arrangements with the regional officer and asked him to inform the Divisional Executive Secretary in the area. This was done. On the day, three regional officers and some one hundred people awaited the Regional Commissioner, who did not appear. A messenger sent by the Area Commissioner informed the people that the Area Commissioner should have been informed earlier and as he was not he was cancelling the Regional Commissioner's visit to the opening. The next day the Administrative Secretary informed me that "technically" the Area Commissioner was

within his authority, that it was now realized that the Area Commissioner was "touchy", and that although the Regional Commissioner was annoyed the "milk had been spilt" and there was no sense in pursuing the matter further.

85. Interviews with the Divisional Secretaries referred to in note no. 83, above. In August, 1969, six weeks after the Divisional Secretaries took up their post, the Geita TANU and District Council Chairman, in an interview with Charles Bayeka, observed: "Their work is not properly defined. Even if you ask them what their responsibilities are they cannot tell at all." Also in August, 1969, the Mwanza District Executive Secretary of TANU was interviewed by Aloys Rutiahwa on the same point, he responded: "I do not know. We have not received a circular describing the duties of the Divisional Secretaries." When I interviewed the Geita TANU Executive Secretary and District Youth League Secretary of this, on 12 May 1970, they thought the Divisional Secretaries had an "official" tie with TANU, but not a "working" one; it was their impression that the Divisional Secretaries were "most of the time" working for the District Council. In all the Districts the only officials who expressed certainty about the position of the Divisional Secretaries were the Area Secretaries, who thought that they were under the Area Commissioner "through" the Area Secretary. At the Morogoro meeting of the Association of Rural Local Authorities in Tanzania, 1—2 September 1969, many questions were asked as to the duties and authority of the Divisional Secretary. All except the Assistant Commissioner for Local Government and Rural Development claimed to be befuddled. The minutes of this meeting (mimeo.) are a clear explanation of what the Divisional Secretaries should have been doing.

86. In fact it would seem that certain factors—e.g., the gradual build-up of ministerial staffs and programmes in the regions and districts, and better communications with Dar es Salaam—have worked, over the first decade of independent Tanzania, to reduce the ability of Commissioners to participate effectively.

87. The central pressures on or orientation of the Regional Commissioner in 1970 led him several times to telephone the offices of *The Nationalist* in Dar es Salaam to 'order' them not to publish certain feature stories which had been filed by the Mwanza reporter of the newspaper. The stories, which were not published, concerned the Mwanza Development Scheme and the Gallu *Ujamaa* Village, both prestige projects which have taken much of the time of the Region's last three Regional Commissioners, and both experiencing difficulty in staying alive financially.

88. These officials were always, during my time in Mwanza Region, much busier and more difficult to see than the Commissioners. The latter, by sharp contrast, appeared to have an exceptional amount of free time when they were in the administrative centre. On several occasions I came across Commissioners reading books and magazines in their offices, some came regularly an hour or more late to the office and left an hour or so early, and of those who did come early to the office, many departed soon afterwards to take their breakfast at home. They seem to have been underemployed.

89. Rolf E. Vente, *Planning Process: The East African Case*, Munich: Weltforum, 1970, p. 149.

90. See, note no. 41, above.

91. This refers to something more than the British private office, and is much closer to a sort of American White House staff approach. Neustadt, describing Franklin Roosevelt's rationale in creating what was to grow to a 'President's Department' put it succinctly: "he wanted to enhance his own capacity to rule". Richard E. Neustadt, "Approaches to Staffing the Presidency: Notes on FDR and JFK", *American Political Science Review*, LVII (December, 1963), pp. 855—863. Also, Theodore C. Sorensen, *Decision-Making in the White House*, New York: Columbia University Press, 1963, especially at pp. 70—71: "The parochialism of experts and department heads is offset in part by a President's White House and executive staff. These few assistants are the only other men in Washington whose responsibilities both enable and require them to look, as he does, at the government as a whole. Even the White House specialists—the President's economic advisers or science adviser, for example—are likely to see problems in a broader perspective, within the framework of the President's objectives and without the constraints of bureaucratic tradition." Also, Arthur M. Schlesinger, Jr., *The Coming of the New Deal*, Boston: Houghton Mifflin, 1959, pp. 521—528, 533—537, reprinted in, Francis E. Rourke (ed.), *Bureaucratic Power in National Politics*, Boston: Little, Brown, 1965, chapter VIII.

92. This is somewhat true even when committees are set up to look into important regional economic matters. They are usually chaired by the Administrative Secretary—e.g., the three man April, 1970, committee to look into RDF project spending and the seven man March, 1971, committee to look into cotton transport.

The Role of the M.P.

Introduction

The quinquennial parliamentary elections have been the most publicized, recurring political event in Tanzania. In contrast to party elections which are of a somewhat closed nature, parliamentary contests are a visible focus of national political activity. The vote for a Member of Parliament is a constitutional means which rural Tanzanians have for influencing politics. This is not to say that the National Assembly is a powerful or even influential element in the process of decision-making at the centre. Not totally quiescent, and at times a forum for vigorously contending viewpoints, it is nonetheless primarily a legitimizing agency: decisions taken by Government or TANU are submitted to the Assembly so that representatives elected by the masses may give their approval.[1]

Nyerere, in his July, 1970 address to the Parliament elected in 1965, along with noting that "some proposals and Bills, especially those of a technical nature, have found the House at a loss", indicated the two slight deviations from a legitimizing role which the M.P.'s perform: their debates and questions have "enabled Government to improve" and have forced the Government "properly to explain proposed legislation". The explanations, Nyerere pointed out, were necessary so that the M.P.'s could subsequently "explain these things to the people". In his review[2] of what the Assembly had done there was no mention of the representatives representing constituents' views or of their participation in the initiation of legislation. Academic observers have been no more sanguine than Nyerere in describing the activities of the National Assembly. Hopkins begins his article on the role expectations of the Tanzania M.P.'s with the observation that the Assembly has "little influence" on the political processes.[3] Vente, looking at the process of planning, remarks that "there is no question of effective control of the planners by parliament".[4] Bienen refers to the "relative insignificance" of the National Assembly.[5]

Though the unimportance of the M.P. at the centre seems generally accepted, there have been suggestions that this is not repeated in the constituencies. Nyerere's statement to the effect that the M.P.'s explain legislation to the people partially coincides with Hopkins' finding that constituency work was one of the four norms of the M.P.'s role expectations.[6] Hopkins puts the perspective of the man at the centre. There are as yet no similarly systematic studies of the M.P.'s role in the rural areas, although quite a good bit of effort has gone into studying how people come to be M.P.'s.[7] Nonetheless authors have in passing made remarks indicating that the M.P. in his constituency is more important to the political processes at that level than his rather truncated role at the centre would imply. Cliffe and Saul, for instance, see M.P.'s as "TANU influentials" who as members of the Development Committees and as individuals who "can lay claim to representing the wishes of the electorate" are part of the group of "notables within the local party".[8] Bowring mentions that the M.P. within his area is a competitor for political leadership.[9]

The notion that the M.P. is an active and effective participant in the sub-central aspects of national politics is discussed in this chapter. In looking at some of the activities of the Arusha Declaration Parliament (1965—70) M.P.'s in Mwanza Region I attempt to delineate their relationships with government and party and the implications for the balance being struck between hierarchy and participation. The role of M.P. is in a national structure which has some of its roots in mass suffrage constituencies* and most of these are rural; the M.P. is perhaps the best known local political figure in the rural area; and he sits on several committees and boards which at least formally are in the political process of allocating the resources of the national system.

My 1969 peasant survey indicated that the local M.P. is a widely recognized political figure in the rural areas of Mwanza Region. Contrasted with the findings for local TANU leaders, and given an M.P.'s long absences and comparatively extensive constituency, and the "key role"[10] in the penetration process attributed by some observers to the local party leaders, the difference is impressive.

---

* For the 1965—70 Assembly, there were 107 seats for members elected from mass suffrage constituencies, and 97 others. The others comprised fifteen nominated by 'national' institutions and elected by the Assembly, seventeen Regional Commissioners appointed by the President and sitting *ex officio*, ten nominated by the President, thirty-two members of the Zanzibar Revolutionary Council, and twenty members from Zanzibar appointed by the President in agreement with the President of Zanzibar, and three Zanzibar Regional Commissioners appointed by the President of Zanzibar and sitting *ex officio*.

144

Table 12. *Percentage of respondents who correctly identified various political figures*[a]

(n = 193)	
Member of Parliament	55 %
Local TANU branch chairman	38 %
Local TANU branch secretary	30 %
Local branch or school Youth League Leader	13 %
One or more local TANU branch Committeemen	15 %

[a] Question asked in the form, "What is the name of your M.P.?"; and so on.

The relative prominence of the local M.P. is partly explained by the tremendous publicity effort which went into the 1965 campaign, as well as by their substantial tenure in office at the time of the survey. More subtle factors than those, however, would seem to give rise to the local recognition of the M.P. First, there is his mass constituency. The M.P. is one of the two individuals whom a Tanzanian peasant selects in an election with an element of competition. The other, the District Councillor, is also a recognizable political figure in the rural areas and it is unfortunate that comparative figures are not available. Yet notwithstanding the importance for the rural dwellers of the Council elections, it would seem that the mass selection of representatives to the centre of the political system was in 1965 an event which generated widespread attention upon the individual competitors.

Secondly, the pre- and post-independence ideological emphasis placed on the value of the democratic election of leaders,[11] and more so the culmination of this continual emphasis in the universal suffrage voting for most of the seats in the National Assembly, appears to have convinced many of the importance of the role of the M.P. This perceived importance is a prerequisite if there is to be a massive enough voluntary turnout on polling day to allow the Assembly to be a credible legitimizing agency.

Thirdly, the M.P.'s role in the estimation of his constituents has had a materialistic aspect. There has been the belief that he might be able to bring development in the way of bridges, clinics, schools etc., to his area. While I was in Mwanza Region those M.P.'s who were not successful in giving the impression that they were trying to bring something back to their electors were not regarded by the people in the rural areas as doing their job properly. An M.P. whose seemingly valiant efforts to pork-barrel for his people were fruitless might be forgiven;

145

those who 'never come back', who were 'too proud' and 'no longer understand our problems' were low in esteem.

The relationship between this type of local development role and the legitimizing role can be antagonistic. In the Geita East by-election discussed below, one of the causes of the extremely low level of participation[12] was the belief that an M.P. was not able to bring development in this materialistic fashion. The M.P.'s, I was informed, obviously had no influence. This perception, brought to the fore in Geita East because of the rather summary dismissal of an M.P. by a central organ of the party, can present a problem for the national system. It contributed to a reduction in the type of voluntary participation in parliamentary elections which is required if the Assembly is to be the legitimizing body which many, including the present regime, consider necessary.

The M.P. and The Government

As popularly chosen representatives the M.P.'s elected in 1965 were to be participation elements within the political system: the people participated directly in their selection and through them the people had hoped to participate in the exercise of power. The first phase in any participation is informational, both upwards and downwards communications. An aspect of the M.P.'s insignificant position at the centre was their ineffectuality as an upwards communications channel from the people to the leaders. The process of relegating the Assembly to a nominal legitimizing role involved the M.P.'s not being considered at the centre as an authoritative source of information on the views and needs of the people. During 1969—70 this was being reflected in interviews with rural leaders and peasants who no longer regarded an M.P. as a viable political contact.[13] Nor were the M.P.'s elected in 1965 a source of information to the people about government policies and plans. In Mwanza Region the M.P.'s spent little time in their constituencies, a pattern encouraged in many ways by both party and government. During 18 months, February, 1969 to July, 1970, no Mwanza Region M.P. held a public meeting; as a general rule they were not invited to address meetings organized by party or government officials. The Regional Commissioner stated that this was "policy" and that it had been thus for an unspecified period prior to my arrival; the reason,

146

he explained, was that there was no need as the people received all necessary information through the government and party.[14] The M.P.'s did of course move around the towns and rural areas meeting people and discussing events as they went, but there was clearly no intention of using them as popularisers or explainers of government policies.

Though not employed as a communications link, nor able to act as a representative at the centre, there remained for the M.P.'s the possibility of acting as surrogate participants representing the people's interests in the resource allocation process at sub-centre levels. Two of the bodies within the Region on which the M.P.'s are members may in this context be quickly dismissed. The Roads Board during the period 1967 (when it was set up)—1970 met extremely irregularly and in its few years of existence was the preserve of Regional Engineer, its actual secretary; in fact, the Regional Engineer in listing the members of the Board in an interview did not mention any M.P.'s.[15] The Prices Board tended, when it met, to be an *ad hoc* body with little impact outside Mwanza town.

The other bodies which M.P.'s sit on and which in principle are involved in the allocative process are the development committees at the district and regional levels. The District Development and Planning Committees (DDPC) recommend projects for funding to the sub-committee of the Regional Development Committee. They were not used by the 1965—70 M.P.'s in their attempts to influence allocations, and their attendance tended to be spotty.

In Kwimba District—which had two M.P.'s—an M.P. was present at four of the sixteen meetings held between 1966 and 1969; in Mwanza the M.P.'s participated even less, and in Ukerewe and Geita the M.P.'s were not members of the DDPC.[16]

It was to the regional level that M.P.'s repaired in trying to gain influence and it was at this level that the difficulties which faced the M.P.'s in the allocative process were most obvious. The three Mwanza Region M.P.'s whom I interviewed agreed that the perception of the Geita East constituents which I earlier referred to was generally well-founded, viz., that the system did not work in such a way as to make an M.P. an effective surrogate participant.

The M.P.'s made specific reference to the Regional Development Committe and the substance of their remarks is reinforced by failure of all the initiatives which M.P.'s made as members of the RDC. All the Mwanza M.P.'s have been members of the RDC since late 1963.[17] Initially they were considered part of the contingent of "community leaders" invited at the discretion of the Regional Commissioner—in practice the M.P.'s were always invited. From May, 1967 they have been recognized as members *ex officio*.[18] The RDC is important because it lays down the principles for the allocation of the monies of the Regional Development Fund,[19] the main source of free floating governmental resources in the Region. The incidents which I mention below are *all* the efforts which got as far as the RDC.[20] Other attempts by M.P.'s in the nature of informal discussions with regional officers were presumably made, but with no noticeable effect.

The first initiative was in late 1966 and early 1967 when J. W. Kasubi (Mwanza West), one of the two regular TANU M.P.'s from Mwanza Region, personally organized a campaign to have motorized transport on the Lake. It included meetings with the Regional Commissioners of Mwanza, West Lake, and Mara, and with the Area Commissioners of Geita, Ukerewe, and Ngara. Kasubi described himself as being encouraged by these officials.[21] In an attempt to rally support for the idea, not to ask for anything in a material way—at least at that time, Kasubi brought his campaign to the Regional Development Committee meeting of late January, 1967. The RDC "ordered" that nothing more be done until the views of "Dar es Salaam" had been heard.[22] As of July, 1970, the matter had proceeded no further. The second instance occurred in the same meeting and again involved Kasubi. The M.P. argued that some of the former residents of Nyakato (the present location of the textile mill) had not been paid compensation for the compulsory demolition of their homes. The Mwanza Regional and Area Commissioners promised to look into the matter.[23] Three and a half years later the RC and the AC (the personalities having changed in the meantime) were still looking into the matter.

The third attempt was made in the RDC meeting of August, 1967. F. L. Masha (Geita East) raised the possibility of siting a milk plant in Geita with assistance from a central government or other outside organization, for instance, the Association of Rural Local Authorities of Tanzania.[24] Two meetings later in January, 1968, the RDC received a report that the research which they had ordered undertaken by civil servants was continuing, but that the probe was no longer restricted to Geita District but was rather looking into various other sites.[25] The matter was resolved insofar as Geita (and hence Masha) was concerned with a decision taken by the RDC's sub-committee in October, 1968. According to the official "information brief" it was "unanimously decided that a dairy industry should be established and that it should be run by the NCU ...".[26] Representatives from the NCU (the co-operative union), the Mwanza Town Council, and the Mwanza Area Commissioner were present when the decision was taken, and the implication was that the industry should be established near Mwanza town in Mwanza District. (The current Plan refers to a "milk centre" to be set up "within a radius of about 20 miles of Mwanza town"; it makes no mention of a dairy industry for Geita.)[27]

Of the 14 meetings of the Mwanza RDC held during 1966, 1967, and 1968, the eight M.P.'s were completely absent from five, and in the remaining nine an average of two attended. Although M.P.'s at times could not attend because of other duties, it seems arguable that their inability to 'use' the RDC, as well as the fact that they received no allowances for attendance,[28] were factors involved with their poor attendance. This inability of the M.P.'s to use the RDC in an initiative for bringing development to their constituencies is a concomitant of the arrangement of allocative power in the Region. The allocative process is dominated by government bureaucratic structures[29] and the RDC's role is one of legitimizer. The case of the Sengerema school is a clear, and not unusual, example. The RDC meeting of February, 1967, was attended by 21 of the 51 invited. The 21 comprised 17 civil servants (including the Principal Secretary of the Ministry of Education), one TANU staff official, the Geita Area Commissioner, and two Geita M.P.'s. This was the first meeting which these two M.P.'s attended; in fact, four meetings were held after their 1965 election before they were put on the regular mailing list.[30] At the meeting the Principal Secretary explained that the RDC was to decide the site for the Region's new secondary school, although "it is the intention of the Ministry to build either in Geita or Kwimba". Ukerewe District was excluded, he further explained, because it is an island, and Mwanza District because it had a sufficient number of secondary schools already. As there were no representatives from Kwimba, the only other competing District, the RDC decided that the school was to be built in Geita at Sengerema, located in the constituency of one of the attending M.P.'s. Rather than the M.P.'s manipulating the allocative machinery, it seems the decision reflects the manipulation (albeit willingly) of the two M.P.'s by the machinery.

The difficulty an M.P. faces in trying to influence this allocative machinery is accentuated by his stance outside the information flows of government and party. On the government side the position was made clear by a circular letter from State House to Regional Commissioners in May, 1968. It began with a review of a decision by the Cabinet two years earlier on the distribution of regional monthly reports and other documents, viz., that instructions from Dar to Regional heads be copied to State House, Regional Administration, and to the "Administrative Secretary of the Region for the Regional Commissioner's attention", and that reports from regional officers to Dar be similarly distributed; the circular then noted:

It has now come to light that one or two of the Regional Commissioners have ordered that monthly (and other) reports should also be copied to Members of Parliament in their Regions. The purpose of this circular letter is to make it clear that the decision explained above did not embrace Members of Parliament. It is feared that if these reports are distributed to Members of Parliament they may be used as a basis of attacks against Ministers in Parliament.

It is, however, realized that Members of Parliament as representatives of the people and members of Regional Development Committees need to be well-informed about the problems of development in the various Ministries to be able to participate fully in the discussions and to be able to answer questions competently in their constituencies. Whenever, therefore, a Member of Parliament wishes to have certain information there would be no objection for a Regional Commissioner to use his discretion to authorize an extract of that particular information to be given to the Member of Parliament.[32]

This instruction, coupled with the generalized caution of the bureaucracy in releasing information on their activities, put M.P.'s in the position of being, at best, only marginally better informed about current or proposed activities than interested citizens. It is partly why M.P.'s found it difficult to "exercise tireless revolutionary leadership", to take a "critical look at Government actions, and correct government where it goes wrong", and why at least some of them later in 1968 were judged guilty by the *Nationalist* editor of resorting to "outrageous" and "random accusations".[33]

The effort required by an M.P. who is to persist until successful in trying to influence allocations in the Region can be observed in the only case which, to my knowledge, did have a happy ending for the M.P. In 1967, the Mwanza Regional Roads Board was set up to "make estimates and plans for spending all road money".[34] All M.P.'s were named as members with one of them to sit as chairman in the absence of the Regional Commissioner. Other members were officially designated as: Regional Secretary as secretary, all Area Commissioners, all

District Council Executive Officers, the Regional Agricultural Officer, one representative each from the cotton marketing organization and from the co-operative union. At its first (the only meeting which M.P.'s attended) meeting in July the M.P. for Kwimba North, M. Mabawa, spoke of the need for a bridge over the Simiyu river. The Regional Engineer undertook to consider the matter. In the RDC meeting that August, in Mabawa's absence, it was announced that the Regional Roads Board had discussed the bridge but there was no further elaboration or discussion.[35] Mabawa proceeded to collect 40,000 shillings from the people in the area and from Mwanza merchants towards a bridge fund. In early 1968 this money was handed over to the Ministry of Communications and Works in Dar es Salaam. In an interview with Sokoine, the Junior Minister, Mabawa claimed that the RDC had set aside 50,000 shillings for the project. Whether the M.P. was unsure of the actual functioning of the RDC, or whether he was applying a sort of pressure is not clear. In fact, the RDC had not set aside any funds for the bridge and when the issue was considered by the usual decision making body, the RDC's sub-committee, in August, 1968, the decision was made not to fund the bridge project.[36] In September the sub-committee received a letter from the Junior Minister requesting that money be set aside for the bridge. The sub-committee met the following month without the Regional Commissioner. The intervention of Sokoine made the whole affair a bit too 'political' and the sub-committee sent it on to the Regional Commissioner for a decision, although noting,

Much as the bridge appears necessary ... we should discourage the M.P.'s method of by-passing established bodies ... The money should have been channelled through the RDC. Direct dealings with Ministries on matters falling under our purview can only cause confusion if not misunderstandings.[37]

In refutation of the above observation of the bridge falling under the purview of the RDC, the sub-committee went on to remark that the building of the bridge was "too big a project" and should be "completely" under the Ministry.[38] Three meetings later the Regional Commissioner again put the Simiyu bridge on the agenda; the sub-committee decided to allocate the money in 1970, "if the funds are available".[39] This was not satisfactory to Mabawa who urged that it be put on the agenda once more and that he be invited to attend the meeting. This was done and at the August, 1969, meeting of the RDC's sub-committee Mabawa, along with Kwimba's other M.P. and the Executive Officer of the Kwimba District Council, argued the case for the bridge. The sub-committee's decision was a reiteration of its earlier, now designated as "final", decision—if available, funds would be allocated in 1970.[40] The decision, however, was not all that final; in the following meeting the Regional Commissioner "informed" the sub-committee that 50,000 shillings had been allocated for the bridge[41] and in April, 1970, a team investigating development expenditure in the Region reported that the money was well-spent, the bridge completed and officially opened by the Comworks Minister, Job Lusinde.[42] The arguments that Mabawa was able to marshal to convince the Regional Commissioner to over-rule the sub-committee could only be guessed at. What is definite is that the M.P. required more than two years of fairly dogged effort to win his bridge, and in the end it depended on the unusual intervention of one man. The Regional Commissioner for many reasons very seldom over-rules the sub-committee, and in this sense the M.P.'s victory appears to have been fortuitous.[43]

The M.P. and The Party

The Simiyu bridge case is interesting because it is unusual—the M.P. won. However it also demonstrated the way in which the official dominated RDC sub-committee was able to resist various forms of political pressure emanating from elements in the political system: the popular contributions to the bridge fund, a letter from a Junior Minister, the personal pleading of two M.P.'s. The sort of leverage which an M.P. might find helpful if he is to participate effectively in the allocation process in a more continuous and reliable fashion is the support of a rival organizational structure. The role of rival organization officially belongs to the party, and in Mwanza Region and in their individual constituencies the majority of the M.P.'s elected in 1965 were not of the more regular or long-standing TANU organization.[44]

In some cases the M.P. had been a departed former resident of the area recalled to stand in the election on the basis of an educational qualification and without having done any obvious canvassing (Geita East and Geita North). Others, (Kwimba North, Kwimba South, Mwanza East, and Ukerewe) after being convincingly outvoted in the party's preference balloting at the district conference, went on to soundly defeat the 'regular' candidate in the open election. In only two of the eight elections did a regular party man win.[45] The allocative influence of some of these defeated regulars became greater than that of most of the elected M.P.'s. One, Bomani, sat on all the main committees of the party in Dar es Salaam and was appointed to a Cabinet post by Nyerere.[46] Another, Mpanduji, after becoming Regional Chairman of TANU in 1969 sat *ex officio* on the most important allocative body—the RDC's sub-committee; at the same time he became a member *ex officio* of the party's National Executive Committee, the group which in 1968 demonstrated their power to decide who shall not be permitted to sit in the National Assembly. A third, Budodi, the District Chairman of TANU in Geita, was three times invited to participate in the deliberations of the RDC's sub-committee. The elected M.P.'s rarely entered such corridors.[47]

Another product of this non-regular position of most of the Mwanza M.P.'s is that they were not used as middlemen between Dar and the Region.[48] Bomani, on the other hand, performed this function as a matter of course.[49] It was he or the Regional Commissioner who quite often was given the honour of announcing new schools,[50] hospitals, and so on in the Region. Bomani was also the favourite choice as the main promotor for the larger TANU fund raising drives. In the event of a dispute arising between representatives of the centre and popular elements in the Region, or even amongst elements within the Region, Bomani was at times pressed into service.[51] It is exceedingly difficult to identify the impact and scope, or even the identity, of all the middlemen whom one might suppose are operating between Dar and Mwanza; this is especially true because of the "closed" style of politics.[52] The elected M.P., however, seldom becomes involved.

This was underscored by what came to be protocol in the region. When V.I.P.'s visited the region, and even when they visited the member's constituency, precedence was given to district and regional heads of departments, NCU officials, Area Commissioners, District party chairmen, members of the TANU regional executive committee, and, in the rural areas to the chairman of the local TANU branch. The M.P., when present, was normally heard from only very briefly in the round of speechmaking. Geita District party headquarters, and in some places local branch officers allocated office space to M.P.'s and in this symbolic way the M.P.'s were tied in with the party structure. Yet the Geita headquarters had an excess of office space and the allocation to the M.P. was not part of a scarce resource. In some local branches individuals have suggested that the office was allocated to encourage the M.P. to spend time in it listening to people's problems. Others have suggested the reverse of this, namely that it was to embarrass the M.P. by vividly demonstrating to the people how little time he spent in the constituency.

The distribution of allocative power and the ways of protocol combined over a period of time to weaken the status of the M.P. in the estimation of his constituents. The credibility of his national role of legitimizer stems from his mass base,[53] and his mass base stems ultimately from his presumed function as a representative of his people.[54] Yet as a representative with little influence in party or government, the mass base of an M.P. is especially sensitive to actions which highlight his lack of influence. An example of the extreme form of such an action was the 1968 dismissal of seven M.P.'s from TANU (and automatically, by statute, from the Assembly) by the National Executive Committee for reasons not subsequently explained to their constituents.[55] (Except, to my knowledge, in Karagwe where the West Lake Region's member of the National Executive Committee made a nine day tour of the constituency of the expelled M.P. 'explaining' the reasons for the expulsion).

The official announcement of the National Executive Committee said that all those expelled had "grossly violated the Party creed both in their actions and attitude, all of which sum up to a very clear opposition to the Party and its policies". All were, in the elaboration by the official Party newspaper, "extremely vocal ... remarkably outspoken". And although *The Nationalist* specifically denied that this characteristic was related to the expulsions ("it is one thing to criticise. It is another thing to oppose."),[56] a *Nationalist* editorial of three weeks earlier does give some weight to the notion that in being vocal an M.P. is well-advised to be extremely circumspect:

It is true that evidence about allegations is sometimes difficult to acquire by an M.P. But the fact that this may be so is no excuse for indiscriminate allegations, some of which are quite obviously aimed at personal politicking. On the contrary this underlines the need for holding one's tongue in the absence of concrete evidence.

By uttering some wild allegations, problems are created which in fact are not there, and public attitudes may be forged—based on misconceptions of socialism and so-called facts which in reality have no foundation. The sum effect of this trend is clearly subversive. For this reason words must be weighed carefully so that the evidence does suit the intention, and is seen to suit it. Unless there are those who do not care for truth or the success of our political and economic system, and if there be, they should by quickly dealt with.[57]

In response to this editorial Masha, the subsequently expelled M.P. from Geita East, spoke in the Assembly in a manner which one can probably presume *The Nationalist*, and later a majority of the National Executive Committee, found distasteful. *The Nationalist* reported Masha's speech:

Mr F. L. Masha ... launched a scurrilous attack on the Party English newspaper, *The Nationalist*, and Radio Tanzania, alleging that they were being misused ... [and] were being used to vilify Members of Parliament. He added that the policy of TANU and the Government on Parliament was not understood.

He said *The Nationalist* ... described Members of this House as subversive. Radio Tanzania has been carrying out a campaign to discredit Members of Parliament.

Mr Masha ... said the Party newspaper was making pretences at 'ideological direction' contrary to the country's democratic principles.

[He] said Editor of *The Nationalist* and the Commentator on Radio Tanzania were drawing much higher salaries than he and his fellow M.P.'s. 'I don't see why they should make a lot of noise', he added.[58]

Masha's attack in the Assembly was rebutted by Richard Wambura, Junior Minister in the Second Vice-President's Office, who pointed out that "TANU was supreme and the comments of *The Nationalist* belonged to the Party"—Wambura went on to observe that the Party had the duty to "correct" any leader, and ended by congratulating *The Nationalist* staff for their "revolutionary spirit".[59]

The tone, content, and public nature of Masha's speech were an indirect challenge to the Party and some of its individual leaders. The expulsions are perhaps explainable in terms of the Party victoriously meeting this sort of challenge[60] from the Assembly—the expulsions being a resolution of a contradictory formulation of the Commission on the One Party State which seemed to confer supremacy on both the National Assembly and the party's National Executive Committee.[61] Why Masha was included amongst the group expelled, however, can not be explained merely by quoting from his Assembly speeches. *The Standard* reporter at the time thought the action against Masha a surprise.[62] Saul has written that Masha's case is "less clear" and suggests a somewhat guilt-by-association explanation: "his prominence in TANU head-quarters during the heyday of Kambona and Anangisye may have been a factor".[63] One can not hope at this time to know the precise incidents which led up to Masha's expulsion, but in looking at some of the underlying factors in his situation and at some of the possible incidents one can, I think, gain some insight into the relationship between the M.P.'s and the party.[64]

In 1965 Masha was called back from his post as Publicity Secretary for East African Airlines by the Geita District party organization to stand in the parliamentary elections. He was called back because, in the opinion of individuals whom I interviewed who had participated in the 1965 preference balloting at the district conference, his bachelor's degree in journalism was a desirable qualification for an M.P. Also he had met many people and impressed them favourably during a brief period in which he worked for the Geita District Council. Masha's opponent in the election was the undisputed leader of Geita's TANU organization. Within Masha's Geita East constituency his election victory made him a potential rival for the District's second most powerful TANU regular who was chairman of one of the constituency's TANU branches (Sengerema) and later elected by the party to its regional executive committee. The Sengerema chairman gave one of his branch's unused rooms to Masha for use as a constituency office, a move seen by some, including Masha, as designed to embarrass the M.P. who was confined to Dar by official duties. Masha made a partial counter by starting to build a permanent house in the area to demonstrate his close ties.[65] It is difficult to accurately categorize Masha's relations with the Geita TANU organization after his 1965 election—that is whether he was seen as an opponent or as merely a marginal political figure. It was obvious, though, in interviews with several Geita TANU officials that he was not considered one of the more regular organization, and hence had no legitimate power base to mobilize in his confrontation with the national party organization.

At the national level Masha was at first considered one of the party's bright young men; some have suggested that his abilities impressed Nyerere. He was appointed Publicity Secretary of the party and a managing director of the company which publishes *The Nationalist* soon after his election to the Assembly. He was dismissed from both positions in 1967. (The most credible explanation of his dismissal is that older elements within the TANU leadership had apparently taken a disliking to certain qualities of his—specifically, that he was not sufficiently quiet and respectful. Nyerere's initial good impression may have altered as Masha, in the opinion of Dar es Salaam observers, did not appear to have been applying his abilities with hard work.) By the time of the 1968 expulsions Masha had few supporters in the regular party organization at the centre and was susceptible in the purge of the M.P.'s. Having aligned himself in the Assembly with the group which posited the supremacy of parliament, and without a political base in either the national or district party organizations, Masha was vulnerable to the "self-criticism"[66] (although he was not present) at the meeting of the National Executive Committee and to the affirmation of the normative theme of party supremacy.

Masha's Geita East constituency has traditionally been a problem spot for both colonial and independent governments. This has been well documented by Maguire,[67] and within the Region parts of Geita District have a certain renown in this regard. The problem was demonstrated by the low voter participation in the 1965 parliamentary elections. Of the 101 contested constituencies in the nation, Geita East ranked 101st in percentage of registered voters voting (43.4 % *versus* a national average of 76.1 %).[68] It is an area which has not been very amenable to attempts to elicit greater mass participation in the national system.

The by-election necessitated by Masha's expulsion was a political activity which put into sharp relief the several strands in the relationships between the M.P. and the party and the government. Masha by this time was not highly regarded by many. There was a general discontent among his more politically aware constituents with his lack of ability to bring development. Since mid-1967 Masha had been left out of the V.I.P. groups which visited the District from time to time, and his lack of stature in government and TANU circles was apparent to all. His expulsion, however, in being too obvious a triumph of the principle of hierarchy, made the problem of increasing participation greater. People seemed to think that the idea itself of electing representatives was useless if the representatives were to do nothing but "eat salaries" and in the end be judged not by the people but by "Dar es Salaam".

Soon after the expulsion police visited people in Geita who were thought to be friends of Masha. This may have heightened what administrative officials have considered the recalcitrance of the peasants of Geita East. I was made well aware of this quality by the resistance which the residents of Mayuya put forth to the proposed research

157

project of the University College, Dar es Salaam. In spite of persuasion by local and district TANU and government officials in a series of four meetings, with the fourth distinguished by the threat of force by the Area Secretary, the Mayuya people refused to co-operate. In interviews at the time, just after the Geita East by-election, eleven Mayuya cell leaders were cognizant of Masha's expulsion and seemed quietly hostile, commenting that the whole affair was not their responsibility as their task was completed by voting in 1965 and adding that they had not been "officially" informed of the reasons for the expulsion or indeed of the expulsion itself. None of these cell leaders voted in the by-election.

By-election day, May 5, 1969, was dry and sunny as it had been for the previous few days. The 84 polling stations were the same ones as used in the 1965 election; I visited nine of them, some of them two or three times, between 7 a.m. and 5 p.m. on the day. Opening and closing times were irregular, but polling generally went on from about 9 a.m. to 4 p.m. In four of the stations which I visited nobody was voting. In the others, there was no queuing, and aside from one or two officials (and at times not even them) and perhaps a policeman, the stations were empty. This was particularly striking in stations located in busy centres—the ones at the Sengerema TANU office next to the market and at the Sengerema hospital for instance were doing no business at all early in the morning, at mid-day, or in the afternoon. The turnout was no more than nominal in the upper part of Kasungamile Division, the home of Masha's family. The only area where the numbers voting appeared to be significant, according to information which I later received from the Geita Area Secretary, was around Bulela where one of the candidates, Bunuma, is well-known. The general attitude of many people in Geita East on by-election day seemed to be one of studied non-concern.

There have been to my knowledge no reports on the 1969 by-elections which would be helpful in analyzing their overall significance for Tanzanian political development. The tables above set out the returns for the six constituencies which were contested; one of the expelled M.P.'s was a National Member. It is perhaps noteworthy that the highest turnout was in Karagwe and neighboring Ihangiro as it was in Karagwe that the expulsions were publicly explained. In Geita East at the time of the by-election there was a general profession of non-understanding of the National Executive Committee's action against the M.P.'s; local and district TANU leaders as well claimed no knowl-

Table 13. *Comparative election statics: 1965 General elections and 1969 by-elections*

	Registered Voters (1965)	Voters (1965)	Voters (1969)
Nzega East	54,142	40,652	11,415
Ihangiro	37,060	22,701	11,384
Karagwe	29,695	20,311	11,737
Mufindi	22,059	17,303	3,659
Iringa South	31,865	25,681	6,807
Geita East	34,247	14,849	5,327

	Percentage of Registered Voters Who Voted in Election	
	1965	1969
Nzega East	75.1 %	21.1 %
Ihangiro	61.3 %	30.7 %
Karagwe	68.4 %	39.5 %
Mufindi	78.4 %	16.5 %
Iringa South	80.6 %	21.3 %
Geita East	43.4 %	15.5 %

edge of the reasons behind the expulsion. The small number of campaign meetings is another possible factor in the low level of voting. There were about ten meetings contrasted with the 24 held in the 1965 campaign, and the campaign meetings which were held seem to have aroused little interest. Questions on the reason for the by-election were ruled out of order; speeches were devoted to the relative worth of the symbols (hoe and house) and statements by the candidates that they would work for the people. More generalized discussion about the election seems to have been discouraged by statements by supervising officials that "interference" with another's vote was criminal, and posters to the effect that "interference" would lead to prosecution. As has been remarked elsewhere, "interference" in this context is not uncommonly interpreted to cover any discussion at all.[69] The candidates themselves when not speaking at public meetings during the campaign were secluded in their lodgings so as not to give either an advantage which might accrue from the establishment of a more informal contact with the voters. This was, according to informants, different from the situation in 1965 when Masha very effectively moved around greeting all and sundry throughout the campaign.

The candidates Wilson Bunuma and Ezekiel Ng'wishemi were the first and second choices at the district conference balloting on January 25, 1969; Bunuma received 237 votes while Ng'wishemi the eventual victor received 39 with 96 other votes being distributed amongst the seven remaining nominees. Bunuma was the first chairman of the Geita District TANU organization,[70] whereas Ng'wishemi was a much lesser figure in the early years. The latter claimed to have been doing TANU work "at night" from the late 1950's, and had been an unsuccessful nominee for the Geita East candidacy in 1965. Both Bunuma and Ng'wishemi were regular party candidates, but Bunuma was obviously the party's favourite. This seems to have been a factor which worked against Bunuma in the election as some felt that he was being forced upon them. This was reinforced by the fact that Bunuma was considered an outsider by many Geita East constituents. He was born in Kwimba District and after moving to Geita in 1965 became associated with the Geita South and Geita town areas. Ng'wishemi, on the other hand, was born in the constituency and except for short periods outside for education had spent his time working as a medical aide (eventually he became a Senior Rural Medical Assistant) in clinics scattered throughout Geita East. Bunuma's contacts within the area were mostly confined to the Kasamwa-Bulela section where he was a trader. Education—Bunuma with Standard VII and Ng'wishemi a Standard IX leaver with a considerable number of medical courses afterwards—may have been to Ng'wishemi's advantage being mentioned by several of the people whom I interviewed. Age does not seem to have been an influence—Bunuma was 44 and Ng'wishemi was 38. A factor mentioned by many as being decisive was the symbol: the winner had the hoe, the loser had the house. In the context of the low-level of participation, who won and who lost was perhaps irrelevant; of the 70,000 adults in Geita East old enough to vote in parliamentary elections, 5,327 went to the polls.

Conclusion

The role of the M.P. by mid-1970 was not viable as a vehicle for popular participation in Mwanza Region. Although the 1965 election campaign was instrumental in bringing many into a position where they could be influenced by national ideas, those who were elected to the Assembly were not able to significantly influence national political processes; also they were not used as a means for influencing the people. The 1969 by-election campaign had a negligible amount of participation and thus the winning candidate became neither a surrogate participant nor a credible legitimizer of government policy. The most striking feature of the Geita East by-election was not that the more regular TANU candidate was again defeated by a sizeable majority in Mwanza Region—3,426 to 1,689. Indeed, in the 1970 general election Bunuma was nominated again by the party for a constituency covering a different area and he won,[71] while Ng'wishemi was defeated. Rather, it was that only about 7 % of the adult population voted. Even for a by-election that is a low figure and, in fact, shorn of the organized push for voters which has become characteristic of a Tanzanian general election it may be a fair representation of the number of people who both wanted to participate and who saw voting for an M.P. as an effective way of doing so. The M.P.'s elected in 1965, generally ineffectual as they were in the political processes, were in 1969 joined by a new member from Geita East who lacked a mass electoral base.

That the activities of the M.P.'s were peripheral to the political system is not a phenomenon peculiar to Tanzania, although it may well have progressed further than in, say, Kenya.[72] Tanzania, whose republican constitution enshrined the "sovereignty of Parliament" was rightly included in the observation of Engholm and Mazrui that "the institution of Parliament seemed to be losing its centrality in African political systems".[73] On the historical continuum this is towards the restructuring, quite forthrightly in Tanzania, of the political institutions inherited from the colonialists and an adjusting of the relative saliences of these institutions.[74] The reduced impact of the National Assembly was reflected in Mwanza Region in the intentional restriction of the M.P.'s in the communications and allocative processes and in the low protocol status accorded them in tours, meetings, and other political events. That the success of these moves was well understood at one point in time by the people in the rural areas was indicated by the disregard with which those interviewed held the prospect of electing a replacement for an M.P. who had been centrally dismissed from his seat without prior or even subsequent reference to his constituents.

I was not in Mwanza Region during the October, 1970, general elections and have not had the opportunity of studying any of the as yet unpublished reports on the sort of participation which occurred. The reportedly high voter turnout would seem to mean that, as was

161

the 1965 election, the 1970 event was successful in bringing people into a situation where they were influenced by national ideas.[75] The number of individuals who submitted their names as possible candidates for Mwanza Region constituencies, 15 and 16 for some seats, shows that there remains a desire to be an M.P.; the position still carries a salary and for some it has served as a stepping-stone to appointed positions. The degree of participation which the role of M.P. brings to the Tanzanian political system is not, however, determined only by highly organized quinquennial events; it is as well determined by the activities of M.P.'s and others in the on-going political processes at the centre and in the regions. Barring radical changes the future of the M.P. seems clear, he will continue as a ceremonial figure, a throwback to the "influence of symbols and institutions surrounded by the authority of the ex-colonial power".[76]

Notes

1. Raymond F. Hopkins, *Political Roles in a New State*, New Haven: Yale University Press, 1971; *idem*, "The Role of the M.P. in Tanzania", *American Political Science Review* (September, 1970), pp. 754—771; William Tordoff, *Government and Politics in Tanzania*, Nairobi: East African Publishing House, 1967, pp. 1—53. *Cf.*, Newel M. Stultz, "Parliaments in Former British Black Africa", *Journal of Developing Areas*, II, 4 (July, 1968), pp. 479—493; M. Lofchie, "Representative Government, Bureaucracy and Political Development: The African Case", *Journal of Developing Areas*, II, 1 (October, 1967), pp. 37—55.

2. *The Standard*, 7 July 1970. Although Nyerere did not mention it, on a very few occasions M.P.'s have introduced private motions which were successful or which gave rise to subsequent government bills.

3. Hopkins, *op.cit.*, 1970, p. 754.

4. Rolf E. Vente, *Planning Processes: The East African Case*, Munich: Weltforum Publishing House, 1970, p. 143. Vente also mentions that questions in the Assembly put pressure on the planners to be concerned "to a greater extent than before with questions at the local and regional levels". Similarly, Hydén: the "electoral system undoubtedly increases the responsibility of government authorities to pressures from the environment". Göran Hydén, *Political Development in Rural Tanzania*, Nairobi: East African Publishing House, 1969, p. 56. Neither author provides material to substantiate this view.

5. Henry Bienen, *Tanzania: Party Transformation and Economic Development*, Princeton: Princeton University Press, expanded edition 1970, pp. 201—202n.

6. Hopkins, *op.cit.*, 1971, p. 232: "M.P.'s have tended to emphasize

working in constituencies to support and explain government policy." This chapter should make clear that in Mwanza Region this expectation was not met during 1965—70.

7. For the 1965 election see, Lionel Cliffe (ed.), *One Party Democracy*, Nairobi: East African Publishing House, 1967. Less comprehensive treatments are, Belle Harris, "The Tanzanian Election", *Mbioni*, II, 5; Göran Hydén, *op.cit.*, pp. 228—233; Bienen, *op.cit.*, pp. 382—405; G. Andrew Maguire, *Toward 'Uhuru' in Tanzania*, Cambridge: Cambridge University Press, 1969, pp. 371—384.

8. Lionel Cliffe and John Saul, "The District Development Front in Tanzania", Dar es Salaam, 1969 (mimeo.), p. 15.

9. W. J. W. Bowring, "Competitive Politics in East African Local Government", *Journal of the Developing Areas*, V (October, 1970), p. 49.

10. Hydén, *op.cit.*, chapter 10; Belle Harris, "Survey of Agricultural Training Institutes: Implications for Producing Ujamaa Vijijini Extension Workers", presented to the East African Academy, Sixth Annual Symposium, Dar es Salaam, September, 1968, p. 5.

11. For instance, Nyerere in 1958: "government by representatives in whose selection most of the governed have no part is not rule but repression", in his "The Entrenchment of Privilege", *Africa South*, II, 87 (January—March, 1958); and Nyerere in 1970, explaining the "fundamental reason" for having elections: "without free elections the people of an independent country do not govern themselves, they are governed by masters", *The Standard*, 7 July 1970. Also, see, *The Nationalist*, 30 October 1970. Others have observed the saturation of pre-independence nationalism with "liberal democratic dicta . . . which gave the legislative council a special mystique in the colonial political system". G. F. Engholm and Ali A. Mazrui, "Crossing the Floor and the Tensions of Representation in East Africa", *Parliamentary Affairs*, XXI, 2 (Spring, 1968), pp. 137—154.

12. In the 1965 elections some three-fourths of the registered voters, accounting for one-half the adult population, participated. Cliffe, *op.cit.*, appendix 1B.

13. The interviews upon which much of this material is based are the following (except in a few cases an undertaking of confidentiality was given): T. M. Budodi, Geita District TANU chairman, April 15, 1970; Francis Kisenga, Geita TANU leader, 5 May 1969; one Mwanza Region M.P., a non-regular TANU member, 16 May and 17 July 1969; two Mwanza Region M.P.'s, one a regular and the other a non-regular TANU member (see the section "The M.P. and the Party", below), individually, 10 January 1970; Geita District Area Secretary and the Acting Village Executive Officer of Mayuya, Geita District, together, 29 May 1969. Also a group of interviews were carried out in the Geita East constituency during and immediately after the 1969 by-elections. Thirteen 'leaders' who were identified as such either by their neighbors or by the interviewer, or by both, were interviewed in an informal fashion at some length, usually two to three hours, over the period May 5—17, 1969. The interviewer in these thirteen instances was Mbeti Musiyi, a sometime research Assistant of mine, who had five years of experience in assisting various social scientists doing

research in Sukumaland and one year as a member of the evaluation unit of the UNESCO literacy project; at the time he was on loan to me from a sociological survey being carried out under the auspices of the East African Community's Medical Research Centre in Mwanza. Mr Musiyi's help was invaluable. Seven of those interviewed by Mr Musiyi were again interviewed by myself, May 28—30, in discussions normally lasting about an hour. These seven are indicated with an asterisk.

(a) Farmer; Standard IV education; 30 years old.

(b) *Farmer; Standard IV education; 40+ years old.

(c) Herbal doctor; illiterate; about 25 years old.

(d) *Farmer; Standard IV education; has reputation as being especially wise and well-informed; reputed head of family (father is dead) although not the first born; early 20's.

(e) Secretary of local primary co-operative society; former Veterinary Field Assistant; one of the unsuccessful nominees in the TANU district conference primary of January 25, 1969; 40+ years old.

(f) Cell leader; farmer; age?

(g) *Councillor; cell leader; hotel owner; participant in the 25 January 1969 primary balloting; 40+ years old.

(h) *Farmer and herbal doctor; no formal education; has herbal certificate from South Africa; particularly keen on hearing "information"; 30+ years old.

(i) Carpenter; travels almost continuously in Geita District on jobs; Standard IV education; 40+ years old.

(j) *Councillor for six years; shopkeeper; was considering contesting 1970 parliamentary election; former agricultural instructor; locally identified as a "TANU leader"; about 45 years old.

(k) Ex-chief.

(l) Early official of TANU and, later, TAPA in Geita; building contractor; Standard X education; 40+ years old.

(m) *Councillor; early member of TANU; formerly in army; participated in January 25, 1969 primary balloting; Standard IV education; farmer; 40+ years old.

14. Interview, Mwanza Regional Commissioner, 6 March 1969.

15. Interview, Regional Engineer, Mwanza, 14 March 1969. In June, 1969, the M.P.'s were reminded by a government spokesman in the Assembly that they were members of the Regional Roads Board in their respective regions and that questions on roads should be raised there. *The Standard*, 14 June 1969.

16. This is based on a reading of all the minutes of all the DDPC meetings in the four districts for 1966 through 1969. Whether they were members or not depended in practice upon the opinion of the Area Commissioner as to whether the M.P.'s were local leaders.

17. Letter of 30 August 1963 from the Junior Minister in the Vice-President's Office to all Regional Commissioners, in file C.5/47.

18. See note attached to the minutes of the Mwanza RDC meeting of 26 May 1967. It is interesting that after the election of a new M.P. in the 1969 Geita East by-election, the Administrative Secretary omitted to add the

new name to the list of RDC members until, after two meetings had passed, the new M.P. specifically requested to be included. See, the M.P.'s letter of 8 November 1969, in file C.5/84.

19. Presidential Circular No. 1 of 1968, "The Decentralization of the Regional Development Fund", 19 April 1968.

20. The period covered by this discussion coincides with the 'Arusha Declaration Parliament' up to July, 1970.

21. See, Kasubi's letter of 26 January 1967, to the RDC, file C.5/47.

22. Minutes, Mwanza RDC Meeting, 26 January 1967.

23. Ibid.

24. Minutes, Mwanza RDC Meeting, 25 August 1967.

25. Minutes, Mwanza RDC Meeting, 26 January 1968.

26. Minutes, Mwanza RDC Sub-committee Meeting. 25 October 1968.

27. *Tanzania Second Five Year Plan*, Dar es Salaam: Government Printer, 1970, Vol. III, chapter 14.

28. This factor was suggested by M.P.'s in interviews.

29. This is a general conclusion to be drawn from this study. It is also a conclusion drawn from, Vente, *op.cit.*; and, Paul Collins, "The Working of Tanzania's Rural Development Fund: A Problem in Decentralization", IDS Communication No. 62, University of Sussex, 1971.

30. Letter from the Administrative Secretary to all members of the Mwanza RDC, 18 January 1967, file C.5/47.

31. Minutes, Mwanza RDC Meeting, 24 February 1967. The administrative decision not to consider Ukerewe is interesting because since early after independence the Ukerewe M.P.'s have urged that a secondary school be built on the island.

32. Letter of 6 May 1968 from the Principal Secretary of State House to all Principal Secretaries, Heads of Independent Divisions, and Regional Commissioners, in Devplan file MDPC/C.60/4.

33. *The Nationalist*, 1 and 23 October 1968, 7 January 1969. The lack of information at an M.P.'s disposal is evident in the report of the following exchange in the National Assembly: "Mr M. Mabawa (Kwimba North) asked how far the study of Simiyu River had finished as carried out by 'Alexander Gibbs' of Nairobi. He also wanted to know the purpose of the study. Mr Sokoine told him: 'I am sorry to say that the Ministry has never employed Alexander Gibbs to carry out a study of the Simiyu River'." *The Standard*, 16 July 1970.

34. Minutes, Mwanza RDC Meeting, 29 April 1967.

35. Minutes, Mwanza RDC Meeting, 25 August 1967.

36. Minutes, Mwanza RDC Sub-committee Meeting, 30 August and 5 September 1968.

37. "Information brief", 6 November 1969, file C.5/83.

38. Ibid.

39. Minutes, Mwanza RDC Sub-committee Meeting, 30 May 1969.

40. Minutes, Mwanza RDC Sub-committee Meeting, 19 August 1969.

41. Minutes, Mwanza RDC Sub-committee Meeting, 30 September 1969.

42. Report of April, 1970, file C.5/69.

43. In interviews with the Regional Commissioner and Regional Engi-

neer (6 and 14 March 1969, respectively) it was stated that the bridge in question very definitely needed to be built, and would be built immediately funds were made available. I had the impression that they were eager to "work the money loose" from Dar es Salaam. Ultimately there may have been a degree of collaboration or manipulation between officials who had already decided on professional grounds that the bridge needed a high priority and politicians who were representing popular demands.

44. Maguire, *op.cit.*, pp. 371—384. The M.P.'s are officially members of the TANU executive committees at the district and regional levels, but they did not often attend the meetings.

45. This point is made in, *ibid*. It is also made in, Ganja Geneya, "Sukumaland: Traditional Values and Modern Leadership", in, Cliffe (ed.), *op. cit.*, pp. 186—207.

46. During the time of this study Bomani was Minister of Economic Affairs and Development Planning, a Presidentially appointed member of the TANU Central Committee and National Executive Committee, the chairman of the Central Committee's five man sub-committee on financial and economic affairs, and elected (along with another defeated parliamentary candidate and the non-elected Speaker of the National Assembly) by the TANU national conference in June, 1969, as one of the trustees of the party. In the 1970 parliamentary elections Bomani won a seat in Mwanza and was subsequently appointed Minister of Commerce and Industries. Nyerere relieved him of his Cabinet post in February 1972 and later appointed him Ambassador to Washington.

47. Aside from the attendance of the two Kwimba M.P.'s at the meeting of the RDC's sub-committee which discussed the Simiyu bridge project referred to above, there is one other recorded attendance of an M.P.— Mageni (Kwimba South)) at the sub-committee meeting of 28 May 1968. (Mageni, who was not at the time of his 1965 election considered a regular of the local party, was in February, 1972, appointed to a Cabinet post by Nyerere.) In the general and correspondence files of both the RDC and its sub-committe there appears no mention of M.P.'s in other than the few instances which I have noted. In June, 1969, in reply to a question in the National Assembly put by Imerzi, the Ukerewe M.P., a government spokesman said that requests for water supply projects should be presented to the Regional Development Committee. *Sunday News*, 15 June 1969. Presumably aware of the allocative process and of the role of the RDC, Imerzi did not subsequently raise his request there.

48. 'Middlemen' is used as a comprehensive term covering communications and dispute settlement ("mediator") in a situation of a degree of encapsulation. See, F. G. Bailey, *Stratagems and Spoils*, Oxford: Blackwell, 1969, p. 184n.

49. See, *The Standard*, 19, 20, 21, 22, 25 and 27 August 1969, for the reports of Bomani's nine day tour of Mwanza Region which was intended, according to official announcements, to launch the fund raising drive for the new regional TANU headquarters building. Throughout his tour Bomani, Minister of Economic Affairs and Development Planning at the time, announced projects which would be undertaken during the upcoming

Plan period. (Bomani was successful in the 1970 general elections and one factor may have been his ability to identify himself as capable of bringing material aspects of development to his area.) In January 1969 Bomani spent 3 days in Mwanza town as the 'Guest of Honour of the Revolution Day' and was engaged almost continuously in meetings with local TANU leaders. The Geita Rural Development Officer made a special report on Bomani's tour, dated 29 August 1969, District Rural Development Officer's file RDR. 6/11/161.

50. The work is sometimes duplicated. The Sengerema secondary school which was announced by Bomani in his August, 1969, tour had been announced by the Regional Commissioner in a public meeting which I attended at the same place (Sengerema) the previous May.

51. In August 1969 the Regional Commissioner told an estimated 500 members of a traditional Sukuma cultivating society in Busega that they were being "exploited" and that he was "banning" their activities. Bomani arrived for an unscheduled 8 hour visit the following week, explained the matter to the Regional Commissioner, and the ban was not heard of again.

52. Hopkins, op.cit., 1971, passim.

53. The importance of mass turn-outs in parliamentary elections for establishing the legitimacy of the Tanzanian regime, can be seen in this extract from The Nationalist editorial of 1 June 1970. "The importance of this year's general elections cannot be overemphasized. The elections will yet be another milestone in Tanzania's consolidation of her chosen democratic principles. The elections will also set the pace at which our chosen socialist goals will be implemented in the future. Whether or not we respect and uphold our democracy will be judged by the way Tanzanians turn out to vote in the next elections." The Nationalist of 23 May 1969, quoted the Director of Elections as saying, "The success of elections does not depend on who is elected but on the number of peasants and workers who actually go to the polls to vote". The Second Vice-President, Rashidi Kawawa, stated in the Assembly late in 1969 that election turn-outs may be considered an indication of "the standard of political advancement Tanzania has reached". The Standard, 18 December, 1969.

54. See, also Kenneth Prewitt and Göran Hydén, "Voters Look at the Elections", in Cliffe, op.cit., pp. 296—297.

55. A persistent and widespread lack of understanding of the expulsions and of the role of the National Executive Committee can be seen in the letters to the editor of Kiongozi (Tabora), 15 June, 1 August, and 1 September 1969; and, to the editor of The Standard, 16 July 1970. A discussion of the general background to the expulsions is in, H. U. E. Thoden van Velsen and J. J. Sterkenburg, "The Party Supreme", Kroniek van Afrika, 1969, 1.

56. The Nationalist, 19 October 1968.

57. The Nationalist, 1 October 1968.

58. The Nationalist, 2 October 1968. With regard to Radio Tanzania Masha was referring to the "Mazungumzo baada ya Habari" (commentary after the news) programme which in September and October, 1968, often dealt with the functioning of the National Assembly with M.P.'s some-

times characterized as donkeys and monkeys.

59. *Ibid.* The Second Vice President, speaking at the end of the same debate, referred to the perceived need to alter the institutional arrangements inherited at independence. He said a "revolution" was necessary "to wipe out this colonial mentality" whereby some M.P.'s claimed not to understand the supremacy of TANU. He added, "it should be taken into account that M.P.'s were not the only people who represented the people".

60. This is van Velzen's and Sterkenburg's interpretation, *op.cit.*

61. See, the *Report of the Presidential Commission on the Establishment of a Democratic One Party State.* The Assembly was to be "primarily concerned with the more detailed task of giving effect to Government policy through appropriate legislative measures and exercising vigilant control over all aspects of Government expenditure", while the National Executive Committee of the party would "be concerned with the formulation of the broad lines of policy". Then, in referring to the Assembly's mass electoral base, the Commission observed, "we regard it as a basic principle that the supreme law-making body in the State should be directly elected by universal suffrage and we could not contemplate any major departure from this principle". The relevant extracts are conveniently reprinted as Appendix IV of, Lionel Cliffe, *op.cit.*

62. *The Standard*, 19 October 1968.

63. John Saul, "Background to the Tanzanian Election 1970", presented to the 1970 University of East Africa Social Science Conference, Dar es Salaam, December, 1970, p.v.

64. A credible explanation of Masha's expulsion would appear to be that he was a "deviant" who was "punished" for not complying with the norms of the "closed system of politics" in which Tanzanian politicians are expected to not discuss publicly any differences over "fundamentals", policies, timing or priorities, but are rather to devote their efforts to "constructive criticism". Presumably this would be the conclusion which would be drawn from the findings of the only major study on the norms and rules of elite politics in Tanzania. See, Hopkins, *op.cit.*, 1971, *passim*, and especially, p. 38. It should be pointed out that there was no suggestion that Masha, or any of the other expelled M.P.'s, lost their seats because of failure to comply with the leadership requirements of the Arusha Declaration. In October, 1969, it was announced in the Assembly that since the Declaration twenty Tanzanian leaders had failed in leadership because of the leadership code. They were listed as three Ministers, one Parliamentary Secretary, Six Regional Commissioners, five Area Commissioners, three TANU regional chairmen and two members of the National Executive. *The Standard*, 23 October 1969.

65. The uncompleted house was sold soon after Masha's expulsion.

66. The TANU expression for the process through which the M.P.'s were found deserving of expulsion. It is taken from the title of an essay by Nyerere, "*Tujisahihishe*".

67. Maguire, *op.cit.*, *passim.*

68. The 1965 election statistics are in, Cliffe, *op.cit.*, appendix 1B.

69. Hydén, *op.cit.*, p. 231.

70. For Bunuma's early role in nationalist politics in Geita, see, Maguire, *op.cit.*, pp. 212, 223—226.

71. Both the defeated candidates brought successful election petitions thus necessitating a by-election.

72. In general, see, C. Gertzel, *The Politics of Independent Kenya 1963—8*, Nairobi: East African Publishing House, 1970, especially pp. 125 —143. Malcolm Wallis who has recently completed a research project in Kenya has enlightened me on the pork-barrel role of some of the Kenya M.P.'s. Also Stultz, *op.cit.*; and, Engholm and Mazrui, *op.cit.*

73. Engholm and Mazrui, *op.cit.*

74. See, note no. 59 above.

75. There was some difficulty in mobilizing the people to register for the 1970 elections and the scheduled fifteen day registration period was consequently extended by an additional fifteen days. *The Nationalist*, 15 July 1970. A study of the election was carried out by members of the Political Science Department of the University of Dar es Salaam: *Socialism and Participation: Tanzania's 1970 National Elections*, Dar es Salaam: Tanzania Publishing House, 1974.

76. Bienen, *op.cit.*, pp. 201—202n.

The Continuing Problem

One of the problems which confronts countries as they attempt to pattern their development is the balance to strike between, to use Nyerere's phrase, freedom and development.[1] Organizationally this presents a conflict between the imperatives of goals premised on the basic dignity and equality of men, and goals premised on the increased use of modern technology. The former implies some form of mass participation in decision making; the latter has led historically to increases in operational size and the use of bureaucracies which, by definition, restrict participation in decision making. A major stated goal of the Tanzanian leadership is the increased participation of the citizenry in the decision making of the national political system. Arguing that popular participation, along with being inherently valuable, is more productive of material output, they have consciously designed organizations with the intention of enhancing participation at the expense of the bureaucratic structures and methods inherited from the colonial period.

The balance to be struck in organizational design between participation and bureaucracy has become more and more central to discussions in and of Tanzania. Though sympathetic to Tanzanian's egalitarian goals there are some who have challenged the efficacy of a participative organizational strategy at this conjunction. They assert that given the historical process of underdevelopment, the current state of class relations in Tanzania, and the "low level of consciousness" of the Tanzanian masses, reliance for the present must be placed upon "benevolent" leadership rather than participation in decision making.[2] The only solution which they see to this "administrative solution" is the long term one of raising the level of consciousness of the people— "educating them to a heightened awareness of the context of imperialism and 'historical backwardness' within which the development effort must take place".[3]

In contrast, others have asserted that Tanzania's goals necessitate a much more participative approach now. The University of Dar es Salaam, for instance, which perhaps more than any other university in free Africa has been responsive to the requirements of the national goals, has discussed a major research project on district and regional planning based on the notions that the Tanzanian leadership desires a "developmental process in which the people as a whole are regarded as agents of their own progress and not as passive recipients of government policy"; and that one of the "imperatives" of the February, 1971, TANU Guidelines is "for the government to adopt new methods that would encourage broader participation and to adopt the formal bureaucratic procedures which are consistent with these new methods".[4]

While the debate continues, and while many continue to credit the Tanzanian leaders with sincerity in their desire for popular participation, some have gone further and concluded that a viable balance between participation and hierarchy is actually in the process of being attained. Rene Dumont has described Tanzania as one of the two countries in Africa which is *not* becoming entangled in "bureaucratic socialism".[5] Maguire has written that Tanzania is "unique" in the success it has had in maxing competing organisational principles.[6] The verdict of an academic close to the Tanzanian leaders is that "there is in Tanzania a high degree of openness in public and national matters".[7]

The findings of pre-1972 empirical studies, however, indicated that such conclusions were in substantial conflict with the Tanzanian reality, that far from being unique Tanzania's hierarchical organizational approach was basically similar to that of, say, Kenya, which in terms of economic ideology, differs greatly.[8] After a close examination of the Regional Development Fund it was reported that, "although it was intended to meet popular needs as expressed through the District Councils, [it] was in most cases an example of 'bureaucratic decentralization', rather than 'democratic decentralization'".[9] Another study found that planning at the regional and district levels was mainly concerned with implementing central decisions and that there was a tendency in all the East African countries, but especially in Tanzania, for planning to be from above.[10] As for the Tanzanian ombudsman, the Permanent Commission of Enquiry (PCE), Kjekshus reported that it was part of the "antiburcaucratic" idcology of Tanzania, that it was intended to establish "on a national scale the same kind of balance between ruler and ruled that operated in the tribal societies", that it was charged with "restraining the state and party bureaucracy". But after a close study of its activities he found that it had not reached the "masses"—"know-

171

ledge of and utilization of the PCE is the treasure of a tiny [educated, urban] minority".[11] Perhaps even more significantly, Hopkins found that the politics of Tanzania were "closed" and restricted to a few people. The panapoly of committees and conferences in which decisions are officially made are in fact merely laudatory and ritualistic ceremonies; decision making actually occurs in a "small and private" arena. When wider participation is sought, it is a "preemptive move to have it [a decision from above] ratified at all levels".[12] Finally, Mapolu concluded that though TANU is responsible for workers' participation in industry, in fact it is a no-party which through being responsible for everything permits specific responsibilities to be taken up by bureaucrats and management.[13]

In this study I have contributed additional material to this pre-1972 literature. The Village Development Committees and the TANU cell leaders in Mwanza Region were decidedly hierarchical and penetrative in their connexions with the national polity.[14] In their final years (1967 —69) the VDC's were not viewed as vehicles for participation in decision making over the allocation of nation resources at local levels; rather they were viewed by government workers and central TANU functionaires as exhortation points and possible vehicles for the implementation of central government programmes. Few of the committees were willing to take-up these essentially administrative responsibilities; many simply stopped meeting altogether thus contributing to neither participation nor output. Their successors, the Ward Development Committees were, during their first year of operation (1969—70), no different in these aspects from the village committees. The M.P.'s during 1965—70 were ineffective as surrogate participants representing their constituents in decision making at any level. This was an element of the process of firmly relegating the National Assembly to a ritualistic role *vis a vis* the central party, and it entailed the M.P.'s not being considered in Dar es Salaam or in the Region as authoritative spokesmen for the electorate. This was gradually realized by the people, especially after the summary dismissal of a Geita M.P. by the centre for reasons unexplained to his people. Of the eight Mwanza Region M.P.'s six were not regulars of the local TANU. The goals of the 'party supreme' proponents of the central party, and this non-regular local status ensured that most of the M.P.'s were neither accorded the deference nor given the opportunities which would have enabled them to assist in representing or mobilizing (i.e., enthusing, penetrating) the rural societies. The Regional and Area Commissioners (we will come

172

back to their positions in the following section) had few connexions other than formal ones with the local party. Also, they had very limited and insufficient resources with which to exert political control over or to coordinate the local activities of the central government ministries. Moves to strengthen the role of the Commissioners through the provision of line and expert staff were ineffective. The major part of the time of the Commissioners was spent in exhortative tours and the overseeing of relatively large government projects which held out the possibility of gaining them central recognition.

A study of roles and organizations in one part of rural Tanzania obviously cannot provide the breadth and depth of insight necessary to permit of a macro-societal analysis as a conclusion. But examined along with other reports one can hope to gain some understanding of the nature and direction of events. My findings considered with other studies indicate quite clearly that the participation of the general citizenry in the decision making of the national political system had not notably increased nor changed in nature since the last decade of colonial rule, the ideological and rhetorical images arising from a fairly intense amount of intraelite participation in discussions about what to do with the general citizenry notwithstanding.[15]

Politics in the sense of the politics of diversity,[16] of individuals and groups conflicting for national resources was not permitted the people of Mwanza Region. With the tendency on the part of the national leadership to consider as national some of those resources which formerly were regarded as local (e.g., those of the co-operatives and of the District Councils), and to rely almost exclusively upon indirect methods of skimming the economic surpluses out of the rural areas (sales taxes rather than local rates and produce cesses), the participation of the rural population in making decisions about those activities which affect them directly and which link them with the national polity has lessened.

This lessened politics of diversity was not replaced by an increase in the politics of mass enthusiasm. In many ways this also lessened as witnessed by the party's difficulties in raising money from its rural members, the poor attendance at meetings and self-help projects, and the continued refusal of the overwhelming majority of Mwanza peasants to accept central government and party urgings to change the pattern of social and farm organization (i.e., to become members of block farms or *ujamaa* villages), or even to accept central advice in respect of specific agricultural improvement techniques (fer-

173

tilizers, insecticides, etc.). A concomitant of the bureaucratic approach to development in Tanzania was that the small elite, mostly concentrated in the government bureaucracy, was satisfied with the maintenance of their relatively better-off socio-economic position while the peasant masses continued to be uninvolved in the application of more productive technologies.

The paradox is that Tanzanian peasants were often influential in that by not participating they removed from the bureaucratic elite the opportunity of persuading them to change their ways.[17] In many ways it appears that the rural people, perhaps aware of the influence over their own lives which they retain by not being mobilized, avoided participation. The participation revolution, to the extent that there was one at all, was not from below but rather from above, national leaders trying to devise organizations to bring rural Tanzania into the nation along productive lines determined by the national leaders. Participation in this situation inevitably became nothing more than a management technique, a political Theory Y in which leaders manipulate followers in the hope that they would undertake specified activities, in certain ways, and attain predicted results.

Since the imposition of colonial rule in the 1890's one of the objectives of all the different regimes which have claimed suzerainty over what is now called Mwanza Region has been to bring 'development', however variously defined, to the people. The colonial attempts were openly premised on the idea that the officials knew what was developmental while the people had only to change. The nationalist government formally rejected this approach, but in practice, during the time of this study, they adhered to it. In the continued reliance on bureaucratic rule and the absence of a substantial politics of either diversity or mass enthusiasm Tanzania resembled the Tanganyika of the Germans and the British and other independent African states of today. Underdevelopment, however, persisted. The inherited bureaucratic approach, although permitting in Tanzania the investment of resources in infrastructural investments with good possibilities of productive long-run payoffs, did not lead to any great surge in rural agricultural development. The slowness of agricultural development remained Tanzania's most glaring shortcoming. It was this shortcoming which led in 1972—73 to a major organizational restructuring.

An Attempted Solution: Bureaucratic Decentralization

The field materials on which this study, and the others to which I have referred, are based are all pre-May, 1972. At that time the Tanzanian government began implementing a massive decentralization programme in the hope of rectifying the participation and productivity difficulties which we have outlined; put more positively, the decentralization was undertaken so as to attain "more democracy, more efficiency".[18] In concluding this study I analyze the decentralization and delineate the reasons for thinking that the new arrangements comprise a bureaucratic solution.

One of the difficulties in discussing any decentralization is that it is so often commended as a panacea—"almost nobody is against it".[19] Following the analytical framework of this study, and to get around this problem, it is helpful to distinguish between problems of low public participation and, on the other hand, low productivity administration stemming from deficiencies in government-client or intra-governmental arrangements. We bear in mind, however, that increases in 'participation' are quite commonly suggested as a therapeutic, human relations method for improving productivity. In such cases participation is seen as a method for coopting horizontal, popular resources and supplying them to the implementation processes of administrative hierarchies at their deconcentrated or agency levels so as to increase the productivity of such agencies in terms of the centrally set goals.[20]

Part of the background to the Tanzanian decentralization is the increasing concern of the leadership with the balance of power, the division of functions, between the two national hierarchies of state and party. It is at least partly dictated by their participative ideology which in stressing the instrumental and ultimate value of participation suggests a drastic shift away from the bureaucratic authoritarianism of the colonial and, at a lesser extent, initial post-independence periods. To its own thinking TANU has been relatively unsuccessful in increasing popular participation in decision making. The thrust of much of the discussion in TANU's 1970—71 regional and national conferences was that the people, through the party, must have a much larger say than theretofore in resource allocation decisions. In this context, the 1972—73 decentralisation followed from the party's awareness that with some 93 per cent of the population living in the rural areas, a significant portion of decision making must be sited at regional and district levels if Tanzanians generally are to participate.

In most developing countries democratic decentralization as envisaged by the TANU conferences has not been possible. There is a severe difficulty in meeting popular demands if people are permitted to participate and if people are permitted to choose they (so the national leaders think) may not always "exercise common sense and choose in their own best interests".[21] Also, bureaucracies, based as they are on expertise, tend to become more salient in a political system as a government expands its development programmes. What has made Tanzania somewhat unusual though is the series of factors which have permitted experiments in counter-balancing such centralizing factors with methods designed to increase participation in decision-making. One might point out the gradual articulation of a coherent ideology (albeit this has set the limits within which popular participation can influence decisions), a comparatively stable political climate including the lack of divisive regionalism, and a leadership which views organization as a crucial variable in increasing both productivity and equality and which is sincerely committed, it has been argued, to the interests of 'the people', even at the expense of the economic interests of would-be members of an elite, including themselves.

There was, however, another very different argument which contributed to the Tanzanian decentralization, namely that there are now sufficient trained and experienced staff to permit 'rational' and 'efficient' decisions to be made at sub-centre levels. This argument, made consistently by Nyerere himself,[22] underpins the administrative approach to decentralization which has accompanied the TANU demand in Tanzania for increased participation. Whereas the party conferences concentrated their attention chiefly on relationships between the people or their counter-organization (the party) and government decision making, Nyerere's explication focused mainly on intra-government organization and productivity. He posits that with decentralization decisions will be better informed and quicker because they will be made by the men on the ground; morale, enthusiasm, and co-operation within the bureaucracy will increase as officers at the lower levels make more decisions about their own work; planning and critical decision making will be more effective as men at the top find they are dealing less with day-to-day affairs and more with the broader problems and strategies of development. Administrative decentralization will also permit of more useful co-ordination in the field of the dif-

176

ferent departmental units involved in the multi-faceted process of rural development. The political aspect of this 'rational' approach would seem to be that decentralization will make more viable the attempt to 'politicize' peripheral areas, to bring villages into the nation; therapeutic participation of citizens will attach them to the goals of the nation, as defined by the leaders, and to the not yet well entrenched institutions of the new state.

It should be clear that these management rationales do not necessarily lead to popular control of the state apparatus in the field (as suggested by the TANU conferences) but rather to a deconcentration of departmental authority to lower levels, a better meshing of administration at these lower levels, and a 'human relations' approach to clients. And it is certainly true that many of the problems outlined and solutions put forward in Tanzania's present decentralization programme do follow these lines. For instance:

Problem A:
"it is sometimes difficult for local people to respond with enthusiasm to a call for development work which may be to their benefit, but which has been decided upon and planned by an authority hundred of miles away".

Solution A:
Bring power "closer to the people"; at the ward, district and region levels local representatives now comprise approximately, 95 %, 75 %, and 45 %, respectively of the membership of development committees which "lead the work of direct consultation with the people". Their actual powers are left undefined except "to hold frequent meetings with the people to answer their questions and to explain".[23]

Problem B:
"Officials . . . find all their ideas—and enthusiasm—buried in the mass of papers flowing backwards and forward to Dar es Salaam. For at present these officials have in reality very little local power."[24] "A civil servant in a region cannot spend even a single cent of Government money without asking and receiving authority from his Principal Secretary who is in Dar es Salaam. This system causes a great deal of delay in our development".[25]

Solution B:
Give regional and district officials of the central government increased responsibilities. Approximately 40 per cent of development expenditures, rather than the 4 per cent previously is now be allocated at sub-centre levels and it is the officials who are designing and selecting projects within policy guidelines established at the centre and at the district level. It is now possible to shift funds between programmes or projects within

a region or district, and any project cost savings revert to the region or district and not to Dar es Salaam.[26]

Problem C:

"Each functional officer is responsible only to his own Ministry in Dar es Salaam so that it is extremely difficult to work out a regional or district development or problem-solving scheme which calls for co-ordinated action."[27]

Solution C:

Organize on an areal basis. Under the new system the eight functional officers in each district and regional centre are responsible to the District and Regional Development Directors.[28]

One might predict that these solutions will have their own costs—duplication of facilities, competition for central resources, inter-regional policy discrepancies and differential rates of development, and the time of scarce technically skilled personnel expended in co-ordination and consultation in the field. After the first year of decentralization there were complaints about misunderstandings between the staff who are "decentralized" (that is, the Development Directors and their staff aides) and the officials of the functional departments, competition amongst regions (although some saw this as a positive result), financial losses, and the "arrogance" of the officials.[29] It is much too early to evaluate the decentralization or these complaints. But judged on the basis of most organizational histories it is not unlikely that these costs will lead eventually to 'rational' demands for more centralized control. In the meanwhile, what of the other problem—participation? As the official statement has it, the new system "is to increase the people's participation in decision making ... and to ensure that future economic planning stems from the people and serves the people directly".[30]

The decentralization scheme embodies three strategies for asserting this popular role. The first two are structural and relate to TANU —its centre and branches—*vis a vis* the government. Both have been tried since independence, with no great success. The questions in discussing these strategies are thus why were they unsuitable before, and what has been altered to make them potentially more effective in ensuring participation in the future?

The first is the practice of appointing political prefects—Regional and Area Commissioners—who as representatives of the President and central TANU are intended to co-ordinate the government bureaucracy in a manner consonant with national political goals and, within the parameters set by those goals, local political demands. They are ideally to ensure that the broad interests of the people are not subverted by departmental localism, and that development plans are people's plans when "the initiative for this is lacking at the local level".[31] In the past they have been unsuccessful partly because as representatives of the centre and as outsiders it was difficult for them to become a focus for the input of local demands. More crucial perhaps was their relative lack of resources with which they might influence the actions of civil servants in their areas. They had no control over expenditures, their regard was of little moment to a civil servant's career prospects, force was largely ruled out by a 'national ethic' of persuasion and was impracticable given the lack of a developed coercive apparatus, and an ideology supportive of national goals had not became a significant normative factor which a Commissioner might manipulate.

Aware of the Commissioners' relative lack of resources President Nyerere in 1968 moved to buttress their role by instructing that staff aides—an economist and an *ujamaa* village adviser—be assigned to each Regional Commissioner. These aides, the President hoped, would provide Commissioners with independent sources of specialist information to assist them in evaluating and controlling the projects and officials of the 'functional' ministries. The positioning of these aides within the administrative structure, however, was a decision made by civil servants within the regional administration headquarters in Dar es Salaam. They instructed that the aides were to report to the Commissioner through the senior civil servant in each region—the Administrative Secretary. In practice this resulted in the Commissioners not receiving countervailing advice.

In another move, attempts were made during 1969 to provide Commissioners with line staff (Divisional Secretaries) in the rural areas directly responsible to them. This was hampered by confusion as to the exact duties of these officials, by what had come to be protocol arrangements which strictly defined a Commissioner's territorial rights (thus causing some friction between Area and Regional Commissioners), and by the very nature of the role of the new staff in the rural areas which charged them, much as the Commissioners, with co-ordination and control but which provided them with almost no resources with which to carry out these functions.

When the positions of the Commissioners were established in 1962, they were assigned the essentially political half of the political-administrative role of the colonial Provincial and District Commissioners. The administrative half was charged to the Administrative and Area Secretaries. And up to the decentralization it was these Secretaries who were most effective in controlling the departmental officials. This was a pattern not much affected by whether a Commissioner had a civil service or political background. The Secretaries allocated official houses (a crucial authority when, as is often the case, housing is in short supply), they served as the effective executive officers of the development committees at the regional and district levels, they were the warrant officers for regional administration and often deputized for a Commissioner at public functions, they managed the flow of official information to the Commissioners, with all the other bureaucrats reporting through them. Their capacity for information management was enhanced by their practice of not travelling out of the regional or district headquarters, thus providing them with a continuity which was a key asset in what bureaucratic infighting there was, and which was an asset unmatched by the other officials, including the Commissioners, who spent a good part of their time in the rural areas or outside of the region. The Administrative Secretaries also had the authority, which was used with good results, to write directly to an officer's Principal Secretary in Dar es Salaam in the event of clear failure to pay the expected deference to their status as the most senior civil servant in the field.

In reviewing the resources of an Administrative or Area Secretary relative to that of his Commissioner, one does not wish to stray too far from what was the primary feature of pre-decentralization Tanzania: that is that the process of resource allocation was highly centralized tending to sectoral and departmental rather than areal inputs, and national rather than local priorities. In the periphery this meant that government officials were responsible directly to their departmental headquarters in the capital while with respect to the Commissioners, the civil servants were induced mostly not to give the appearance of being unco-operative or obstreperous. The corollaries of this pattern were that there was a critical lack of co-ordinating power at the regional and district levels and the small amount which did exist tended to be dominated by the Administrative and Area Secretaries.

The lack of sufficient co-ordinating power at the regional and district levels has been attacked by shifting from a functional to a more areal and prefectoral form of administration. To the extent that there was an element of prefectoral control before it should be clear that it was exercised by Administrative and Area Secretaries; the Commissioners were largely excluded from resource allocation processes. Under the decentralization, the Regional Commissioners' major new resource is that they are now full Cabinet members, and those appointed have in most cases been more senior and experienced than their predecessors.[32] Yet the role of the Secretaries has also been given additional resources which, one might predict, will ensure that in most instances that portion of the control of government operations that is permitted to be exercised outside of the capital will continue to be controlled by them and not by the Commissioners. The Secretaries' role has been renamed and they are now styled Regional and District Development Directors, they are now appointed by the President (at the least, a prestige resource), they head the development team of eight functional officers (who formerly were responsible to their various Dar es Salaam headquarters), they are directly assisted by three highly paid, specialist staff aides, they are charged with the implementation of the annual plans for their areas, the Regional Directors transfer officials within the region without reference to Dar es Salaam ministries and, most significantly, all Directors are responsible for the expenditure of government monies in their areas in a situation in which the notion of "sacrosant 'vote'" is castigated and the Directors (particularly the District Directors) are being enjoined to use their "discretion on District development matters" so as to permit "sudden opportunities [for development] to be seized".[33]

The decentralization arrangements have the Directors accountable for policy implementation to both their Commissioners and to Dar es Salaam; for financial accounting they are responsible only to Dar es Salaam. These dual lines of accountability make possible, especially given the apparently strong emphasis on the direct financial tie of the Directors to Dar es Salaam, the maintenance of the prefectoral role of the Secretaries, who at any rate will have increased resources not dependent upon their Commissioners. As enterprise organizations have long realized, lines of accountability are the key aspect of decentralizations and it would seem that Tanzania's attempt is based on the accountability of the senior civil servants at the decentralized levels not to centrally appointed politicians, and not to local representative bodies, but rather to officials in the Prime Minister's office in which the regional administration's head office is now located.

The decentralization is premised on a particular distinction between policy making and administration. With the Directors formally responsible to both "Dar es Salaam" and the Commissioners for policy implementation, this distinction is a crucial factor in deciding the kind and degree of the decentralization, and the relative power of various roles. At the broadest level (socialism, self-reliance) policy will continue to be centrally determined. But within the centrally established guidelines, who will make which categories of decisions? Before answering this, we might note the second structural strategy for participation applied to Tanzania's decentralization.

At every level—ward, district, regional—there will be development committees composed of people's representatives and officials to "lead the work of direct consultation with the people so that this decentralization really does result in the people themselves having a say in their own development and in their own affairs".[34] At the two lowest levels, the TANU chairman is the chairman of the committee (at the District level it is a called a Council), while at the regional level the Regional Commissioner is the head. The District Development Council has under it a committee composed of an approximately equal number of officials and representatives whereas on the Council the representatives dominate by about three to one. The district and regional team of functional officers sit on the committee at its respective level, and it is these teams who will be drawing up the plans (i.e., making allocative decisions) for development.

Except for some fairly minor altering of personnel and the simultaneous demise of the locally elected District Councils, which formerly did control certain functions, none of this is new. Under the development committee system which had been in operation since 1963, official sub-committees of the somewhat representative committees had carried out the work of co-ordination and, in those cases where some spending authority was decentralized, as from 1967 with the Regional Development Fund, they effectively allocated most of the monies available. There is some reason to believe that the current decentralization will not alter this. President Nyerere, in an early reference to the decentralization, before perhaps its public rationalization had been devised, stated that "regional teams" would be making "decisions concerning regional activities".[35] When announcing the measures Nyerere specified that it would be the district staff (team) who would have "full responsibility ... for ensuring active local participation in all development programmes".[36]

The superior power of the bureaucratic staff in the decentralized decision making is even more likely in view of the distinction made between policy and administration. The popular representatives on the development committees are all TANU leaders in that they are selected through TANU electoral processes. The party also has its own bodies and it is through both sets of institutions that TANU hopes to redress the balance of power between government and party. At the district level, where most project selections are intended to be made, it will be the TANU bodies who will provide guidance on "policy" for the district team. And it is in discussing this policy role of the local TANU organization that Nyerere gives a practical and illuminating example of the policy/administration demarcation. Plans for the district, drawn up essentially by the team, will be submitted to the TANU District Executive Committees who,

... will consider the policies being implemented ..., not the detailed project. For example, the Party could say to the District Development Committee, that their proposals give too much emphasis to schools and not enough to water, but they would not argue about whether a water project should go to one village rather than another.[37]

The distinction is interesting, first, because up to now the party at any level and popular representatives generally have not been too successful in influencing this type of "policy" decision. In September, 1971 the party's biennial national conference called for priority to be given to water, health, and education projects. In checking into the implementation of these priorities in January, 1972, the party's National Executive Committee expressed great dissatisfaction with the 1972/73 allocations which the government had made and called, unsuccessfully for water, health, and education allocations to be doubled.[38] In a time of severe financial shortage and of increasing demands, Tanzania was yet again confronted with the conflict between service and productive projects with the leadership asserting the priority of the latter. Perhaps even more striking in this policy/administration distinction is the attempt to ensure that politicing for projects (pork-barrelling, the who gets what) does not involve the politicians at the decentralized levels. Project selections will be done on a 'rational' basis by specialised bureaucrats who (at least by definition), know what is needed and who would be rendered less efficient and rational by the intervention of popular (by definition, non-rational) elements.

Put another way, individuals or groups who want projects will find that much as before it is to government officials, and not to TANU leaders, that their representations must be made. Development committees and local TANU units were ineffective in the past in increasing popular participation; as the people gradually realized that these representative bodies had nothing much to allocate in a material way (though they did of course allocate some of the positions within their own organizations and, at times, recruit for positions in other bodies), the indicators of mass participation (attendance at meetings, self-help projects, campaigns) showed a sharp decline. While on the face of it the decentralization intends to reduce this problem of low participation, its structural strategies would not appear to alter the prevailing pattern of giving allocative power to the bureaucratic rather than popular elements.

The administrative or bureaucratic approach to development has dominated in Tanzania. It has taken hold in the absence of a strong party organization. Though Nyerere's outline of the decentralization does observe that it "will provide a new opportunity for local TANU leadership", and that the accordingly "necessary strengthening of the relevant departments of TANU is now under consideration",[39] the main thrust of the decentralization is extremely cautious with regard to shifting away from the bureaucratic approach. The structural strategies are administrative solutions to administrative problems which contradict the 'mass line' spirit with which civil servants are being encouraged to act.

It would seem that if more participation in decision making is indeed to come out of this decentralization, it will be a function not so much of the structural strategies, but of the 'spirit' or ideological consciousness of the bureaucratic officials themselves. This is in effect the third strategy applied and the linchpin of the attempt to gain *both* 'more democracy, more efficiency'. In warning about the "one danger which must be guarded against", President Nyerere made clear the critical role of this 'spirit' strategy.

The transfer of power to the Regions and the Districts must not also mean a transfer of a rigid and bureaucratic system from Dar es Salaam to lower levels. Nor is it the intention . . . to create new local tyrants in the persons of the Regional and District Development Directors.

These officers will have overall responsibility; but the Decentralization exercise is based on the principle that more and more people must be trusted with responsibility—that is its whole purpose. We are trying to erase the thicket of red tape and the tyranny of 'the proper channels' . . .

What this really means is that the spirit of *Mwongozo* must permeate the entire implementation and operation. Personal responsibility for duties assigned will, of course, exist. But it must be recognized as responsibility to lead, to guide, and to help; officers are intended to be servants entrusted by the people with certain duties, not Gods whose orders must be obeyed for fear of damnation.[40]

Students of Tanzania would agree, I think that Tanzania's civil servants have been hardworking and sincere in their attempts to implement socialist and self-reliance policies set by the leadership, and that they have for the most part been willing to forego the conspicious elitism and consumption of similar officials in neighbouring and other African countries. But these same officials, with a number of notable exceptions, have not been able to avoid the bureaucratic imperative to consider citizens as clients with its concomitants of a bias in favour of the better-off members of the community[41] and a lack of responsiveness to the aspirations of, in particular, poor peasants. In the long run, it is hoped that through schools and the mass media a humanist attitude will be inculcated in all members of the society; in the short run a continuing series of seminars for civil servants has been the major vehicle for altering the status quo and imbedding a 'mass line'—the "spirit of *Mwongozo*"—in the minds of the officials. Without prejudging the probality of success of this political education, and it should be noted that much of the difficulty in implementing "*Mwongozo*" has centered on clause 15 which calls on officials not to treat workers and citizens in a 'commandist' fashion,[42] it is clear that what is being called for is a spiritual revolution in the behavior and ways of thinking of the government officials.

In Nyerere's view of the organizational problems of Tanzania, in order to "make a reality of our policies of socialism and self-reliance, the planning and control of development . . . must be exercised at the local level to a much greater extent". The people at the local level who have been given the increased power are the civil servants; to again quote Nyerere, the intention has been "to decentralize the control and decision-making now exercised from Dar es Salaam, and also to centralize local control, decision-making and responsibility".[43] The decentralization is an administrative deconcentration in the form of a return to the district team approach of the colonial days; it is, to use the Zambian expression, 'decentralization in centralism'. The wheel structure of the District Commissioners' days has returned with the Development Directors in the centre post position.[44] For administrative efficiency the result may be excellent—coordination should improve, bureaucratic morale should go up, and, assuming a fair degree of regional self-containment, Tanzanian's government machine could very well become especially in the short run vastly more rational in a bureaucratic way.

Whether a more internally efficient bureaucracy will in turn elicit higher levels of rural agricultural production is another question altogether. The Tanzanian experiences and those of other countries present serious objections to any suggestions that more or better bureaucracy is the solution to low production levels in this sector. Reviewing Tanzania's first decade of independence, Nyerere pointed out that attempts to introduce productive agricultural techniques had failed, those production increases which were attained were achieved through the extension of area under cultivation while the methods remained "those of the past".[45] In a review of Nyerere's review, Claude Ake observed that the first decade's "logic of leadership was the logic of colonialism", that those at the top in Tanzania were "very suspicious of the ability of the Tanzanian masses to rule themselves", and that in general there was "too much bureaucratization and centralization".[46] This "colonial logic" and "bureaucratization and centralization" would seem to be contributing factors to the failure to adopt more productive methods of agriculture. A case in point would be the take-over of the very successful Victoria Federation of Co-operative Unions based largely in Mwanza Region.[47] This was an attempt to lessen the exploitation of the members by their leaders and bureaucratic officials and to increase the co-operatives' capacity to facilitate increased production. The latter has not happened, and by the 1972/73 cotton harvest much of the crop was lost through the failure of the parastatal sector to provide transport in time.[48] In retrospect a more productive approach may have been to try to undercut exploitation through a direct and vigorous campaign to politically educate the members while continuing to allow the VFCU as an organization to manage its own affairs. The decentralization measures do go a long way in removing difficulties derived from too much centralization in Dar es Salaam, but they do not attack the basic structure of bureaucratization and its colonial logic. And after a year of decentralized bureaucracy, with Tanzanians facing various commodity shortages, Nyerere reported that the "greatest enemy" was the *deterioration* of production".[49]

As for 'more democracy', in so far as process is concerned the outcome could be to lessen popular participation still further and in the long run impede administrative efficiency and raise doubts about the attainment of an acceptable, in terms of Tanzania's goals, degree of social equality. The administrative efficiency of wheel-structured, district teams has often been at the expense of 'democracy'. For example, the colonial district team in Uganda was similar to what it is hoped the team will become in Tanzania: an "entrepreneurial committee" concerned with local development and welfare, "identifying the most publicly sought projects and schemes and finding local means for going ahead", whose "excellence... [was] often at the expense of the district council which is technically responsible for many of the matters for which the district team determines policy".[50] Pessimism on this point is reinforced by the fact that the discussions which resulted in the decentralization were *in camera* rather than in public, while the changes themselves were designed by an American management consultancy firm rather than the party.[51]

Decentralization of administration is however a move which can accompany an intention to increase community participation in decision making.[52] Thus the Soviet substitution of the territorial or area for the functional or production principle in the organization of the state in the 1950's was done with the

aim of moving the non-party state bureaucracy away from Moscow, so that senior civil servants should not be more powerful than the local communist party bosses ..., for the party was, as all political parties, organized territorially... so when the political or ideological need arose to subordinate the state even more fully to the party, it was a good move to reconstruct the state on the territorial principle ...[53]

In other cases, such as public school decentralization to community level in New York, administrative deconcentration, though perceived and designed by bureaucrats as a rational response to the bureaucracy's need to find quicker and more effective ways of making decisions, has as a by-product 'triggered' participation.[54] Whether this will occur in Tanzania, and there is some indication that at least some leaders hope that "failures" in the decentralization will serve "to stimulate a sense of political consciousness",[55] is a question which can only be addressed after some time as passed and evaluation studies undertaken.

The bureaucratic approach to development, which is being varied not abandoned in Tanzania's decentralization, is not of course unusual. It seems almost forced upon governments by the immediate economic and political problems which confront most poor countries.[56] The crux

187

of the problem is that the desire to rationally allocate a nation's scarce resources seems to lead invariably to a dependence upon the judgement of 'rational' individuals and a certain distrust of popular participation in other than a therapeutic or implementory way. The pitfalls of this approach—the difficulty in mobilizing support from those who have not participated in decisions, and the inaccuracy of bureaucratic estimates of the "price" people will demand to be induced into producing differently and more,[57] seem to be considered by most leaderships as less odious than the problems which might accompany increased participation.

Popular involvement, Nyerere hopes, will come indirectly as the people become aware that it is the field officials who are in many instances the decision makers and as the field officials, in the correct spirit, respond to the insights and demands of the people. This of course presupposes that officials and citizens will employ a common framework in establishing priorities and criteria for decision making, and that will depend upon the success with which both are ideologically educated. As the recurring allegations of official "arrogance" and the recurring popular insistence upon service projects now indicates,[58] the campaign to educate the people and the bureaucrats to the wisdom and implications of the government's policies of socialism and self-reliance has a long way yet to go. And in all probability the campaign to educate the people must succeed before the leaders will insist that the bureaucrats take some of the 'mass line' from the masses as opposed to taking it from the leadership. It is when the people's demands somewhat coincide with the leadership's estimation of the nation's needs that, one may speculate, devolution will be possible.[59]

It is essentially the task of TANU to bring the people to the requisite level of understanding, but post-independence TANU, especially in the rural areas, has been neither a strong mobilizational vehicle nor composed of an ideologically committed vanguard. These weaknesses were undoubtedly factors which ensured that the present decentralization would rely upon the state apparatus rather than the party. Given that organizationally and ideologically TANU is one of the least weak parties in Africa one begins to get an intuition as to just how strong popular forces must be at sub-centre levels before their strength will be expressed in the organizational design of a decentralized resource allocation system.

Tanzania's decentralization will be interesting to observe in coming years not because it aims directly at increasing production through popular participation in resouces allocation, although in this regard the success or otherwise of the programme of politically educating Tanzanians will merit watching; but because it is based on the premise that a more rational way, a more productive bureaucracy will result from deconcentrating substantial authority, including budgeting and project selection, to teams of officials in the field. This approach follows the advice of some of the best thinking in the discipline of development administration and the results may provide us with a measure of its usefulness.[60]

Notes

1. Julius K. Nyerere, "Freedom and Development", an essay published in, *The Nationalist*, October 18, 1968; *idem, Freedom and Development*, Dar es Salaam; Oxford University Press, (forthcoming).

2. John Saul, "The Nature of Tanzania's Political System", *Journal of Commonwealth Political Studies* X, 2, 1972.

3. Lionel Cliffe and John Saul, "The District Development Front", in "Tanzania", Dar es Salaam (mimeo), 1969; see, also, J. R. Nellis, *A Theory of Ideology: The Tanzanian Example*, Nairobi: Oxford University Press, 1972.

4. "Research Prospectus", paper prepared by the Dar es Salaam Department of Political Science for the Workshop on Development Planning in Tanzania, held at the University of Dar es Salaam, December, 1971.

5. Rene Dumont, "To have and have not", an article published in, *The Guardian*, August 26, 1971.

6. G. Andrew Maguire, *Toward 'Uhuru' in Tanzania: the Politics of Participation*, Cambridge: Cambridge University Press, 1969, p. xvii.

7. K. E. Svendsen, "Development Administration and Socialist Strategy", paper presented to the Conference on Comparative Administration in East Africa, Arusha, Tanzania, September, 1971.

8. *Cf.*, Göran Hydén, Robert Jackson, and John Okumu (eds.), *Development Administration: the Kenyan Experience*, Nairobi: Oxford University Press, 1970; Edward Feit, "Military Coups and Political Development", *World Politics*, XX (January, 1968); R. B. Charlick, "Participatory Development and Rural Modernization in Hausa Niger", *The African Review*, II, 4 (1972).

9. Paul Collins, "The Working of Tanzania's Rural Development Fund", IDS Communication No. 62, University of Sussex, 1971.

10. Rolf E. Vente, *Planning Processes: The East African Case*, Munich: Weltforum Publishing House, 1970.

11. Helge Kjekshus, "The Ombudsman in the Tanzania One-Party System", *The African Review*, I, 2 (September, 1971), pp. 13—29.

12. Raymond F. Hopkins, *Political Roles in a New State*, New Haven:

Yale University Press, 1971, pp. 38, 241.

13. Henry Mapolu, "The Organisation and Participation of Workers in Tanzania", University of Dar es Salaam, Economic Research Bureau, 1972.

14. A study in rural Pare District resulted in a similar conclusion. See, Jean R. O'Baar, "Cell Leaders in Tanzania", *African Studies Review*, XV, 3 (December, 1972), pp. 437—465. In Tanga Region it was found that except for their greater numbers the cell leaders differed little from the colonial headmen; see, Clyde R. Ingle, "The Ten-House Cell System in Tanzania", *The Journal of Developing Areas*, VI (January, 1972), pp. 211 —226.

15. In a sense this study underscores the great difference between the picture of rural Tanzania often delineated in official discussions and in the national newspapers with the situation on the ground. For the exact same problem in Dodoma Region, see, the discussions occasioned by the reports of Walter Rodney and G. Kamenju after their visits to *ujamaa* villages in that area, in, *The Nationalist,* 25 September, 3 and 6 October 1970.

16. For the notions of the politics of diversity and mass enthusiasm, see, Bernard Crick, *In Defence of Politics*, Harmondsworth: Penguin, revised edition, 1964, esp., p. 164.

17. *Cf.*, S. M. Lipset, *Political Man*, Garden City, N.Y.: Doubleday, 1959, pp. 179—180.

18. This is the description of the government newspaper, *The Standard*, 28 January 1972.

19. Harold J. Leavitt, "Applied Organizational Change in Industry", in, Victor H. Vroom and Edward L. Deci, *Management and Motivation*, Harmondsworth: Penguin, 1970, p. 366.

20. See, Philip Selznick, *TVA and the Grass Roots*, Berkeley: University of California Press, 1949; Henry Maddick, *Democracy, Decentralisation and Development*, Bombay: Asia Publishing House, 1963; B. C. Smith, *Field Administration*, London: Routledge and Kegan Paul, 1969.

21. Antony Rweyemamu, "The Preconditions for Regional Planning", presented to the Conference on Comparative Administration in East Africa, Arusha, Tanzania, September, 1971.

22. Julius K. Nyerere, *Decentralization*, Dar es Salaam: Government Printer, 1972. These management rationales also led to the 1972 breakup of Tanzania's state Trading Corporation into individual corporations for each of the eighteen regions.

23. *Ibid.*

24. *Ibid.*

25. This is taken from President Nyerere's initial public description of the decentralization which was published in *The Standard*, 27 January 1972.

26. Nyerere, *Decentralization.*

27. *Ibid.*

28. *Ibid.*

29. See, *Daily News*, 26 June 1973.

30. Nyerere, *Decentralization.*

31. Tanzanian Cabinet Paper No. 70 of 1967.

32. The Regional and District Development Directors who have been appointed are generally more senior and more often trained in technical fields—Agriculture, Veterinary, etc.—than the Secretaries whom they replaced.

33. Nyerere, *Decentralization.*

34. *Ibid.*

35. *The Nationalist,* 11 December 1971.

36. Nyerere, *Decentralization.*

37. *Ibid.*

38. *The Standard,* 11, 17, and 24 January 1972.

39. Nyerere, *Decentralization.*

40. *Ibid.*

41. P. M. van Hekken and H. V. E. Thoden van Velzen, *Land Scarcity and Rural Inequality in Tanzania,* The Hague: Mouton, 1972; Michaela von Freyhold, "The Government Staff and *Ujamaa* Villages: The Tanga Experience", presented to the East African Universities Social Science Conference, Dar es Salaam, 1973.

42. A post-decentralization study of the implementation of the rural water supply system indicates quite clearly that it is the structural strategies and not the spirit strategy which have the upper hand. The bureaucrats and their 'techniques' are still very much in command. See, G. Tschannerl, "Rural Water-supply in Tanzania: Is 'Politics' or 'Technique' in Command?", presented to the East African Universities Social Science Conference, Dar es Salaam, 1973. For a similar Finding after Mexico's decentralization, see, C. E. Grimes and Charles E. P. Simmons, "Bureaucracy and Political Control in Mexico: Towards an Assessment", *Public Administration Review,* XXIX, 1 (January/February, 1969), pp. 72—79.

43. Nyerere, *Decentralization.*

44. See, Jon Morris, "Administrative Penetration as a Tool for Development Analysis: A Structural Interpretation of Agricultural Administration in Kenya", presented to the Conference on Comparative Administration in East Africa, Arusha, Tanzania, September, 1971.

45. Julius Nyerere, "Tanzania Ten Years after Independence", *The African Review,* II, 1 (June, 1972), pp. 1—54.

46. Claude Ake, "The Progress of a Decade", *The African Review,* 2, 1 (June, 1972), p. 60; Nellis, *loc.cit.*

47. Norman Long, "Co-operative Enterprise and Rural Development in Tanzania", in, Raymond Apthorpe (ed.), *Rural Co-operatives and Planned Change in Africa: Case Materials,* Geneva: UNRISD, 1970, pp. 287—361. See, also, the discussion of co-operatives in chapter 2.

48. *Daily News,* 29 June 1973.

49. *Daily News,* 3 July 1973 (my italics). The different organization requirements of different rural production situations is the core of my forthcoming volume, *The Organization of Rural Development.*

50. David Apter, *The Political Kingdom in Uganda,* Princeton: Princeton University Press, 1961, p. 41.

51. Mapolu, *op.cit.*

52. Selznick, *op.cit.,* p. 19.

53. P. J. D. Wiles, *The Political Economy of Communism*, Oxford: Basil Blackwell, 1964, pp. 43—44.

54. Hans B. C. Spiegel, *Citizen Participation in Urban Development*, Washington: Institute for Applied Behavioral Science, 1969, Vol. 11, part b.

55. See the remarks of Prime Minister Kawawa, *Daily News*, 27 June 1973.

56. For a very interesting study of the effects of a participatory approach in a poor country, see, Ichak Adizes, *Industrial Democracy: Yugoslav Style; the Effect of Decentralization on Organizational Behavior*, New York: Free Press, 1972.

57. See, Colin Leys, "The Analysis of Planning", in, Leys (ed.), *Politics and Change in Developing Countries*, Cambridge: Cambridge University Press, 1960.

58. *Daily News*, 26 June 1973; Christopher Mulei, "The Predicament of the Left in Tanzania", *East Africa Journal*, IX, 9 (August, 1972), pp. 32—33. See, also, William Tordoff and Ali Mazrui, "The Left and the Super-left in Tanzania", *The Journal of Modern African Studies*, X, 3 (October, 1972), pp. 425—427.

59. This view would seem supported by the Chinese experience. See, James R. Townsend, *Political Participation in Communist China*, Berkeley: University of California Press, 1967: Franza Schurmann, *Ideology and Organization in Communist China*, Berkeley: University of California Press, 1968, second edition.

60. Bernard Schaffer, "The Deadlock in Development Administration", in, Leys (ed.), *op.cit*. Also, Morris, *op.cit*; and, Guy Hunter, "Development Administration in East Africa", *Journal of Administration Overseas*, VI, 1 (January, 1967), pp. 6—12; *idem, Modernizing Peasant Societies*, London: Oxford University Press, 1969.